PEACE STUDIES IN THE CHINESE CENTURY

Peace Studies in the Chinese Century
International Perspectives

Edited by

ALAN HUNTER
Coventry University, UK

Routledge
Taylor & Francis Group

LONDON AND NEW YORK

First published 2006 by Ashgate Publishing

2 Park Square, Milton Park, Abingdon, Oxon OX14 4RN
711 Third Avenue, New York, NY 10017, USA

Routledge is an imprint of the Taylor & Francis Group, an informa business

First issued in paperback 2017

British Library Cataloguing in Publication Data
Peace studies in the Chinese century : international
   perspectives
   1.Peace 2.Peace-building 3.Conflict management 4.Peace -
   Study and teaching
   I.Hunter, Alan, 1953-
   327.1'72

Library of Congress Cataloging-in-Publication Data
Peace studies in the Chinese century : international perspectives / edited by Alan
Hunter.
      p. cm.
   Includes index.
   ISBN 0-7546-4794-3
   1. Peace-building--China. 2. Political stability--China. 3. Conflict management--
China. I. Hunter, Alan, 1953-

   JZ5584.C6P43 2006
   303.6'60951--dc22

                                                                          2006012015

ISBN 978-0-7546-4794-2 (hbk)
ISBN 978-1-138-26260-7 (pbk)

Contents

List of Figures

List of Tables

List of Contributors

Johan Galtung	Professor of Peace Studies, Dr hc mult Founder and Co-Director, *TRANSCEND:* *A Network for Peace and Development*
Hu Chuansheng	Editor, *Xuehai* (Academia Bimestris) Jiangsu Academy of Social Sciences, Peoples' Republic of China
Alan Hunter	Centre for Peace and Reconciliation Studies, Coventry University, UK
Jørgen Johansen	Freelance peaceworker and researcher, Visiting Scholar at Centre for Peace and Reconciliation Studies, Coventry University, UK
Lin Yuan	Doctoral Candidate, Macao University of Science and Technology
Liu Cheng	Associate Professor of History, Nanjing University, Peoples' Republic of China
Paddy Meskin	World Conference on Religion and Peace, Durban, South Africa
Pan Zhichang	Professor of Sociology, Nanjing University, Peoples Republic of China
Úrsula Oswald Spring	Concurrent Professor at National University of Mexico and United Nations University, Bonn, Germany (MRF Chair in Social Vulnerability)
Qian Chengdan	Director, Centre for European Studies, Nanjing University; Concurrent Professor of History, Beijing University, Peoples Republic of China
Carol Rank	Centre for Peace and Reconciliation Studies, Coventry University, UK
Stuart Rees	Director, Centre for Peace and Conflict Studies, University of Sydney, Australia; Director, Sydney Peace Prize Foundation

Andrew Rigby   Director, Centre for Peace and Reconciliation
                         Studies, Coventry University, UK

Kazuyo Yamane   Lecturer in Peace Studies,
                         Kochi University, Japan

Translations

Acknowledgements

Sincere thanks are due to many people who contributed to the writing and production of this book. I would especially like to convey the gratitude of all concerned to Professor Qian and Dr Liu of Nanjing University and Professor Andrew Rigby and Dr Carol Rank of Coventry University for their steady and gracious support for a programme of collaboration in peace studies over a five-year period. Their hard work has already resulted in significant original publications and translations, an international conference hosted in Nanjing, new teaching programmes and opportunities for dialogue between peace researchers inside and outside China. Thanks also to all other contributors of chapters to this volume. Each and every one made a personal commitment, sometimes under difficult circumstances, to participate in a conference in Nanjing in 2005, subsequently to write and rewrite chapters, and always to make a positive contribution to academic co-operation in this field of study.

Important financial support for the academic link between Coventry and Nanjing universities was received from the British Council, the Macao Foundation, Amity Foundation and from both universities: we are very grateful for the generosity without which the projects would not have been possible.

I would also like to thank Mary Savigar, editor at Ashgate, for her prompt and expert advice; and to Chas Morrison and Paul Marshall for their expert assistance with editing and bibliographic work.

I first went to China as a student in 1981, and have since visited the PRC on numerous occasions, as well as staying in Hong Kong, Taiwan and Singapore, several times with my wife and sometimes with my children. I remember hardly any occasion when we were treated badly, and on the contrary, I have frequently been overwhelmed by hospitality, friendship and generosity. It is difficult to single out individuals when so many people have been so kind, but for their sympathy towards a foreigner struggling to understand the great civilization, I would especially like to thank Dr Chan Kim-kwong of Hong Kong, Mr Li Xudong of Shanghai, and Professor Wang Yao of Beijing.

List of Abbreviations

ACCORD	African Centre for the Constructive Resolution of Disputes
ANC	African National Congress
BME	Black and Minority Ethnic
CCP	Chinese Communist Party
CCR	Centre for Conflict Resolution
CEPAL	Comisión Económica para América Latina y el Caribe [The Economic Commission for Latin America and the Caribbean]
CLAIP	Consejo Latinoamericano de Investigación para la Paz [Latin American Council of Peace Research]
CND	Campaign for Nuclear Disarmament
COPRED	Consortium on Peace Research, Education and Development
ECC	End Conscription Campaign
FAO	Food and Agricultural Organization
FARC	Fuerzas Armadas Revolucionarias de Colombia
FBO	Faith-based organization
HUGE	Human, Gender and Environmental Security
IFP	Inkatha Freedom Party
IMF	International Monetary Fund
IMSSA	Independent Mediation Service of South Africa
JWRC	Center for Research and Documentation on Japan's War Responsibility
LCS	London Corresponding Society
NGO	Non-governmental organization
NRLF	National Religious Leaders Forum
PAC	Pan African Congress
PJSA	Peace and Justice Studies Association
PMW	Peace Museums Worldwide
PSA	Peace Studies Association
PSAJ	Peace Studies Association of Japan
PRIO	Peace Research Institute Oslo
IPRA	International Peace Research Association
SACC	South African Council of Churches
SAR	Special Autonomous Region (referring to Hong Kong or Macao)
SIPRI	Stockholm International Peace Research Institute
TRC	Truth and Reconciliation Commission
WCRP	World Conference on Religion and Peace
WILPF	Women's International League for Peace and Freedom

Introduction:
The Chinese Century

Alan Hunter

China's phenomenal rise to wealth will make a global economic, political and perhaps cultural and even religious impact far beyond the modernization of its smaller neighbours. In the early 1990s analysts frequently referred to the rapid economic growth of Japan and the 'four little dragons' – South Korea, Singapore, Hong Kong, Taiwan – as the main evidence of the shift of economic power to the Asia Pacific region. It was almost unthinkable then that China would soon become the world's second economic power; yet that is likely to be the case by 2010. It is now more appropriate to compare China's rise with that of the USA in the first decade of the twentieth century. Another relevant point of comparison is with India which, despite a different configuration of resources and social ordering, is a huge economy expanding in numerous sectors. The terms 'Chinese Century' and 'New Chinese Empire' are gaining currency as the rest of the world reflects on the statement, attributed to Napoleon, that 'when China wakes, the world will tremble'.

Opinions differ as to whether this rise will be a sustainable and positive phenomenon. Some writers stress negative features of the economy, government and social system, believing that China's new-found power makes it an unstable and fundamentally flawed nation-state. Among problems they highlight are an ambitious but outmoded and corrupt form of government by the Chinese Communist Party (CCP); massive if hidden unemployment that is only tolerable because of the short-term boom; and unsustainable predation of the environment. Terrill, for example, presumes that the Beijing government wants a dominant role in Asia, similar to that of the USA in Latin America. However his overall assessment is that the CCP will be simply incapable of fulfilling its ambitions, so China will become a vindictive, frustrated power.[1]

Other writers are much more optimistic, and point out that so far China's ascendancy has been remarkably successful. Shenkar, for example, believes that we are witnessing the dramatic growth of a future world power, with excellent resources at home, and the international financial and technological clout of a sophisticated diaspora.[2] China's economic success has lifted perhaps half a billion people out of poverty, while the CCP has managed reforms that are unique in the communist

---

1   Ross Terrill, *The New Chinese Empire: And What It Means for the United States* (New York, 2003).

2   Oded Shenkar, *The Chinese Century: The Rising Chinese Economy and Its Impact on the Global Economy, the Balance of Power, and Your Job* (Philadelphia, 2004).

world, apparently aiming for cautious moves towards democracy in the next decade. Human rights have improved immeasurably compared to the 1970s. Its government has avoided major conflicts both internally and internationally, since the maintenance of a peaceful international environment for several generations was established as a basic principle of the modernization programme by its architect Deng Xiaoping in the late 1970s.

Nevertheless, however one assesses the reforms, such a major power-shift has inevitably created new risks: the maintenance of international peace in this changing environment needs to be continually addressed and re-assessed. Until 2004 there was no dedicated peace research institute or university faculty in China. Of course, leading Chinese politicians receive advice from think-tanks and international relations specialists, who are usually based in a handful of institutions in Beijing. In a positive development, Nanjing University, rated among the top four or five in China, has now established peace studies as an academic discipline. In March 2005 Nanjing University and Coventry University jointly organized an international symposium in Nanjing where, for the first time, several leading international peace researchers shared ideas and perspectives with Chinese colleagues. This volume is an edited collection of the papers presented at that conference.

Perceptions

Relations between China and the rest of the world are based partly on factors, like economic or military strength, that can to some extent be measured. However, another important component is less tangible: how do Chinese perceive the rest of the world, and vice versa?

From publications over many decades one sees various strands in Western approaches to China. As a generalization, the West has never been well informed about China. For example, at the time of the Enlightenment, European thinkers formed an impression of the Confucian tradition which they compared favourably with European clerical and aristocratic rule. However, the information on which they based this opinion was fragmentary, gleaned from reports by a few travellers and missionaries. China was more open in the first few decades of the twentieth century, and more systematic reporting by visitors and journalists began to emerge; but it was a period of colonial attitudes, where China was seen partly as a huge market, partly as a backward or degenerate part of the world. From the Japanese invasions of the 1930s until the end of the hard-line communist period in 1978, China was again virtually closed to outsiders. As well as the practical difficulties of staying in China and visiting its regions, non-Chinese were also faced with a complex writing system, a profound and for most people obscure élite culture, and a spoken language which had no connection with any European one. They were obliged to gain most of their information at second- or third-hand, through intermediaries, translations, compradors and interpreters.

Stereotypes which seem crude in the 21st century dominated Western perceptions for decades, sometimes for centuries. One such was of timeless China, a country stagnating under the deadweight of ancient, obscure traditions, where nothing ever changed: picturesque river scenery, silks and magic martial arts on the one hand; illiterate, doomed peasants and rickshaw pullers on the other. A more sinister and perhaps more durable view was the 'evil empire'. Some sociologists – including Weber and Wittfogel – concluded, without having ever visited the country, that China had an almost uniquely oppressive social system, for which they coined the phrase 'oriental despotism'. Such negative evaluations were easily assimilated into two myths that haunted Western popular perceptions for much of the twentieth century: the 'yellow peril' and the 'red hordes'. Conflated with US and UK anti-communist propaganda, they would easily be manipulated into anti-Chinese sentiment during the Cold War.[3]

Recently the rest of the world has had more exposure to the realities of Chinese life, with hundreds of thousands of people going to the country for study, sport, tourism and business, especially since the mid-1990s. Consequently, hundreds of books are available to the interested reader, as well as a plethora of films, newspaper articles and websites. There is less excuse for ignorance now. Hopefully the Western public are gaining a more balanced and better-informed picture of the sub-continent and its billion people. Nevertheless, anti-Chinese sentiment can be stirred quite easily: new villains may not be communist hordes, but they might include triads, illegal immigrants, industrial polluters and cheap labour.

Westerners also have positive feelings about China and its culture, so the picture is by no means entirely negative. For example, people from all walks of life appreciate Chinese art and design, although its music is yet to catch on. Millions enjoy Chinese martial arts and traditional medicine. People read books on Daoism and Buddhism, and some practise their techniques as part of the diffuse spirituality available in today's mostly post-Christian societies. As an immigrant community, at least in the UK, Chinese are regarded as relatively law-abiding, industrious and successful. Parents, who often survived in the UK by taking low-paid manual jobs, have encouraged their children and grandchildren to gain a good education and move into professions. And the community, and China itself, is not perceived as associated with religious fundamentalism or terrorism.

How do Chinese view Westerners? In 2005 I heard a Chinese person on a train journey say 'I hate and despise the English, they go around the world bombing and killing other people. The Americans are worse, but the English always support their wars'. I believe this statement summarized one aspect of Chinese perceptions of the West, particularly of the USA and the UK: that they are belligerent, arrogant and hypocritical nations – the same point is made in Liu's chapter in this collection. Many Chinese take an interest in international politics, and they are not slow to point out catalogues of double-standards: nuclear weapons for Israel, not for Iran; routine

3 See Alan Hunter and John Sexton, *Contemporary China* (Basingstoke, 1999), pp. 123–5 for further discussion of this point.

invasions of independent states; use of torture; bombing of civilians, and so on. For many Chinese the invasion of Iraq encapsulated the real agendas of the US and the UK leaders.

Nevertheless, the picture is much more nuanced. First, it is unusual in my experience for Chinese people to blame individuals for the behaviour of their governments. It is much more common for them to give a shrug and say in effect, 'Well, all politicians are like that, what can you expect?' Also, even where they may dislike the governments, many Chinese have a fond and often knowledgeable appreciation of Western culture. Depending on the age and interest of the Chinese you might speak to, he or she will usually speak favourably of Western literature, fashion, music, human rights, democracy or technology. Millions of Chinese have spent time in Europe and other parts of the world and have come to their own conclusions. On the one hand they are inclined to be sceptical about a crude anti-Western propaganda emanating from Beijing, on the other for the most part they do not buy into the Voice of America self-presentation as the voice of freedom. They know too much about Vietnam, Iraq, Guatemala, Guantanamo.

What is Peace Studies?

One purpose of this collection is to provide analysis of the scope, approaches and topics that may be included under the rubric of peace studies. Peace studies has sometimes been critiqued in the academic world as being 'soft', too value-laden, or subjective, or lacking intellectual rigour, and of having too diffuse a focus. Writers from Mexico (Oswald), Japan (Yamane), the USA (Rank), South Africa (Meskin) and the UK (Rigby and Hunter) help readers to understand the dimensions of peace research that are prominent in their countries. In her chapter Carol Rank cites the following definition of peace studies from the USA:

- Central propositions. 1) The traditional belief in the inevitability of war and injustice is questioned, based on data and insights from peace research and movements for social change; 2) The pedagogical purpose of peace studies is to provide students with appropriate intellectual tools with which to examine this traditional belief and inquire into possible alternatives to war and oppression.

- Fundamental core. 1) The central questions Peace Studies asks are: What is the nature of peace? What are the conditions that make peace possible? How are these conditions achieved? 2) The minimum areas of concern are: organized lethal violence among social groups at all levels of organization (war) and structural violence (systemic discrimination, deprivation, and oppression). 3) The basic values of Peace Studies are a world-wide human perspective, desirability of achieving peace and justice, and recognition of the possibility of their achievement.[4]

The scope of peace studies is also influenced by different national cultures and priorities. To take three examples from this book, the chapters of Yamane, Oswald and Meskin show how their respective countries' histories deeply influence the peace studies agenda. For the Japanese, the 1937–45 war remains very much alive at the heart of current controversies. Yamane shows how museum exhibitions can range from radical assessments, educating the Japanese public about Japanese war crimes, to nationalist representations of Japan as victim. Oswald's article comes from a part of the world with completely different political agendas. The peace movement in Latin America grew up in the turbulent period of US-sponsored dictatorships supported by brutal para-militaries, and in the heady climate of intellectual challenges typified by Liberation Theology, urban guerrillas and dependency theory. In the new wave of democratization in the region the focus of peace activists has shifted to the intertwined issues of gender and environmental security in the context of sub-state ethnic violence and acute economic disparities. South Africa is different yet again. Meskin shows that the new state emerging from the anti-apartheid struggle appeared to embody many ideals, making unique contributions to international theory and praxis on reconciliation. However, new challenges seem almost as intractable as former ethnic ones. The struggle against AIDS, for example, connects with the daily violence against women that has become part of the way of life.

Prospects for Peace Studies in and on China

Peace studies is now an established discipline, with dozens of universities and research institutes working on a variety of issues. How may it develop in China? Peace studies or peace research in the West and Japan broadly stated arise from connections, interactions and oppositions between various groupings, particularly the academic world, peace movements, NGOs and governments and government agencies. Such connections can be quite complex; for example, many or probably most individuals in peace development agencies and academic institutions were outspoken opponents of the UK government's attack on Iraq, while at the same time reliant on UK government funding for some of their activities. As we try to delineate 'peace studies in China', one issue is that the relations between academia, grassroots movements and the state may not be a mirror image.

Although peace studies is a relatively young discipline in the West, it still has forty years' experience; in China, as a named discipline, it is virtually new in the past two or three years. In the West, peace studies is closely associated with a number of other disciplines or sub-disciplines, for example international relations, psychotherapy, legal studies or development studies. An important factor in China will perhaps be

---

4   'The Juniata Consultation on the Future of Peace Studies', *COPRED Peace Chronicle* (1986): 3–4, cited in Chapter 6 of this collection.

to discover a similar set of associations. A third element is the cultural heritage. Chinese scholars and writers are familiar with the Western socio-political tradition, and are accustomed to writing articles and books in more or less Westernized social science formats. However, thinking about issues of peace, harmony, conflict and related topics inevitably springs from deep cultural traditions embedded in different scripts, linguistic patterns, philosophies and religions.

China of course has its own intellectual and cultural heritage on peace and reconciliation which Lin and Hu explore in their chapters. Although he adopts a rather negative stance towards his own culture, Pan also initiates a debate on the concept of forgiveness and its roots in Chinese culture. Hopefully Chinese scholars will continue to explore and interpret for the rest of the world the pro-peace resources in the work of individual thinkers like Mozi and Huainanzi, and within the traditions of Daoism, Buddhism and Confucianism.

Another peace resource, if an ambivalent one, is the legacy of memories from the 1937–45 war, the 1945–49 civil war and the Cultural Revolution. China has perhaps suffered more casualties through violent conflict in the twentieth century than any other country in the world except Russia: there are estimates of some ten million casualties at the hands of the Japanese alone.[5] One would expect these tragedies to lead to a great consciousness of the futility and destruction of war, and commitment to more peaceful methods of resolving conflicts. And without doubt, one meets many Chinese who are openly committed to peace and opposed to war as a matter of principle.

Anti-war, or at least anti-Japanese, sentiment is memorialized in various places, but nowhere in a more moving fashion than in the city of Nanjing itself, where there is a Holocaust Memorial museum dedicated to the Japanese atrocities there. This museum immediately raises the question of the purpose of memorializing the massacre of Chinese civilians that took place in the city in 1937–38: is it a warning against repetition, an attempt at constructing a different attitude for the future, or a way to reproduce distrust, hatred and fear? The question is important, because China certainly also has pro-conflict as well as pro-peace heritage. On the level of common-sense or popular wisdom, the idea of nonviolence probably seems completely bizarre to the great majority of Chinese. Although Buddhism has some residual influence, it certainly did not penetrate the society in the same way as, for example, Hinduism did India or Christianity some Western cultures. There would be no real call to religiously-inspired nonviolence. On the contrary, most Chinese would probably have a common-sense, utilitarian approach to the issue, and assume that violence is unavoidable in many situations, as a lesser of two evils.

Traditional Chinese scholars did not place a high value on military valour. Chinese élite thinking distinguishes between *wen*, culture, and *wu*, military activities. The former is considered more refined, befitting a gentleman, worthwhile. However, ter

---

5　　Statistics in 'Wars, Massacres and Atrocities of the Twentieth Century' at <http://users. erols.com/mwhite28/war-1900.htm>. Other gross estimates are Soviet Union, 20 million deaths; Poland and Germany, 5 million each.

Haar, a Dutch sinologist, argues that in practice violence was and is an intrinsic part of Chinese culture, even at the élite level. Lower down the hierarchy there was a balancing concept of the *haohan*, the valiant fighter, and considerable admiration for outlaws and gangsters. The exaggerated respect for the *wen*-ideal was more a self-representation by groups of literati than a realistic reflection of society.[6] However, the army itself was rarely seen as a particularly glorious or admirable career path, nor is there much myth or literature about knights or noble warriors: in fact, soldiers are usually depicted in traditional novels as uncouth riff-raff.

The development of the Communist Party in any case radically challenged anti-military sentiments even among intellectuals. The Chinese felt deeply humiliated after the foreign invasions staged by European and then Japanese armies. Peaceful political movements failed to secure national independence, and it was only the brilliant military successes of Mao Zedong that finally led to the expulsion of first the Japanese and subsequently the pro-American nationalists. From about 1950 to 1980, and especially in the Cultural Revolution, the Red Army was in the forefront of Chinese politics, society and culture, glorified in literature and film. Many Chinese are still proud that their armed forces can ensure national independence, stand up to the USA and Japan, and ensure that China has a strong voice in the world.

Since the mid-1990s the Chinese government has invested heavily in education, including the tertiary sector. At least the top hundred universities are well up to international standards in many disciplines, although probably stronger in natural sciences than social sciences; and the dozen or so leading universities, including famous ones like Beijing University, Fudan and Nanjing University, produce a cutting edge international standard of research. In addition to universities, the state also supports a number of academies and research institutes, of which the most prestigious is the Chinese Academy of Social Sciences in Beijing.

So what might be the prospects for, and constraints on, peace studies in this academic environment, in the newly resurgent China? I would divide an answer into three components, broadly to correspond with mainstream activities of peace research in the West: 'pure' research, for example on the history and theory of conflicts and peace movements; applied research, for example training programmes in conflict management or peacekeeping, or policy recommendations; cross-fertiliion with grass-roots movements, for example with anti-war activists.

With regard to the first, I believe the prospects for research in China are excellent. Many, or most, universities have programmes in international politics, modern history, law or related areas, and I think many of them would be happy to introduce peace or conflict research onto their agendas. Westerners who have never visited China, or who do not read Chinese, often seem to be under the impression that a heavy-handed censorship operates, preventing all but the most pro-government publication from appearing. In fact, on the contrary, Chinese authors publish on a vast range of topics,

---

6   Barend J. ter Haar, 'Rethinking "Violence" in Chinese Culture' in Göran Aijmer and Jos Abbink (eds), *Meanings of Violence: a Cross Cultural Perspective* (Oxford, 2000), pp. 123–40.

ranging from studies of classical Greek philosophy or Egyptology to nano-science and almost anything in between. It is true that publishers are obliged to apply for permission before they publish a new book, but in most cases it is a mere formality. Much more pressing for authors and publishers are commercial considerations: apart from some prestige university publishing, it is a capitalist market place and authors must sell to survive. Similarly, universities are reasonably free to offer new under- and post-graduate programmes of study; the main issue is whether they can persuade students to take them. These days the impetus to study and publish in business studies, or closely related areas with good career prospects, is intense. So, the extent to which peace research and peace studies takes off in Chinese universities is, I would say, mainly a question of a level of public interest.

What kind of topics might be open to this kind of research and teaching? I believe the Chinese government and education authorities would, and in some ways already do, actively encourage the study of Japanese invasion and imperialist aggression in Asia. Likewise there should be no objection to theoretical issues, like the theory of pacificism in other countries, religious dialogue, conflict resolution skills and peacekeeping in various parts of the world. In fact such research is already going on, for example in the works of Wang Zhicheng, who has made available a thorough evaluation of the phenomenon of interreligious dialogue in numerous original works and translations; and those of Han Hongwen, who has published a substantial analysis of European and the US peace studies literature.[7] Nevertheless, it is true, admittedly, that some conflicts within China – for example social unrest in major cities or government intransigence – would need to be analysed with discretion, and it might not be easy to report research findings in formal publications.

Chinese universities are increasingly subject to funding regimes similar to those in the West, obliged to bid for financial support and to prove their worth by various kinds of output. However, for the most part, they have not yet taken the step into 'applied research', consultancies or training that many Western universities have already had to do. Their teaching is generally confined to students in the traditional age range, with adult education programmes in the evenings. Therefore we may perhaps not expect to see a large number of conflict management courses, for example, offered through universities in the near future. There are, however, exceptions to this. The most important is that a small number of key academic institutions, mostly based in Beijing, feed ideas and policy recommendations into central government, through a variety of formal and informal mechanisms including newsletters, internal reports, think-tanks, seminars, and meetings with political leaders. Likewise the same institutions train young people who are destined within a few years to join policy-making political units in the capital. It is probably in this inner circle of senior academic/political connections that peace research could perhaps make some

---

7   Wang Zhicheng, *Hepingde kewang: dangdai zongjiao duihua lilun* [Eager for Peace: Contemporary Theories of Interreligious Dialogue] (Beijing, 2003). Han Hongwen, *Ershi shijide heping yanjiu: lishixing kaocha* [Peace Research in the Twentieth Century: A Historical Investigation] (Beijing, 2002).

impact; in the same way that sophisticated models of economic development have been fed through from scholars with international expertise.

I mentioned above that the perception of some outsiders about censorship and surveillance is exaggerated or unfounded. Nevertheless, there are definite constraints on publications, and on activities that academics or researchers could undertake. I would suggest that three areas of peace studies which have featured quite prominently in the West could not at present be adopted in Chinese institutions. First, some Western peace research arises from close cooperation between academics on the one hand and mass movements or protests on the other. For example, many conferences or e-groups explicitly bring together students, peace activists, NGO workers and professors. Rees' chapter in this collection illustrates the case in Sydney. The situation of Chinese scholars with regard to cooperation may be more parallel to the big state-funded institutions in Scandinavia like the Stockholm International Peace Research Institute or the Peace Research Institute of Oslo, which are more closely tied to government agencies than to grass-roots groups, and which focus on security studies.

Second, an important aspect of peace research in the West has been the calculation and subsequent critique of government military spending, as well as monitoring of military human rights abuses, support for conscientious objectors and so on. Third, peace activists have often supported peaceful movements for regional autonomy, where an ethnic minority has demanded more independence or rights from a central government. As far as I know, Chinese academics would not feel able to take part in either of these areas of activity, at least not at present.

The case of Tibet, widely publicized in the West, is probably the best example. The issue has aroused much passion in international media, partly because of the objective facts of the situation such as human rights violations, religious persecution and environmental destruction; partly because of resonance of a mythical Shangri-La and the projection of all kinds of dreams and spiritual aspirations by often ill-informed outsiders; partly the skilful use of the media by the Dalai Lama's devotees and the political supporters of an independent Tibet. The latter also generally fail to acknowledge the tremendous gains in living standards and life expectancy under communist rule, and some make irresponsible statements about an alleged genocide of Tibetans – a claim for which there is no evidence. The historical context of Sino–Tibetan relations, complicated by English and Russian rivalry in Central Asia, the political history of Mongol–Tibetan–Han control over the Tibetan plateau, the nature of the Tibetan theocracy before 1949, and, in short, the legitimacy of various forms of government in that vast region, are in reality extremely complex issues. It would be foolish to expect a simple solution to them. I have no solution either, but my main point here is that, in my view, Chinese peace researchers would simply find this whole topic 'off-limits' in current circumstances. I do not believe any university or research institute in China would undertake research directed at finding a peaceful solution, nor would they allow staff to participate in international research projects. The Chinese government views this particular issue as a threat to territorial integrity and national sovereignty, and as such fundamentally closed to comment. If a deal is ever to be made, it will be made by the central government, not brokered by outside observers.

On balance we can expect that Chinese scholars will make important contributions to conceptualization of peace and security. Several of the chapters in this collection begin to point out some themes. To anticipate for a moment, Oswald's report notes that Brazil, Russia, India and China form a new economic configuration known as BRIC, the impact of which on geo-politics suggests that the Chinese leadership has been making a partial re-think of traditional security concepts. Hu's chapter on reconciliation shows a typically Chinese concern for balance and compromise, in this case between liberty and stability; and Lin's discussion of Hong Kong and Macao is a case-study on a similar topic.

How might Western peace researchers approach questions related to China? First, given the general profound ignorance about China in Western academia, one hopes that much of it will be conducted as joint Sino–Western projects or programmes. Two issues for research stand out immediately. One is the inevitable tension arising from China's remarkable economic growth. In 2005, for example, there was a crisis in EU–China relations owing to textile imports from the latter, cheaper than EU products, which threatened European manufacturing. There are bound to be continuing disputes about intellectual property, market access and many other questions that will have to be decided by negotiation. On a favourable note, Western academics are starting to analyse China's development trajectory, to see how it might become a role model for other developing countries.[8] More than that, China will become a major aid-donor and possibly a provider of serious numbers of peacekeeping forces to the UN. All these activities will mean that Chinese policy-makers will have to face many of the issues arising in donor politics, nonviolent troop deployments and so on.

Finally one cannot rule out serious military confrontations between China and other countries, despite China's good track record so far of avoiding them. As we see in the next section, there are a number of unstable positions in Asian politics. The study of international peace management may be a high priority for East Asia.

Conflict and Peace Potentials in China

Assuming peace and conflict studies develop in China, which actual situations or potentials may they take up as research areas? It would surely be meaningful and interesting for non-Chinese to read about Chinese philosophies and their views on peace and related topics, as raised by some chapters in this collection. There must also be a rich heritage of case-studies to reveal, of processes of peaceful change and conflict management both from classical China and from contemporary society.

Another area for research could be the question of regime change, or at least of political process. The Chinese government itself is well-informed and politically

---

8   For example, the Institute of Development Studies at Sussex University has a major research programme in this area.

sophisticated, aware of the events that shook East Europe and the Soviet Union since the late 1980s. It has frequently used the media to persuade the Chinese population that such change is not always for the best: there have been numerous TV reports of civil war in the former Yugoslavia, terrorism and economic chaos in Russia, and so on. The Chinese government seems to be willing to undertake a process of gradual, incremental change in the direction of democracy, painfully slow, flawed perhaps, but carefully managed. Despite periodic setbacks, this process has been going on for several years, leading already, for example, to elections at local level for official positions. Given the overwhelming preponderance of the CCP in all walks of life remotely connected with politics, though, one expects this process to last for a long time. Any eventual regime change, in the sense of relinquishing power to a different party, would take place in the indefinite future, barring surprise events. Nevertheless, it will surely be a process worth studying.

A more immediate question is how the Chinese government handles the numerous contradictions and conflicts inherent in the business of governing a 1.3 billion population. Some issues are already apparent, while others must be about to appear soon. One is the stark increase in polarization, with rapidly growing disparities in wealth, education, health-care, housing and other indicators. It is true that almost the whole country has seen a rise in living standards, with hundreds of millions of people lifted out of extreme poverty in the past two decades. But real affluence is still restricted to key groups, for example successful urbanites; farmers with access to land, water and markets; and often local politicians and power-brokers who have been able to cash in on the economic boom. There are still gross inequalities, with some of the poorest people being migrants to cities, peasants who have lost their homes, minority peoples who have been chased off to sub-standard land, and those who live in drought regions. Other victims of the economic boom have been, for example, the countless thousands who have suffered illness or accident in appalling working conditions.

As well as dealing with issues of social exclusion and poverty, the government may increasingly have to deal with conflicts over access to resources like water or land, and over environmental protection issues. The dramatic growth of economic activity, especially manufacturing, has already led to intense pressure on farming land. One sees numerous reports, letters and complaints in China about farmers selling land to industrial concerns – either freely, to make money; or under pressure from local bosses – leading to significant shrinkage of prime agricultural land. Similarly, there is and will increasingly be intense competition for power and natural resources including water. As in other countries, the state will have to mediate between different sectors of the economy, some of which are extremely powerful.

Internationally China already has to handle trade disputes, for example tariff and quota negotiations. Perhaps more tendentious will prove Chinese business activities in regions which were previously regarded as US spheres of influence. Two obvious cases are Latin America and West Asia. In the past few years Chinese investment in Latin and South America has increased greatly, particularly in mineral extraction to feed China's manufacturing boom. Similarly there has been talk of a new 'alliance' of some kind, with China to become a major partner of Saudi Arabia and other oil-producers in West Asia. It is hard to foresee if the USA would be willing to allow China to displace it in these parts of the world where it has dominated the scene for such a long time. On a more traditional security agenda, China also has to handle acute military tensions in Asia, for example the probable collapse of North Korea, the China–Japan dispute over territory and resources, Sino–Russian and Sino–Indian border disputes, and the political conflict with Taiwan. Many of these issues could be compounded by US antagonism to Chinese economic growth and political influence.

Finally, environmental issues such as resource competition and eco-degradation may have an impact not only internally but also on China's relations with neighbours: for example, there has been talk of diverting rivers flowing from the Tibetan plateau which would impact water supplies into India or Vietnam. On a more general note, of course, there is world-wide concern at the growth in greenhouse gases and other pollutants in China, India and other industrializing countries.

The Rationale of this Collection

As mentioned at the start of this introduction, these chapters derive from papers presented at a conference in Nanjing, the main purpose of which was for Chinese scholars to share peace studies perspectives with other researchers. Scholars contributed to this process by providing an overview of peace studies as a varied international discipline. It would be ideal if one could include similar reports from all countries which engage in peace research, but with the current range of institutions involved, that would mean studies from at least a dozen other countries: Germany, India, Spain, Sweden and many others. The present selection provides a starting point, a wide ranging analysis of research in Mexico, Japan, the USA, the UK and South Africa. Professor Úrsula Oswald goes beyond her Latin American theme to present a wealth of information both about the history of peace studies and about cutting-edge research on new security concepts. Since peace research is well represented on the internet, readers could further pursue the theme for themselves.

These overviews are complemented by three short articles of a more reflective nature. It was a particular honour that Professor Johan Galtung agreed to attend the Nanjing conference. His contribution offers a unique personal insight into peace studies from the person who, most estimate, founded the discipline in its current form nearly fifty years ago. Johansen, a Scandinavian researcher and activist presents an issue that lies close to the heart of many successful social movements: nonviolence. And at our request, Stuart Rees, Director of the Sydney Peace Prize Foundation, writes an account of the practical issues involved in setting up a successful centre and a prestigious peace prize.

The study of peace, conflict management and related topics may be crucial for Chinese and international security, so this collection presents a number of articles by Chinese scholars, selected to show a range of ideas and approaches. Liu shows his remarkable grasp of British politics, explaining fine details of the Cook/Blair PR manipulations – illegal invasion in the name of ethics – that led to the disastrous war in Iraq. Qian, from a case-study of British parliamentary reforms, argues that negotiated peaceful transitions from absolutism to democracy are feasible. Lin provides a comparative analysis of developments in Hong Kong and Macao, raising an issue that should be, but is not universally self-evident: that China may develop forms of governance that are liberal, effective and acceptable to its population, but not necessarily democratic in the Western sense.

Finally, two rather unusual reflective chapters on forgiveness and reconciliation are included – by Professors Pan and Hu respectively – to show how these ideas, with inputs from East and West, appear to contemporary Chinese thinkers. Chinese writers and academics today do enjoy a large measure of freedom of expression. But quite apart from any residual political sensitivities, they write in a cultural environment that is different from the West. As readers will know from traditional Chinese art and poetry, there is a certain Chinese subtlety that prefers to leave things unsaid, that enjoys ambiguity and irony, and that writes apparently about one situation in order to turn the reader's attention to another. Readers of these chapters can decide for themselves whether the 'Hong Kong', or 'Britain', or 'Christian forgiveness' of these chapters are literal, allusive or both.

Several authors used internet sources, including reports on the Chinese-language BBC news website. They are referenced in footnotes but not in the Bibliography, and were all accessible at time of editing, November 2005, unless otherwise stated.

The study of peace takes many forms and is continually evolving, as evidenced by the diversity of chapters in this collection. One thing that would be very valuable to the discipline would certainly be more cultural diversity. Peace studies has mostly, although not exclusively, emerged from Western universities and movements. Among other things, Western society is often perceived as valuing the individual rather than the collective, the material rather than the spiritual, formal rather than informal processes. An example sometimes given is that two Westerners in dispute would usually rather have a third-party mediator who is a stranger to both of them, perceived as 'neutral'. People from many other cultures would prefer to have a trusted and respected person known to both parties, perhaps a community elder. Another example is that rural populations in many countries may perceive violent conflict as caused by evil spirits which need ritual exorcism by traditional ceremonies. Westerners may know little or nothing about how to operate in these environments: abstract talk about forgiveness and reconciliation could be completely incomprehensible and meaningless in the particular context. As seen in this collection, the theory and practice of peace-making is now a global undertaking. One of the most hopeful developments, in my opinion, is that Chinese scholars take a deep interest in the theory and practice of peace studies, conflict transformation, reconciliation and related areas. The world undoubtedly has much to learn from both traditional and contemporary China, with the heritage of its religion and philosophy, the subtleties of Chinese interpersonal skills and the – hopefully continuing – commitment to non-interference in foreign countries' internal affairs.

Chapter 1

Peace Studies: A Ten Point Primer

Johan Galtung

The world's biggest country, based on one of the world's oldest civilizations, soon also with the world's biggest economy, is having a serious look at peace studies. That will be a small step for China, but a major one for us who have been working in this field for almost fifty years. In this chapter I have been given the task of reflecting on the field of peace studies, something I will do with the warning that what you get from me is one person's perspective. Others will have other perspectives. We can enter this field from many angles, and it is important that we do so. Peace studies, like anything else, is a process. It has to be born and reborn, again and again. Our colleagues in Coventry University have entered the field via reconciliation. No doubt China will put its particular imprints on it, and I cannot wait! How will the Daoist, Confucian, Buddhist and other traditions find their ways into the field, and how will the daunting task of coming to grips with peace conceptually, theoretically, practically reshape them? How will the experience of China, between the Tundra, the Gobi desert, the Himalayas and the China sea, with almost no military excursions outside, but the subject of several incursions, with the Nanjing massacre by the Japanese Imperial Army as a major example, impact on peace studies?

So, here follow five short descriptions, and five elaborations:

1. Peace studies explore handling of conflict by peaceful means.

Another word for peace is equality. And other words for equality are equity, symmetry, reciprocity, equal rights, equal dignity. You can see them as part of the definition of peace, or of the peaceful means. As such they are necessary rather than sufficient conditions. Equality, equity, symmetry do not guarantee peace. But inequality, lack of equity, and so on almost guarantee the opposite: direct violence, in one form or another, physical or verbal, directed against the body, mind or spirit of human beings. And inequalities are also parts of structural violence, meaning that absence of structural violence is a necessary condition for the absence of direct violence.

Most people agree that peace is more than the mere absence of direct violence also found in a battlefield after the fighting is over. The word 'justice' is often used for this 'more', as in 'peace with justice'. But 'justice' is ambiguous and has to be supported by adjectives like punitive, restorative and transitional. I can see the pragmatism of giving 'peace' to the political left and 'justice' to the right, hoping to come out neutral, supported by both. But the intellectual quality of such manoeuvres is low.

'Another word for peace is equality' gives to peace a progressive connotation and explains why it is so often resisted on the right, including resisting peace studies. In practice, however, peace is not that radical but rather expresses common sense, a world with less insult to the basic needs for survival, well-being, freedom and identity – meaning with life – and without the inequality, inequity, and so on that generate these insults.

Peace is similar to health, a rich *summum bonum* which we can fill with new meanings. Violence, like disease, is suffering. And peace, like health, is liberation from suffering and fulfilment.

2. Peace studies are empirical, critical and constructive.

As empirical studies, peace studies, like any other field of inquiry, collect data, construct hypotheses, and then compare data and hypotheses to conclude in terms of true, false, both–and, neither–nor. The standards for this activity should be as rigorous as in any other field of study. It is worth noting that empirical studies by necessity are past-oriented as only the past can produce data. Of course, we can make more or less well founded predictions about the future, but they remain hypotheses till the future becomes past with data that can be used to check hypotheses.

As critical studies, peace studies do the same as critics of human behaviour – moral philosophers, priests, criminal judges – do, compare data with values related one way or the other to peace, and then conclude in terms of right, wrong, both–and, neither–nor. For this the criteria have to be explicit and the comparison carried out with the same rigor as in any other field. Art critics are important 'human behaviour critics', an important activity serving as a guide to good art and literature for artists and users. Critical peace studies do the same for politicians and people.

As constructive studies, peace studies would not shy away from making recommendations, the 'therapy' part of the useful diagnosis–prognosis–therapy triangle taken from health studies. Expectations from therapy can then be held against values relating to peace to conclude in terms of adequate, inadequate, both–and, neither–nor.

The peace researcher should ideally be up to all three tasks. The empirical studies should fully respect the canons of research, the critical studies should be based both on adequate reasoning from value premises and on adequate data, and the recommendations both on explicit values and well tested theories. Not always easy.

3. Like health studies peace studies are an applied science.

Imagine a person suffering badly from some disease, barely able to come to the office of a famous physician. The person is duly examined and at the end the doctor expresses his gratitude for offering a case that will be written up in a forthcoming article. 'But what are you going to do to cure me?' the 'case' asks. 'Cure? Nothing, I am a scientist, I am objective, value neutral'.

Fortunately we are better served today by maybe as many as forty-four health professions. The constructive connection between the value of health, well specified and reasonably well grounded hypotheses about what can be foreseen as the result of an intervention has been made; again and again, often successfully, sometimes not. Peace studies should be able to deliver the same, at the same level of adequacy, through conflict transformation, peace-building, peacekeeping, reconciliation to mention some approaches. Let many peace professions grow; mediators, conciliators, and so on and so forth.

But what if we, like health professionals, do not succeed, and even make mistakes? Then we should be accountable and not – like so many economists with misleading diagnosis (because they cut the issue wrongly), prognosis far off the mark (because they take too few factors into account) and highly unsuccessful therapy/remedy (for the above reasons) – get off with impunity. They cannot get off the hook, blaming politicians who execute plans developed by peace or economy specialists. Adding to the predicament come politicians who would rather go wrong with a war than with a peace, like the politician who would rather go wrong with growth than distribution. Growth, like aggressive war, seems to need less legitimatization than peace and distribution. So better be careful, never do what cannot be undone, you may be on a wrong track. Violence is irreversible.

4. Peace studies are trans- rather than interdisciplinary.

As women's studies make women and their conditions of suppression and liberation visible, peace studies make peace visible, understandable, obtainable. No academic discipline has any monopoly on peace, just as little as they have any monopoly of women – but all disciplines have something to contribute.

As a rule, in a good peace researcher the PhD field is no longer visible. There are often four stages on this road.

In the multi-disciplinary stage a university, or a conference, invites specialists from several disciplines to contribute to peace studies from their angle. People or disciplines who never meet because our universities fragment human knowledge, keep us apart fighting for funds and recognition, learn the art of tolerance.

In the interdisciplinary stage a university or a conference encourages dialogue among approaches, an obvious method being to address the same event or phase in history, or the same problem.

In the cross-disciplinary stage this dialogue goes further, into mutual learning. A psychologist may pick up a sociological hypothesis about status disequilibrium (like high on education, low on power) as aggression productive and explore the psychology; a sociologist may explore the social effects of cognitive consonance as 'peace of mind'. Usually such explorations are bilateral.

In the trans-disciplinary stage, based on the preceding three or not, the problem itself determines the choice of intellectual tools, and they will usually have to come from the tool chests of several disciplines, as is the case for health studies. But in this process other disciplines will also learn and change. Historians, for instance, will focus more on peace and on how war could have been avoided; economists more on survival and equity, and so on.

5. Peace studies are trans- rather than inter-national.

Peace studies in Europe, a very belligerent and aggressive continent, emerge mainly outside the big powers' capitals and 'universities of excellence', which study 'security'. The discipline started in the Nordic countries, although Spain (Barcelona), Italy (Firenze), Austria (European Peace University) and England (Bradford) are today more important. But no country has a monopoly, nor does any gender, generation, race, class, nation. As peace belongs to all of us so do peace studies.

This is important because the study of peace is so intimately related to the study of conflict. About conflict we know something for sure: each actor in a conflict has his own angle. The conflict always looks different looked at from different angles. Hence we have to listen to all parties, understanding what they want, to sort between legitimate and illegitimate, using, for instance, human rights as a measure, and then try to bridge the gap between legitimate goals. Such is the approach taught at TRANSCEND, our independent, transnational university. All parties to a conflict have equal rights to be understood, but not the same right to be accepted and supported. That depends on legitimacy.

Ideally a peace research team should be not only interdisciplinary but also international, each participant listening to the other angles in a spirit of tolerance, entering into dialogue. The cross-national stage of mutual learning, reciprocity, will then follow, adding more depth to the analysis of the conflict. And this is exactly what China invites the USA to do in connection with human rights, publishing a yearbook on human rights in the USA, now in its sixth edition. Let us approach such problems cross-nationally, in a spirit of equality, and the way we study peace is already peace. Any pretence at having a monopoly on understanding reality is violence, aggression; in this case cultural violence.

6. Violence, insults to the basic needs of body, mind and spirit, is caused by unresolved conflict and polarization = dehumanization of human and social relations.

That is a basic hypothesis linking conflict and peace. Conflicts have to be solved; human and social relations to be depolarized = humanized; and the cycle of 'violence breeding violence' to be controlled, basically nonviolently, also with healing of traumas and closure through reconciliation. Toward this end peace studies train mediators for conflict resolution and transformation and conciliators for reconciliation, to mention two specialties in the field of peace work. We know a lot about this.

And there is an enormous demand for such peace workers, more than for peace researchers, and much amateurishness and denial that there may be something to study and learn before leaping into practice. One example, often found in Anglo-American approaches, is an inability to distinguish between conflict and violence. Both are seen as shocks to be managed and controlled. Thus there is talk about 'post-conflict reconciliation' where 'post-violence' would be appropriate. Conflict is ubiquitous, forever, violence is not.

The two concepts are different. Violence is to hurt and harm, insulting basic human needs. Conflict is a state of incompatible goals, within and between persons, societies, regions, the world. Another word is contradiction. That is a challenge, and the Anglo-American tradition is unwilling to assume that there could be contradictions even in their social and world orders. Their term 'dispute' does not cover the depth, nor does, indeed, 'trouble'. Anglo-Americans lay down rules and demand that people follow them.

So there is conflict before violence, and more easily solved before than after. And ceasefire, armistice is not peace; peace is much more complex. Politicians and journalists, please take note.

7. In security studies violence is seen as caused by evil forces, like dangerous classes and inferior races/religions/ideologies 'out to get us', and the remedy is to have enough strength to deter or destroy those forces.

A parallel in traditional health studies was disease seen as caused by Satan or God's punishment for evil. The remedy was strength as faith, to resist all evil, and to believe in God, the Church and in authorities in general. One problem with modern hygiene and simple rules to stay healthy was less need for the Church. We have something of the same in today's struggle between peaceful conflict transformation and the reliance on court systems, governments and the UN Security (not Peace) Council.

This security discourse stands in the way of a rational approach to peace. The remedies offered are two: to be strong enough to deter and/or to crush those forces of evil, as we see it all over the world in the Anglo-American effort to deal with terrorism or tyranny. The net result is a security state like a fortress and much, much killing, all over. Very primitive.

8. Disease can be seen as an unresolved contradiction between exposure to pathogens and the resistance capacity of an organism, and violence as unresolved contradictions among the goals of parties in a conflict.

Equilibrium/disequilibrium thinking was basic to Chinese medicine. Then came the idea of some microbes hiding somewhere, 'out to get us', and the remedy was to be strong, building up our immune system, if necessary through outside assistance in the shape of inoculation. I guess most of us believe in that. But I wonder if health studies could not learn something by studying the phenomenon also from the micro-organism point of view? Chinese medicine saw health as natural and many thinkers saw peace = harmony the same way. These are very important perspectives.

9. Major sources of violence in the twenty-first century are globalized, privatized, monetized capitalism; the US empire expanding that system also by military means including the encircling of Russia–China–India (40 per cent of humanity); the contradiction between 2,000 nations, 200 states and 20 nation–states basically with one nation; violence against women through selective abortion, infanticide, discrimination; and among the Abrahamic religions Judaism, Christianity and Islam, and them and other world views.

Peaceful solutions include better distribution/alternative economic systems; boycott of the US empire; confederations (East Asian Community) among states and federations (like Switzerland) inside states; gender parity; civilization dialogue.

There are many pointers in such directions in the *China Daily* these days, coinciding with the 10th National Committee of the Chinese People's Political Consultative Conference. There is talk of social development, gender equality, social harmony, how to calculate ecological costs (cutting China's growth rate by 2 per cent) all over the Chinese newspapers. The many people standing in line to deliver protests and suggestions to authorities come to mind, and it is not obvious that 'idea democracy' is inferior to 'arithmetic democracy', but it depends, of course, on who in fact has the last word.

I also welcome the White Paper 'Regional Autonomy for Ethnic Minorities in China'. And I deplore the hypocrisy of countries criticizing an anti-secession law. How would Washington react to a declaration of independence from Hawai'i? Or Paris to Corsica; England relative to Ireland or parts of Ireland we already know. And yet I feel China would be better off as some kind of decentralized federation linking Beijing to Taiwan, Hong Kong/Macao, Inner Tibet, Xinjiang and Inner Mongolia. Let us have a good dialogue!

10. Peace studies focus less on actors, more on deep cultures and structures and how they affect mediation and conciliation.

I wonder if the next stage in the history of this amazing country may be a turn toward cultural rather than economic development, and in addition to the much needed economic distribution? The focus on economics is also a focus on materialism and a country that seems to change, and even basically so, every nine years (1949, 1958, 1966–69, 1976–80, 1989, 1998 and perhaps in 2007?) might well also turn from material to the more spiritual. As any student of China knows, there is much to draw upon in the historical tradition, and even more important, in the enormous creativity of today's Chinese people.

There has been much focus on the role of structure for peace, particularly of gender and class relations. The time has come for much more focus on culture, and not only in the sense of religion.

Thus, what is the secret behind the outer peacefulness of the 'Kingdom in the Middle', the *Zhongguo*? The USA, following the English tradition of watching the second biggest, has already appointed China its natural enemy, and the 'Project for the New American Century' talks about changing the regime in China. The aggressiveness is unbelievable instead of doing the obvious, which would be not only to act with tolerance but to engage in dialogue and mutual learning like the Chinese do. We are all anxiously watching how the only surviving superpower and the 'Kingdom in the Middle' relate to each other.

If the USA thinks it has the right to create Free Trade Areas in Latin America, China has the same right with Japan and the Korean Peninsula in East Asia. Of course, Japan has to reconcile, revise its textbooks, and apologize deeply for Nanjing. Might Nanjing become a possible centre for an East Asian Community, for peace and prosperity? And the suffering would make some sense.

Chapter 2

Towards a Politics of Reconciliation

Hu Chuansheng

Movements in Modern Politics

The political movement has become the typical vehicle for modern politics, mainly due to the global expansion of Western practices. To contemporary Western readers, the role of the movement – or party, or pressure-group – may simply appear as a natural, intrinsic component of political life. At other periods of history, and in some non-Western cultures, the role and legitimacy of such movements are far from self-evident. This chapter explores two main issues: the role of the political movement, and specifically how it might be harmonized within other political traditions. I use the term 'reconciliation' to discuss an approach to politics which fully appreciates the values of Western liberalism, but which is also alert to some of its risks.

Modern political movements have two aspects, the first of which is ideology. A political movement usually has an ideology in which the basic viewpoints remain more or less stable, although subject to updating. This ideologically-driven politics is different from government in traditional society. In societies like imperial China or feudal Europe, for example, political ideas were essentially in a different category from concepts concerning nature or the cosmos. Traditionally people were permitted, or even encouraged, to hold a variety of ideas about the meaning of life, or the essence of the cosmos, or the philosophy of art. In politics, on the contrary, only one idea ruled: there was a singular answer to such questions as what political system is reasonable? What is the origin of authority? What is public duty? What is the good society? Society for the most part accepted only one obvious, authoritative situation, defining who ought to have the power, who ought to issue orders and execute them, and who must be obedient. Traditional politics were non-participatory: people – usually men – had a share in power because of blood relationship, or in some cases after passing the most rigid selection, for instance in China through recommendations in the Han dynasty and examination in the Tang dynasty. The 'common people' generally understood that politics is the business of governors, and they regarded themselves as the ones governed. Not that government was necessarily morally flawed or conducted with evil intentions, for example in the classical Chinese tradition Confucius regards politics as rule by moral principles (*wei zheng yi de*) and set great store on justice and other virtues. The common people simply had no connection with politics. Then apparently for the first time, in Western societies after the Renaissance, all kinds of political movements arose following the ideals of social visionaries: the desire to realize ideas, the eagerness to change society, and the operation of what Rawls calls 'reason in the free environment', which comprised a main component of Western political history after the seventeenth century.[1]

The second aspect is group orientation. The mode of modern political life is for groups or parties publicly to argue their case to realize reform plans by using social resources; to make points to the political power-holders; or to make the authorities, as well as the general public, hear their demands by means of organized publicity. In Western society, political organizations try to turn their aspirations into reality by competing for power and then controlling it. In less stable areas regime change may be achieved by violence. In general, the more liberal the national community is towards political movements, the more likely the movements will basically be loyal to the community. On the contrary, the more that governments curtail political movements, the more devastating the movements will become. In the West, although political movements may harm society to some extent, their existence is still regarded almost as a sacred right. Typical examples are the tolerance in the EU even for quasi-Nazi and all kinds of religious extremist organizations.

Various kinds of political movements contribute to modern politics. However, generally the main landscape of both national and international politics currently includes movements for human rights, liberal democracy, social idealism, and also for religious dominance. The human rights movement aims to set up democratic systems similar to the EU or the USA: its ideology is liberalism, and it holds that the basis of society is the protection of the common people's rights. Somewhat differing from classical liberalism's concern for life and wealth, modern liberalism places more emphasis on freedom of speech, the right to uncensored political debate, and a robust, free system of elections for political power. Undoubtedly this kind of liberty is the foundation of the European and North American political systems. In the long run political liberty within a democratic system of governance may be the best choice for global society; at least now in the twenty-first century it seems very difficult to argue for an alternative, and there does not seem to be any end in sight for the advantages of democracy.[2]

On the other hand, the liberalist agenda has also become a troublesome, worrying element in modern international politics, because the West, especially the USA, insists on installing clone regimes elsewhere in the world. There are serious drawbacks here. For example, many places may lack basic systemic pre-conditions for democracy; and people may become over-idealistic about US or European ways. In some cases the Western powers, especially the USA, may support various 'citizenship' movements, whose main objective is to set up an electoral system. However, these citizenship groups may also become a kind of secret political movement subject to manipulation. Some élites may turn against their government, undermining relatively

---

1   See John G. Rawls, *Political Liberalism* (Cambridge, 1990), especially Chapter 1.

2   At least it appears so under the *Pax Americana* thesis. The 'The End of History' slogan is a now notorious over-simplification of global dynamics. Francis Fukuyama, *The End of History and the Last Man* (New York, 1992).

effective public welfare systems before any new regime is able to improve them. Their self-sacrifice and high spirit of idealism may have positive outcomes, but they may also deepen social divides and increase the social cost of modernization.

Compared with this, two other ideological trends – utopianism and religious fundamentalism – form a marked contrast to the human rights, liberalist and Western democratic positions. The movement to create a way of life based on the ideal of a perfect society on the one hand represents a continuity, building on all kinds of social ideas of 'saving the world', because almost all civilizations have a rich heritage of ideas about Utopia, the perfect society. On the other hand, it is also a sincere attempt at transcendence of the Western democratic system. In the modern world, however, there has really only been one political movement based on a utopian perfectionist concept, in theory at least, that achieved any measurable power in the 'real world': and that was communism. Communists sincerely believe, to put it very simply, that the capitalist life-style and the totally free political system cannot solve the many problems faced by human society; and on the contrary will make them worse. After a century's combat and experiment, however, the communist movement is at an unprecedented nadir, challenged by citizenship movements both inside countries with Communist Party governments, and more widely in other states.

When the West builds up its hegemony in the world by the power of its ideas and its material wealth, it impacts the life-styles of other civilizations. For example, Western hegemony calls forth the Islamic fundamentalist movements, who demand the right to retain their cultural community and to keep their religion pure. In this active movement they take extreme forms to show their loyalty to the religion and life-style, and their terrorist methodology drives the West to resort to military power. This extreme way to solve the civilizations' conflict – terrorism against massive military deployments – may extend to the inner heart of all cultures and lead to extreme danger.

Ideologies

Various kinds of political movements combine to form a modern political environment. It is true that political movements offer many possibilities for positive well-being in human existence. However, not only anarchy and dictatorship, but also a Western-interpreted liberalism, despite its undoubted benefits, may also endanger our human species' political community. A kind of bottom-lined, coexistent and compromising politics must be initiated in order that the political movements may be active but more constrained. Such a development could extend welfare and open up potentials, but also reduce the harm done to human beings.

Liberalism, seeking equal political rights for all, is the main-stream ideology in modern society. However, it is only one of many political movements in modern history, and by itself cannot provide an adequate political framework for the whole of the international community. Why not? Obviously it is a specific set of political game-rules which developed in Western culture, with a particular background and a very complex historical origin. Certainly it has earned the respect of many outside the Western cultural sphere, but we should nevertheless attempt to analyse liberalism as a historically specific development – and I do not mean doing this only to justify some anti-democratic stance; and we might admit the possibility that in some parts of the world, with massive populations, the majority of people do not at all accept Western life-styles or politics.

One of two peculiar characteristics is that many people in countries all over the world fully support their own nation–state, perhaps seeing it as a symbol of safety or coherence. This attitude seems to have prevailed even in Greece or Rome, at the roots of Western democracy. That is, liberalism's view of the state as 'the necessary evil' and the natural enemy of personal freedom is as far away from Aristotle and Cicero as from Confucius. In the course of history it is difficult to find many examples of citizens' firm belief that they can and should strictly restrain the power of the state, that a system of checks and balances should constrain state authority. For most people such a view would simply contradict common sense. Of course, high officials in Athens or Rome, especially executive officials, might be found guilty of misconduct; or to use an anachronistic expression, they might violate the terms of citizenship. That such individuals should be removed from office, their power removed, is a concept that might not have been altogether alien to their contemporaries. However, it would have been difficult for them to accept that a kind of abstract state-power, a Hobbesian Leviathan, was an intrinsic enemy of the citizens.

For the people of ancient Athens and Rome the state represented public welfare to the benefit of all citizens. The commonwealth, *res publica*, was the ideal, acceptable form of governance. Undoubtedly Roman republicanism did implement some checks on different branches of the state, but they were based on a kind of different political philosophy: not to limit state power because the state is inherently evil, but rather to enhance republican power by mediating between different groupings.

The other point is that some who oppose the West do not agree with the selection of high officials by a competitive process and voting, which is regarded as one of the main principles of modern democracy. Socrates and Cicero both criticized the selection of high officials by a random lottery, but some of their contemporaries did not agree with open electioneering for a variety of reasons.

I also believe that neither utopianism nor religious purism, of any kind, can be a framework for contemporary global politics. These two kinds of movements or ideologies themselves are particularistic compared with the citizenship movement that is trying to establish dominance in the whole world. Back in the nineteenth century fervent supporters of such movements might hold that they would be global masters at some day in the future; but at present, apart from some fanatics, they have to accept realistic limitations, and they can only hope to coexist with other world-views.

Reconciliation East and West

The bottom-line politics that could offer a successful basic framework for the modern world can be called the politics of reconciliation or 'reconciliation politics'. Reconciliation politics would definitely tolerate but would also set some limits on the theories and practices of modern movements. It differs from traditional management or dictatorial politics. It also differs from the extreme liberalist position that unconditionally opposes constraints and that aims for complete liberty. We have to protect ourselves against the high risk factors that have emerged in modern politics. So we seem to be re-visiting old ideas for new understandings. It may be useful to attend to two cultural resources: one, to the ancient 'pure' ideas associated with classical culture, and the other, to turn to daily life, to find some regulatory factors in the everyday world with its ordinary language.

He (harmony) is an important idea in Chinese culture. Like referents to most key concepts in any culture, *he* is an important term in philosophical or religious discourse, and equally an ordinary word in common use. On the interpersonal level in daily life, *he* means that people can get along well with each other, they are prepared to make adjustments and compromises, on the whole they make an effort to enjoy each others' company. Many Chinese novels and films, or better still, the lived experience of daily life at the popular level in China, reveal that Chinese people seem to spend a lot of time socializing, sometimes squabbling, then sorting out their differences, in a more-or-less good humoured kind of way. Of course, the huge population and limited housing stock means that people inevitably live in very close proximity. Social mobility was quite restricted in China until the 1990s, so the majority of families simply lived for decades in the same village or apartment block, cheek-by-jowl with the same neighbours. The same contiguity usually pertained in work-places. We have a rather un-translatable phrase describing this feeling: '*renqing hen nong*', which approximately means a situation where human relationships/feelings run very deep: for example, where a group of people have, for some reason, travelled together down life's road for a while, trying, not always successfully, to help each other out or at least not to be too antagonistic.

The single ideogram *he* is frequently found in two-ideogram collocations, for example *hejie* and *heping*. As is usual in Chinese, the new word formed in this way retains the meaning of the component *he*, but refines and extends it with the meaning of the other component. Let us consider some examples. *Hejie* is probably the closest in meaning to 'reconciliation' in English, conveying the idea of recovering good relationships between persons after quarrels. *Hemu*, friendship between persons or nations, refers to the ideal relationship in the community, so it can carry positive resonances, perhaps similar to concord or amity; or, at a minimum, a recognition of coexistence. The collocation of the two ideograms *he* and *ping* is interesting. *Heping*, harmony and equality/tranquillity, generally used as the equivalent for the English word 'peace', is in my opinion one of the most beautiful Chinese words. When the order is reversed, *pinghe* refers to morality and personal qualities which mean no conflicts in an individual's inner world. *Heqi* means showing a kind attitude towards others. The idea is that if a person holds a high position, is held in public esteem, or regarded as very intelligent and successful, he or she should still be calm and considerate to others, even when they oppose him or hold different ideas. Finally, *wenhe* – leniency – is the political attitude the liberalist might appreciate most. In ordinary life it means that a person is kind, moral and accommodating; in politics it means that a person shows restraint when confronting severe quarrels or violent conflicts.

Thus Chinese has quite a few words containing the meaning of reconciliation. Admittedly, many of these words are modern coinages, and some of them are perhaps directly influenced by the understanding of non-Chinese concepts. However, they have become standard words in modern spoken and literary Chinese, they are embedded in everyday life, and they also perhaps are an example of well-known Chinese characteristics: an effort to be accommodating when dealing with personal relationships, and a certain willingness to accept ideas from other cultures into our own culture. On the more sophisticated level of religion and philosophy, peace in the Chinese tradition develops more the kind of idea that we are a part of the cosmos and participate in its development, and then we become one part of this process. But I feel the concept of peace in politics is in a different sphere of application from religion, so we can better take daily life as a starting point for its conceptualization.

As far as I understand, the term 'reconciliation' originates from Latin and is used in Latin-derived languages. A primary meaning is a transaction to re-establish a close relationship between counter-parts and groups in conflict. Its second meaning is to settle or resolve disputes, which always involves a third party or witness. Similar to the Chinese meaning, to reconcile also means to make compatible or consistent. Even though the word is Latin, we find the concept discussed in Greek philosophy.

Before Socrates many Greek philosophers thought there were two powers in the universe, love and hate. Socrates himself seriously considered how to reconcile this problem. According to Socrates, if brothers quarrelling with each other want to reconcile, they must dissolve their hostility and show kindness. In his opinion, position and wealth are unreliable, so kindness is a more important factor in human relationships. Compared with kindness and concord among people, material rewards are far less important and one should be willing to compromise on them. On this basis Socrates convinced Chaerecrates to attempt reconciliation with his brother.[3] According to Socrates, the best way to convince a clever person is to show him kindness, which is very different from the modern opinion that persuading them of their personal advantage should be the deciding factor.

Political life in the classical Mediterranean did reflect some spirit of reconciliation. In Greece one of the law-makers' important duties was to mediate social contradictions, to invent more tolerant systems to protect or represent various benefits. Because of this mediation Greek city–states frequently invited neutral, talented law-makers, often outsiders, to make laws for their own polity. The reforms

---

3   Xenophon, *Memorabilia*, ii, 3, 15–18 (English translation at <http://classics.mit.edu/Xenophon/xen.mem.html>).

of Solon – a successful Athenian reformer who was invited to legislate in other city–states – were some of the most famous examples. Similarly, Roman republican ideals to some extent originated from Plato, a Greek, whose ideas were explicated by Cicero. In Plato's opinion, the state or republic should be a commonwealth, instead of a violent tool owned by one class or group to dominate others. The commonwealth in Greece ideally represents the public benefit, the common wealth of all people. The republican system of early Rome developed this process, to integrate different classes into the political frame.

Reconciliation or Liquidation

One basic rule of reconciliation politics is that when trying to influence the life of the community any request, suggestion, re-organization plan, political movement, value-claim or appeal, no matter how reasonable it is, must be put forward in a peaceful way. Conversely, the government and the general public must treat peacefully any movement or demand that is put forward in a moderate, peaceful way with good intentions, even if the ideas at first sight are unreasonable or unacceptable. So any peaceful and reasonable movement which aims to extend human cooperation and well-being should operate without fear. Freedom from fear should be the basic rule of political development and the basic promise of an order based on peace and equality.

Reconciliation refuses the extreme of 'liquidation politics'. I am using this term to refer to very severe penalties, punishments, bans and so on being imposed on members of regimes that have been overthrown.[4] The terms 'purge' or 'lustration' are also used in similar contexts. According to reconciliation politics, political life should be a technique or process which is grounded in the real world, which plans for the future, and which can resolve practical problems while allowing freedom.

Some former political systems lacked mechanisms to prevent mistakes that could have been avoided; this characteristic led to terrible, one might say evil, errors. Some leaders attached too much importance to ideals, probably unrealizable ideals, for which they demanded sacrifices; in many cases, the sacrifices became far more important than the ideals, so the ideals became compromised or even degenerated to their opposites, leading to a complete loss of balance. Such leaders would consider that any admixture of kindness or compassion was a weakness, as were practical solutions to practical problems. So we saw the triumph of ideology over rational development.

Certainly, when some regimes come to an end, liquidation politics may seem an attractive option. Without liquidation of abusers can society come to adopt a more reconciliatory approach? Can it even offer a sure footing for a more moderate government? It can certainly be argued that those who have committed crimes must pay a price, while those tortured must be compensated both psychologically and

---

4   This important issue is discussed at length in Andrew Rigby, *Justice and Reconciliation after the Violence* (Boulder, 2000).

materially. Otherwise people will naturally feel there is no justice in the world. However, according to the community, this re-balance, the repair of the abnormal state, which means that those tortured in the past become those torturing others now, is the cost the community pays for its own mistake no matter who are under torture.

In liquidation politics we should make clear what is the result of a national policy, and what is the result of personal choice. In a word, where crimes – or we could call them evil actions – partly stem from systemic enforced brutality, the perpetrators' punishment ought to be less severe than those that stem from personal choice. To give an example from China, Red Guards often committed robberies when implementing policies of the then political leaders during the Cultural Revolution. Their punishment should be less severe than the punishment for simple criminal robbery in the current climate. The reason is that the whole community shares partial responsibility for the mistakes of the Cultural Revolution. The punishment is less severe not because the evil is less grave in itself, but because the evil was diffused through the community. After all, people still have to work together and live together.

To make some general points:

1. reconciliation politics rejects liquidation politics;
2. in practice, replacement of a previous regime must aim at the community's re-direction, reconciliation and solidarity;
3. in theory, the cost of liquidation is the re-cycling of the past;
4. reconciliation politics must uphold the value of the community in theory and give the community priority in practice.

Reconciliation refuses both political crimes and conscience crimes. Political crimes cause disasters in modern society which make reconciliation more urgent. On the one hand, political crimes can often be more catastrophic than any criminal or personal crime. In a specific sense, political criminality is a characteristic of modern societies. In traditional societies certainly there were many incompetent, cruel, tyrannical rulers, but only in modern societies do political movements become formed by opinions and arguments. In modern society we do not have a singular set of values imposed by absolutist rule. On the contrary, modern political actors may argue that their reform programme will bring greater freedom of expression, or faster economic growth. Then, having made such promises, they are eager to devise policies and to implement them.

That is why modern society is highly risky. As liberalism increases its dominance of the political landscape, risks become higher, because in the liberal political framework the state is supposed to be quite neutral with respect to different political ideas, although the state is also supposed to ensure basic security. We have to admit that the phenomenon of German fascism in the early twentieth century was born in the world of liberalism. Likewise fundamentalist and potentially disastrous religious politics thrive in the EU and USA. So in modern society some of the worst political crimes have arisen because political leaders mobilized social opinions and material resources to re-organize society but without a realistically achievable programme. Some leaders felt beyond reach, not frightened by any scrutiny, free to act irresponsibly. It is a peculiar phenomenon that political crimes are organized and pre-meditated, and they thus have very far-reaching consequences, likely to damage people's personal safety, their livelihood and their way of life. It is also a peculiar because the criminals do not regard their actions as criminal; on the contrary, they regard them as a great kindness to society! The simplest examples are terrorist attacks arising from religious extremism, which are totally different from the conventional military tradition of combat with the enemy on the battlefield. In modern society the violence of dying by suicide along with the enemy becomes highly reasoned and deliberate, which undoubtedly heightens the risks.

Therefore, political crimes, promoted by political movements, often cause serious collective violence, providing evidence of a split in modern society. This split originates from conflict among competing ideas concerning the most desirable form of society; such conflict can be more dangerous than that arising solely over material possessions. In modern society this split can only be resolved by a higher level reconciliation. What is more, reconciliation should also be a standard to judge whether the national community, or the political community based on the nation–state, is truly modern or not. The higher level reconciliation implies no political crime. Intrinsically no political movement is evil and every political movement has the right to survive, but there is a limit, a balance. Its right to operate will be restricted when it threatens destructive violence to the community.

Also, anyone promoting a political movement must bear criminal responsibility for any violence it causes. That is, his or her criminal responsibility is measured by violence, even if it is committed against a single individual, when a political movement claims that violent actions are justified. To mitigate the impact of political movements on society, and specifically to reduce the violence of the political movement, does not mean to cancel political activity. Nor does it mean according legitimacy only to those who oppose new movements. There should be a double process: on the one hand political movements should be legalized, and on the other new movements and the society where they are born should come to terms with each other and respect the fundamental security of civic order.

Reconciliation politics thus makes a double promise to appeal to the inner character of humanity. It offers an ever-expanding dimension of experience and ideas, but also personal safety and freedom from repeated violence. Reconciliation politics is an achievement in the search for modernization; but modernization also makes it clear that the exploration of new possibilities always brings risks.

Chapter 3

Peace Research Needs to Re-Orient

Jørgen Johansen

Peace research concentrates on the question of violence. In particular, it has come to focus on organized violence in societal conflicts.[1]

In what is often known as 'peace studies' literature, 'war' is the term most frequently used for violent societal conflicts. War has many varied definitions, but what they have in common is the description of it as an armed conflict with a certain number of deaths. Disagreements tend to revolve around the number of deaths and how to count them, rather than the much more interesting and important aspects of the definitions, namely the almost universal view that war is a form of conflict. I will argue below that war is *not* a conflict, and that this misinterpretation has had serious consequences for the field of study. Although wars have been studied from a large number of perspectives since the first works in this field were published, most research on large-scale conflicts is focused on armed ones. This tradition, started by pioneers such as Lewis Frye Richardson and Quincy Wright, has dominated the field ever since. The exceptions are few but very important.

War Research – Violence Research

I agree completely with Wallensteen that until now the focus in peace research has in fact been research on violence. But I disagree strongly that it should be so in the future. First of all, if the concentration is to be on violence it would be more honest and accurate to call the field 'Violence Research' or 'War Research'. I do not argue so much against the research as such, as against the inaccurate labelling of it. Certainly we need someone to study wars and violence, but should it be the job of peace researchers?

I will argue that the main task for peace researchers should be to help build peace by peaceful means. It therefore seems natural to study the most peaceful cases of conflict transformation in order to learn how to handle similar conflicts in the future. One problem, however, is that most peaceful cases of conflict handling are not even noticed. Most of the large databases on conflicts only count cases in which the numbers of killed are high. The different groups of researchers behind

---

1 P. Wallensteen, 'The Origins of Peace Research' in Peter Wallensteen (ed.), *Peace Research: Achievements and Challenges* (Boulder and London, 1988), p. 8.

these databases use different definitions of the entities to be counted. They do not have the same opinions about what number of dead bodies is sufficient for a war to be considered small, medium or large, or on what period of duration is enough to constitute a war. But they agree and have in common the basis that in order to be included as an interesting case there must be a certain level of violence involved. This focus on the most violent cases is something we also see in the mass media. Journalists and consumers are obviously fascinated by acts of violence and the consequences of these actions. But why should academia in general and peace researchers in particular also focus on only the most violent cases?

War is not a Conflict

Maybe one reason is a misunderstanding of what a conflict is? Is the explanation that researchers do not separate the means used by the actors from the disagreement the conflict is based on? Without making this separation understanding these elements in a conflict will be difficult. The 'conflict triangle' developed by Galtung gives us a very straightforward but important insight into the complexity of conflict. It is crucial not to mix and create confusion about the different components which together make conflict. The sum of A, B and C (Attitudes + Behaviour + Content/Contradiction) is a conflict. And wars belong in the B-corner. War in itself is not a conflict. Wars are simply a way some actors act in some conflicts.[2]

My conclusion so far: a focus on wars is too limited to understand the complexity of conflicts and creates a distorted image through selecting only a limited number of conflicts, i.e. those with sufficiently high casualty rates and use of violence. In order to understand conflicts as such it is necessary to open up the studies to conflicts in which direct violence is not employed. It is also important to be much more specific on the many different means used by the many actors in a conflict.

Modern Peace Research

The last sixty years have seen the establishment of a number of academic institutions for peace research. Some are independent, others have been set up as parts of universities. Most of them have a very strong focus on violence. The Scandinavian research institutions have not been unique in this respect, but rather relatively typical. The independent Stockholm International Peace Research Institute (SIPRI) has focused on arms/weapons, their effects, costs, trade and negotiations of reductions. The best known peace research from Uppsala University is the project of counting armed conflicts based on the number of killings on the battlefield.[3] The Peace Research

---

2   Johan Galtung, *Peace by Peaceful Means: Peace and Conflict, Development and Civilization* (London, 1996), p. 72.

3   Peter Wallensteen and Margareta Sollenberg, 'Armed Conflict and Regional Complexes, 1989–97', *Journal of Peace Research*, 35/5 (1998): 621–34.

Institute Oslo (PRIO) has large programmes on civil wars and on small arms. Patric Brogan in his large work *World Conflicts* tries to cover most armed conflicts with deadly casualties.[4] *An Encyclopedic Dictionary of Conflict and Conflict Resolution, 1945–1996* includes not only wars but assassinations, coups, insurgencies, terrorism, massacres and genocides.[5] Others have different ways of classifying the conflicts, but they all have in common a focus on conflicts in which violent means dominate. One of the few exceptions is the database of the Heidelberger Institut für Internationale Konfliktforschung: the KOSIMO-database. It has four categories of conflicts, two of which account for conflicts in which the actors use little or no violence.

When war is defined as a conflict then the definition in itself creates a number of difficulties for the handling or management of the conflict. A conflict is a complex social, and often political, process and includes a number of components which need to be studied separately in order both to understand the conflict and to deal with it.

Keltner identifies four main elements in a conflict:

- the means used to influence the conflict;
- the questions about which there is disagreement;
- the relations between the parties;
- the aims or possible outcomes.[6]

Each of these elements is of course in itself a complex entity. To use the term 'war' for the whole concept will make it difficult to identify both the different elements and, more important, the range of options other than armed force in the conflict. In other words: if you define war as a type of conflict, then you predefine the means to be used in the conflict. War is of course only one of a wide spectrum of means which are available for those who are engaged in large scale societal conflicts. Two extremes in how to act in such conflicts are nuclear holocaust and complete surrender; between these there are a number of options which have very different implications and effects on the society. Returning to Keltner, I want to stress that different conflicts with identical questions over which there is disagreement, with identical relations between parties and with identical aims can be influenced – or solved – by a wide range of different means. Keltner suggests a spectrum which starts with 'Difference' and ends with 'Fight or War'. Line two of Table 3.1 is Keltner's description of the process leading to resolution.

---

4   Patric Brogan, *World Conflicts* (Lanham, 1998).

5   John E. Jessup, *An Encyclopedic Dictionary of Conflict and Conflict Resolution, 1945–1996* (London, 1998).

6   John W. Keltner, *The Management of Struggle: Elements of Dispute Resolution through Negotiation, Mediation and Arbitration* (Cresskill, NJ, 1994), p. 5.

Table 3.1   Spectrum of conflict types

Difference	Disagreement	Dispute	Campaign	Litigation	Fight or War
Discussion	Discussion	Argument	Persuasion	Advocacy	Violence
	Negotiation	Bargaining	Pressure	Debate	Conflict

Keltner is here mixing the C-corner with the B-corner in the conflict triangle. His classification starts with three varieties of degrees of contradictions. The next three are examples of means (behaviour) to be used in order to influence the conflict. The interesting part of this is the attempt to make a differentiation of how deep the contradictions are.

Active Nonviolence as a Means used to Influence Conflicts

In recent years we have seen a number of large scale societal conflicts in which the level of violence used by the stakeholders has been extremely low, in some cases entirely absent. Regimes have been brought down by massive nonviolent actions in more than twenty cases since 1979. Recently we have witnessed such revolutions in Serbia/Belgrade (October 2000), Georgia/Tbilisi (November 2003) and Ukraine/ Kiev (December 2004). In these cases to use active nonviolence has been the conscious decision of those who organized and prepared the revolutions.

These conflicts have a lot in common with civil wars and armed revolutions, but differ on the choice of means. That they should be omitted from databases on conflicts is a mistake which has serious consequences. Such selection of cases will create a bias which makes the collected material unfit for a number of studies. By picking only the most disastrous conflicts and leaving out the most peaceful ones knowledge about the latter types cannot be produced, only knowledge of those that from my normative perspective 'went terribly wrong'. However the different cases are judged, the consequences of only including the violent ones makes most analytical use of the material very limited. Any conclusions should clearly state that the material used only includes cases of conflicts where at least one of the involved actors used violent means. Any general conclusions about large scale societal conflicts are not possible.

Below I will briefly describe two different sets of means used in large scale societal conflicts and make some proposals for future research in the field of peace and conflict studies.

Definition of Active Nonviolence

Nonviolence is a combination of techniques by which people can address conflicts, including threats to their security, without using violence. It is not an attempt to avoid or ignore conflicts. There are three categories of active nonviolence:

- nonviolent protest and persuasion (mainly symbolic acts of peaceful opposition or of attempted persuasion, extending beyond verbal expressions);
- non-cooperation (deliberate withdrawal of cooperation with person, activity, institution or regime with which the activists are engaged in conflict);
- nonviolent intervention (a class of methods involving the disruption or destruction of established behavioural patterns, policies, relationships or institutions that are considered unacceptable; or the creation of preferred alternatives).[7]

Any combination of these means will in the following be named 'active nonviolence'.

This definition is descriptive and does not take into consideration any aspect of the intentions of the participants or consequences of their actions. The term 'active nonviolence' is used because it has a history within the tradition of struggle for justice and liberation. It is not perfect, especially since the term 'nonviolence' in many cases has been defined in a conceptual way, with a strong normative emphasis, and is therefore not reflective of what is actually happening in nonviolent action. The many definitions of nonviolence can be seen as part of a spectrum. Narayan Desai could be considered a representative from one end of it when, at the War Resisters' International Council meeting in Paris 1983, he defined nonviolence as 'perfect harmony of all life'. At the other end we find it defined as everything which does not include direct, serious physical attacks on human beings. In the following my intention is to stay close to the tradition informing Gene Sharp's classic *The Politics of Nonviolent Action*. That is, closer to 'non-belligerent' or 'non-martial' than to the more philosophical definitions. But rather than introduce a new terminology, I have decided to base my terminology on a well-known concept.

Nonviolent Revolutions

In the following I will try to illustrate some of the possible misunderstandings resulting from the definition of 'war' as an armed conflict. I will use the examples of Poland in the 1980s, the People Power revolution in the Philippines in 1986 and the 'Velvet Revolution' in Czechoslovakia 1989, and compare them with some of the civil wars of the last decades. In all cases the disagreement was over the political control of the territory.

---

7   See the discussion in Gene Sharp, *The Politics of Nonviolent Action* (Boston, 1973), pp. 705–68.

The Solidarity movement in Poland did not accept the contemporary government and its policies. Relations between the parties were more than hostile: the opposition had a long history of violent struggle against the political leadership. Yet after many decades of armed uprisings – the last in 1976 – the Solidarity movement chose in 1980 to try to achieve their aim with nonviolent means. They developed a strategy involving traditional nonviolent actions such as demonstrations, strikes, blockades and occupations; and despite the fact that the government used the military to force them underground for some time, and despite threats of an invasion by Soviet troops they held to their plan.[8]

People Power in the Philippines was similar in many ways. The avoidance of armed means was a deliberate choice. The most visible action was organized mass jogging with yellow T-shirts in the capital Manila. Although it appeared to outsiders to be a spontaneous action, it was in fact the end of a long-term struggle to remove Marcos from the presidency. After a disputed election the armed forces split, and General Ramos supported the demand of demonstrators in the streets to accept Mrs Aquino as the winner. The power of people when they organized and united in actions of protest and disobedience remained, for Marcos, a mysterious force he never understood.[9]

In Czechoslovakia the revolution came as the culmination of an opposition movement that had been active for decades. Charta 77 and other underground groups joined in a movement known as Civic Forum, and mass demonstrations and strikes followed. The opposition had not taken to arms against the Soviet-led invasion in 1968, and the use of violence was never on the agenda in the years to come. According to a parliamentary committee investigation held in 1990, the communist regime tried several times in November 1989 to provoke violence among the demonstrators, but Civic Forum managed to uphold the nonviolent line.[10]

In all three cases civil resistance was only one aspect of a large range of factors leading to the victory for the opposition movements. But the means used had an important influence on the revolutionary process as well as on the outcome of the struggles. Comparing these three examples with what is traditionally called 'civil war' raises serious questions about the connection between means and ends, questions which are extremely significant for development trajectories after the revolutionary process.

Since the end of the Cold War the most typical armed conflict has changed from being one between two or more states with more than 1,000 battle-related deaths a year to being a civil war with fewer battle-related deaths.[11] Examples are Chechnya,

8   Leopold Labedz (ed.), *Poland under Jaruzelski : A Comprehensive Sourcebook on Poland during and after Martial Law* (New York, 1984).

9   Monina A. Mercado (ed.), *People Power: The Philippine Revolution of 1986: An Eyewitness History* (Manila, 1986).

10   Roger S. Powers and William B. Vogele, *Protest, Power, and Change: An Encyclopedia of Nonviolent Action from ACT-UP to Women's Suffrage* (London and New York, 1997).

11   Peter Wallensteen and Magareta Sollenberg, 'Armed Conflict and Regional Complexes, 1989–97', *Journal of Peace Research*, 35/5 (1998): 621.

the Basque country, East Timor and Afghanistan. In each of these cases the 'question to disagree about' was the political control of a territory. The methods adopted to influence the conflict have in all cases included guerrilla warfare as the dominant strategy. The responses from the respective states have been severe military and policing activities from which the civilian population has suffered immensely.

Such civil wars dominate the media, as well as the agendas of peace-researchers and scholars in political science. Casualties among civilians, children, women and elderly people have been broadcast and reported world-wide and no one is unaware of these victims. The terrible consequences of armed conflicts are the focus of political discussions to such a degree that they tend to diminish other interesting trends in current areas of conflict studies.

The discussions on 'democratic peace'; the research on the number and types of conflicts; the studies on specific types of wars or weapon systems are all necessary and important, but there is an even greater need for studies on the ways of creating peace and transforming conflicts effectively and constructively through more peaceful means.

The Future of Peace Research

If peace researchers want to produce new knowledge about how to handle conflicts without the use of violent means, their focus must be to study cases where the stakeholders in the conflicts have not turned to armed struggle. The growing number of issues solved around the negotiating table, or with use of active nonviolence, are much more valuable as sources of information than massacres and other forms of massive violence. Unfortunately the current mode of peace research pays hardly any attention to the majority of peaceful/nonviolent cases, in large-scale societal conflicts as well as all other types.

Conflicts between individuals are only recognized as conflicts when at least one of the actors uses violent means to influence the outcome. In most families there are a number of conflicts every day and they are mostly solved without the use of violence. The few – but still too many – exceptions occur when domestic violence receives attention from police, neighbours, media and researchers. We should study the many successful cases in order to understand the mechanisms and conditions for the peaceful transformation of these conflicts.

In order to understand the mechanisms of peace it seems natural to study peace. Peace, as defined by Galtung in his book *Peace by Peaceful Means*, is having the capacity and skills to act with creativity, empathy and nonviolence in conflict situations. Peace researchers should help us to develop the skills, mechanisms and theories for such actions. And that is not achieved through detailed studies on forms of violence and the consequences of violent actions.

Chapter 4

Forgiveness in Chinese and Western Culture

Pan Zhichang

PART I

On 1 November 1991 Lu Gang, a Chinese student in the USA, committed a tragic multiple murder. Just after gaining his PhD degree in physics from the University of Iowa he shot dead three professors, a Chinese student, Ms Shan Linhua, who had gained her doctorate at the same time as him, and Professor Anne Cleary, Vice President of the university and one of its most respected members. Long ago her father had gone to China as a missionary, so Anne was in fact born in Shanghai. An unmarried woman, she had a special love for the Chinese. She treated the Chinese students as her own children and gave them meticulous care and attention. On each Thanksgiving and Christmas Eve she invited Chinese students to her family home. Pitifully, she was shot dead by a Chinese student.

On 4 November 1991 some 28,000 staff and students at the university stopped work for the day to attend Anne's funeral. On that day, Anne's brothers grieved for her, and they also read out the following letter, full of love, addressed to Lu Gang's family:

> We experienced extreme sorrow through this accident, losing our sister at the best time of her life. She, our greatest honour, had a far-reaching impact on her family, neighbours, her academic colleagues throughout the country, students and relatives. She was respected and loved by everyone who met her. Our family came here from far away, not only to share sorrow with numerous friends of our sister, but also to share the good memories left by her. When we met together in sadness and remembrance, we were reminded of your family and prayed for you, because this weekend must be sorrowful and shocking for you.
>
> Anne deeply believed in love and forgiveness. We write this letter to you when you are sad, because we would like to share your sorrow and we wish that you would pray with us for love for one another. At this moment of sadness, Anne must hope that our hearts are filled with sympathy, forgiveness and love. We know that at this time only your family can be more sad than we are. We are willing to bear this sadness with you together, so that we can get comfort and support from each other. Anne must hope so!
>
> Sincerely yours,
> Doctor Anne Cleary's brothers,
> Frank, Mike and Paul Cleary

When teaching in Nanjing and Beijing Universities and elsewhere, I have mentioned this letter countless times. I always consider this letter to be the most moving I have ever read; and one which could not have been written by a Chinese. There are well-known collections of letters in China, of which three are perhaps the most famous: *Letters between Two Places* by Lu Xun, *Collection of Family Letters* by Fu Lei and *Collection of Family Letters* by Zeng Guofan. However, compared to the Cleary letter, all of these are in the shade. Reading this letter, we should lower our heads and pay our respects to the three Cleary brothers.

However, the real problem has not yet been solved. The last letters written by Lu Gang to his family were full of phrases like 'hatred without any reason' (one would think there might be some reasons for the hatred), 'I cannot hide my anger in any circumstances', and 'I will find several people to go with me even if I die' and so on. Here we will not discuss Lu's letter. What really puzzled me is the unconditional love flowing in the letter of the Cleary brothers. Such love and forgiveness is totally unknown in Chinese cultural traditions.

Of course, there is so-called 'mercy in the heart' in Chinese cultural traditions. But why can this mercy in the heart not lead to love without reason? Moreover, if this mercy in the heart cannot lead to love without reason, is this so-called mercy real mercy? These are difficult issues and we should reconsider this incident and its implications. To be more precise, mercy in the heart should be called forgiveness. Yet calling it mercy in the heart is more vivid than merely saying forgiveness. The heart here implies a kind of sentiment, which has no business with rational or irrational, nor with law which defines crime and punishment (we are not questioning that criminals should be punished by law). This heart is the endowed sentiment – the ultimate care, which makes a human being a human being. So, different sentiments lead to different types of mercy; different sentiments lead to different views about forgiveness in the Chinese cultural tradition and the Western cultural tradition.

A touchstone to distinguish the two kinds of forgiveness – Chinese and Western – is the concept of loyal forgiveness in Confucianism. The core of Confucianism can be condensed in to one word: humanity (*ren*). This humanity can be divided into two parts, loyalty and forgiveness. Loyalty means one's own will. It is to do wholeheartedly one's best; to practise humanity, as indicated by the saying 'you yourself desire rank and standing: then help others to get rank and standing. You want to turn your own merits to account: then help others to turn theirs to account'.[1] Forgiveness means the opposite of one's own ego. It is to treat other people as you would have them treat you; to practise humanity, as indicated by the text: 'Tzu-kung asked, Is there any single saying that one can act upon all day and every day? The Master replied, Perhaps the saying about consideration: "Never do to others what you would not like them to do to you"'.[2]

However, to treat others as you would have them treat you is here confined to the ethical dimension. The meaning of excuse or pardon is not raised, nor does the

---

1   Confucius, *Analects*, Book 6.
2   Confucius, *Analects*, Book 15.

discussion cover such questions as 'what should I do if others force upon me things I do not like?' Confucius once said, 'Justice in return for injustice'. It is obvious that the explanation of loyalty and forgiveness by Confucius basically corresponds to ratio/reason; it is not measured by love. It is real care, a care based on realism; not ultimate care, or false ultimate care. In the philosophy of Mencius, a Confucian scholar, because the main problem studied is how to implement one's own benevolent will, even the word forgiveness is seldom mentioned. The indigenous religious tradition of Daoism largely ignores ethics, including the concept of 'forgiveness'.

The term or concept 'condone', as developed in the Western cultural tradition, barely makes an appearance in China. Chinese 'condoning' developed from the Confucian idea of forgiveness: it is just a rule to deal with ethics. Chinese condoning completely respects conditional rules – distinguishing enemies and friends – and corresponding attitudes – distinguishing love and hatred. At its most crude, it is to defend those who belong to one's own faction and to attack those who do not. 'Putting humanity into government practice' is just makeshift and finesse. It does not come from 'condone' but 'bestow'. 'Men of honour do not remember the faults of flunkies', as the proverb goes, because flunkies are paltry fellows, beneath a definition as enemy or friend, beneath love and hatred. Their defects and offences can be ignored, so men of honour and status might as well show magnanimity! But this does not really mean to 'excuse' their contradictions and disobedience. Even to 'excuse', overlooking the errors of those who are too insignificant to be taken seriously, still has some preconditions. For example, the person should first confess. After this confession, the relationship between 'the one who excuses' and 'the one who is too lowly to be excused' is changed into the relationship between a winner and a loser. As a result, to condone is replaced by 'to absolve'. It is easy to see that condoning does not appear even where it is most needed.

Strange as it may seem at first sight, these ideas about condoning in the Chinese cultural tradition are completely consistent with the concept of original goodness, promoted by the Confucian scholar Mencius amongst others. The Chinese cultural tradition on the whole considers that human beings are born with innate goodness. If a person can follow his own nature, he can achieve the greatest happiness. Human beings can also be saints due to this goodness – as a saying has it, 'those men in the street are all saints'. Questions about so-called free will have also led some Chinese scholars to discuss whether human beings are born with innate evil. In this case, in Chinese thought, human nature is not a developing procedure but an unchangeable blank state, a *tabula rasa*.

In some ways, these beliefs imply and explain an ultra-conservative pattern of belief according to which the growth, development and change of human nature is a sign of ethical decline, which can be avoided only by strict adherence to primary values. The fact that in real life not everyone is a saint is due to external influences. The advocacy of ethics means to clean up the pollution from the outside world, to return to the true human nature and the sincere inner heart. So in the Chinese tradition, the redemption of the soul is not necessary. The only thing needed is the return of human nature to its original state. Here, the fundamental point is that we are our own saviours, and human nature is higher than any deity. So human beings should depend on self-examination and self-redemption, and practise self-help.

So it goes too in the discussion of good and evil. Starting from the point that human beings are born with innate goodness, the Chinese cultural tradition believes that goodness or evil are congenital, and free will cannot get rid of them. A good man does evil things because he has been corrupted into an evil man; while an evil man does good things because he has been uplifted into a good man. That is why Chinese prefer to say 'good will be rewarded with good and evil with evil'. Everything connected to a good man is good. Even when he makes a mistake, he 'makes a mistake by good-heartedness'. Everything connected to an evil man is evil. The whole clan of the evil man may be categorized along with him, and should therefore be killed; or perhaps the evil man is stung by his own conscience and reforms himself.

The Chinese cultural tradition criticizes the weak points of human nature from the starting point of an original, innate goodness, and calls for reform from the perspective of ethics. No shared, human responsibility exists, but personal ethical responsibility does. The criterion seems to depend on outcomes rather than motives. Results influence motives, as reflected in the old sayings 'winners are kings and losers are bandits' and 'the error of a moment becomes the regret of a lifetime'. Because human beings are born with goodness, the person who maintains and develops it can naturally become a saint. If one does not stick to or maintain it, and instead becomes corrupted into an evil man, he should shoulder his own responsibilities. Others should not sympathize with him, but he should 'be treated with fierce brows' and 'be pointed at by thousands of fingers'. The seed of hatred thereby takes root, flourishes and blooms in the Chinese cultural tradition.

If excusing in China is the ignorance of human beings' limitations, condoning in the West is the self-awareness of human beings' limitations. The view of condoning in the Western cultural tradition is in accordance with the doctrine of original sin. As a hypothesis of human nature, the Western, or at least Christian, cultural tradition historically accepts that human beings are predisposed to evil, and they cannot come to goodness naturally. Free will itself is much more fundamental than original nature and can lead to both goodness and evil. But driven by original sin, human beings' first actions can only be to corrupt innocence and commit crimes; and the crimes can never be eliminated. All human virtues and sins stem from this point. Obviously, this original sin is the symbol of human beings' nobility – the idea that they are nobler than animals – and the symbol that they are equal to God. The consciousness of original sin is the consciousness of human beings' absolute right, dignity and duty. In other words, 'original sin' makes the 'sin' absolute and natural, and consequently fashions human beings' actions and thoughts in accordance with this concept.

Free will can lead to both good and evil deeds. This inevitably results in the existence of a criterion for human beliefs: that is, people pursue the infinity of spirit because of the finitude of life, and the sublimation of soul because of the limitation of body. The existence of these criteria is the fundamental guarantee of the change of free will from evil to good. Therefore, unlike in China, the basis of

Western Christian thinking is that God is His own saviour, and divinity is higher than humanity; therefore, human beings depend on God's grace and their own confession. The exploration into the question of good and evil is parallel. Since it has been emphasized that all good and evil come from free will, the exploration must base itself on the foundation of humanity's inherently evil nature.

Therefore, the whole of human history is considered as the history of atoning for human sins. A sinful nature not only marks the beginning of history, but also hopefully points towards the end of history. Evil nature is not a result of the fall of humanity from an innate state, but a consequence of the departure of humanity from divinity. If evil behaviour is essentially a human failing, then people may face crimes and tribulations without much feeling of guilt. But if it arises from the separation of humanity from divinity, people have no excuse to face crimes and pains without guilt. In this aspect, original sin is undoubtedly a fundamental cultural hypothesis aimed at instilling an absolute sense of duty. Through it everybody realises that all crimes closely connect with each other and the same bell tolls for all. And only unconditional love can redeem this tragedy. Therefore, the seed of love takes root, flourishes and blooms in the Western cultural tradition.

Logically, 'forgiveness' in the West is not a rule of moral principle, but a divine standard of spiritual freedom. Forgiveness pursues unconditional principles and unequal attitudes. It means to forgive not only the forgivable but also the unforgivable. In the West, when discussing good or bad people, one is just talking about their deeds. Forgiveness is unconditional, and also aims to turn both friends and enemies simply into human beings. The ultimate aim is to transform human perception into divine perception. Usually Chinese people cannot understand the Christian concept of forgiveness. For instance, when Peter – who perhaps thinks forgiving seven times is already seven times too many – asked Jesus how many times one should forgive others, Jesus answered, 'seventy times seven'. In the Chinese context this attitude is completely inconceivable, because our tradition refers to the human aspect; while in the Western tradition, from the human-divine perspective, the attitude is fundamental. The unforgivable from the human aspect must be forgiven from the divine standpoint.

If people are prepared only to forgive the forgivable, the concept of forgiveness itself will disappear. Forgiveness must incorporate an absolute dimension; otherwise it is not real forgiveness. Jesus said when somebody strikes your right cheek, you should also offer your left cheek. The final judgment will inevitably arrive, so one need not take revenge or require others' confession. All one needs is unconditional love. And so Christ says, 'Love your enemies', and Paul says, 'You can only give others good wishes, never curses'.

PART II

In brief, the phrase 'to bear mercy in one's heart' in traditional Chinese culture obviously cannot lead to 'unconditional love'. Is this so-called 'mercy' actually 'mercy'? My answer is no. Real mercy is not just to forgive those who can be forgiven, but also those who cannot. Only when someone forgives those who cannot be forgiven can mercy exist. However, it is different in China, where the general opinion is that mercy is only valid for those who can be forgiven. This opinion probes into human nature only superficially. If people can be forgiven and they are forgiven, what is the significance of 'mercy'? As for the opinion that mercy cannot be shown to those who cannot be forgiven, it indicates that Chinese 'mercy' is not an absolute 'mercy'. It may include 'pity', a so-called compassion, shame for one's evil, condescension and justification of right and wrong, but there is no real love in it.

Perhaps we can think: I am finite, ignorant and imperfect, but those divine infinite ones forgive me; so why should I not forgive others who are as finite, ignorant and imperfect as me? Of course, this attitude does not mean the total abandonment of criticizing and correcting faults, but is a reminder that we have the same faults as others. That is why Diderot sighed with emotion: a man is half angel and half devil. Thus mercy is a prerequisite when we are finding fault.

However, Chinese mercy averts love by circumventing common responsibility. We Chinese tend to eulogize ourselves on our superb morality, praising ourselves for never associating with evil, declaring ourselves as innocent as angels. Even if we 'made a mistake' (the self-reflection of Mao Zedong on the disastrous Great Leap Forward), we are only doing something incorrect with a good intention. Even if I fail, it is because I am wise while others are stupid. For instance, the evil of the Cultural Revolution is intimately connected with every Chinese person's soul, but after the disaster, all Chinese immediately transformed themselves into victims; everyone was blameless except 'the four evil ones', the Gang of Four.

In the same way, it is because we do not acknowledge common responsibility that we are totally unaware of the crime of conscience as something separate from crime as defined in law. Chinese people of every generation blame everyone and everything except themselves, exculpate their own faults by criticizing others, and intensify their moral superiority complex. We seem totally unaware that evil is internal, not external. Someone once sighed with emotion that we are so sinful as a nation, but we are never concerned with the sense of sin. What a pertinent comment!

Likewise, since we never make mistakes, it must be others who are incorrect; if we refuse to admit that we are evil, it must be others who are evil. Thus the concepts of good and evil, and self and other, are rigorously separated; other people become the scapegoats of our sin. Averting moral responsibility easily reduces other people to evil. As a result, the 'evil ones' become sinners condemned by history, and they have to shoulder the historical responsibility. People are led to believe that evil will leave us if the wicked ones are punished. However, the opposite is true: evil becomes increasingly rampant, and finally ubiquitous.

Max Weber maintained that there were two kinds of civilization, the tragic and the non-tragic. The tragic civilization faces two worlds: the eternal world of God, which is perfect, and the temporal world, which is imperfect and full of crime. People negate the temporal world through the perspective of the eternal one, so they improve and perfect it consistently, finally leading to a noble and beautiful world. Meanwhile, the non-tragic civilization only has a temporal world, which is a morass of sin in which we merely indulge ourselves. What is surprising is that the tragic civilization does not lead to tragedy, while the non-tragic civilization does. The reason is that the non-tragic civilization lacks the perspective of a perfect eternal world. It is the same with Chinese mercy. Due to the absence of a concept of a perfect eternal world, Chinese mercy is not real mercy; instead, it is a self-indulgent and limited approach.

Furthermore, the absence of love inevitably leads to the presence of hatred. Just look at examples from Chinese history. Wu Yuan flogged his enemies' corpses; Gou Jian underwent self-imposed austerities to strengthen his resolve to beat his enemy; Jing Ke tried to assassinate King Qin, even sacrificing his own life. Behind such 'justice' lies hatred. There are numerous Chinese proverbs about revenge, in which we also find hatred. 'A great man can wait for ten years to take revenge', 'I will take revenge even if it is many years later, and I will redress the injustice even if it was a long time ago' and 'if I kill my enemy, I will kill his offspring as well'.

In this sense, it is not an exaggeration to suggest that the Chinese nation is founded on the basis of hatred. Besides hatred, there are other emotions like love, compassion, pity, empathy, admiration, envy … but in retrospect, we find that almost all our history is connected with hatred, a sentiment which dominates our nation. Why? Hatred is a kind of substitution, a way for people to seek self-affirmation in the absence of love. We cannot affirm ourselves through love or our own existence, so we affirm ourselves through evil and non-existence. We fail to see that hatred is not the voice of an angel, but rather a curse of the devil.

It is a pity that few people meditate carefully on the frightfulness and cruelty latent in human nature. We are just used to 'killing the enemy's whole family', 'killing the entire enemy's offspring', and 'killing the enemy at the price of our own lives'. Taking revenge has priority over forgiveness. What is more, choosing to act out of hatred is supposed to be noble. However, hatred is like the delicious but toxic globefish. It may taste satisfying when we eat it, but it poisons us. In the end, hatred will destroy everything beautiful in human nature.

Obviously, hatred is far removed from mercy. An eye for an eye, a tooth for a tooth is characteristic of China. The bloody massacres in Chinese history are unparalleled elsewhere. In China rulers such as Liu Bang and Xiang Yu advocate ideals like 'he can be replaced', and 'a great man should be ruthless'. These words have formed the terrible principles of Chinese emperors and ministers of every generation. Which 'wise rulers' in China did not use massive violence to preserve their place in history? No mercy, love or pity; only slaughter and bloodshed.

Still more pertinent is that such advocacy of violence is not only how the strong rule, but also a way for the weak to snatch power. There are bloody feuds in a constant cycle across generations, with alternating identities of killers and victims. Nevertheless, the bloody tragedies in history demonstrate that justice can never be realised by violence. Instead, violence will lead us further away from justice. A system might force a man to be disloyal, but it cannot make him unfortunate. It is human nature, not the system, that makes him unfortunate. Consequently, if we only change the system and not ourselves, we will merely alter our roles. Nothing will in fact change.

Criminals solve problems in violent ways. If we do the same, we are no different from criminals. So how can we punish a murderer who cruelly kills someone? If we execute him, what do we gain, apart from satisfying the most primitive impulse to take revenge? Violence is violence, no matter how we beautify or justify it. If we replace darkness with darkness, we will never see light; if we replace violence with violence, we still have violence; if we advocate blood for blood, there will be yet more blood; if we punish gangsters in an illegal way, we will become gangsters ourselves. Once the instrument becomes the aim, we can do nothing but use violence repeatedly until we too become its victims. Resistance against evil in any form is no more than the surrender to evil or the duplicate of evil. I conclude that it is unjust to use violence against a human being in any way. Even violence for the sake of justice should be opposed. If violence should be applied to one man, it could also be applied to you; if violence should be applied to an individual, it could be applied to all human beings.

PART III

If we want to reconstruct traditional Chinese forgiveness, we must advocate unconditional love and real mercy. A nation which never knows love but only hatred does not begin with goodness and therefore it will certainly not end with goodness. Such a nation has the right to say 'we are at the heart of civilization' only when it starts to realize the great importance of love, and to reconsider and then reject the concept of hatred. Otherwise, this nation will never be considered truly civilized. Real forgiveness can only be based on love. Of course, such love is not a kind of stimulus, but an intrinsic need. If it depends on external conditions, love becomes an excuse to satisfy oneself, and other people become instruments where to be loved and satisfied are the real goals, to be cared for, cherished and adored are the real motivations. By contrast, the love on which forgiveness is based is the free choice of love. It is intrinsic, without requirements or payments. Eric Fromm distinguishes between:

> 'to be loved' and 'to love'
> 'the target of love' and 'the ability to love'
> 'falling in love' and 'loving each other for ever'
> 'I love because I'm loved' and 'I love so I'm loved'
> 'I love you because I need you' and 'I love you so I need you'.[3]

Obviously, the love on which forgiveness is based accords with the latter phrases cited above.

Anders Nygren, a Swedish theologian, distinguishes between Eros who proceeds from his self-interests and Agape who embodies the interests of the gods.[4] Such divine love is very significant, and is the purpose of human existence. To achieve such a lofty mission in a degraded world is the best way to reveal human beings' essence. In this aspect, Mother Teresa set a wonderful example. Her loving heart moved everyone. In the 1990s, when the war in Kosovo broke out, she went to the battlefield to rescue women and children. When both sides discovered that she was on the battlefield, they ceased fire and only opened fire again after she and the women and children had gone. When she died, people from all over the world came to her funeral. From an individual like Mother Teresa, we can see the essential holiness and dignity of humanity. Therefore, human beings exist for the sake of love, rather than utility.

---

3   Erich Fromm, *The Art of Loving* (New York, 1956), pp. 1–2 and 46.

4   Anders Nygren, *Agape and Eros* [translated from Swedish by Philip S. Watson] (Philadelphia, 1953).

From the utilitarian view, one will undoubtedly harbour the revenge consciousness of 'blood for blood'. When attacked, animals generally make a counter-attack. However, human beings are different from animals. If someone commits an 'unforgivable' crime, the pain cannot be eradicated through revenge. The revenge itself will bring new suffering, as it further damages love. Love is only love which does not care about utility, and it needs no external conditions. An old Chinese saying states, 'One should love one's parents and therefore also love others' parents'. By contrast, Jesus Christ denied his mother in public. Brightness does not simply oppose darkness, but is far beyond it. Likewise, love does not simply oppose hatred, but transcends it.

Obviously, one must persist in loving unconditionally without expecting the world to love oneself in return. To deny and overcome evil is not to fight against evil through evil actions. Rather, one should never tolerate evil in one's own life, but one should declare, 'To exist without evil is the right attitude human beings should hold'. 'To surrender together with Jesus Christ is better than to win with Caesar'. Unfortunately, people always doubt this, for they think that to forgive, in the face of violence, is to commit suicide. But the key lies in that the elimination of evil must begin from oneself. If nobody uses violence, how can it emerge?

One may further argue that some evil people always exist, and they will take advantage of our forgiveness. This argument ignores the fact that the so-called evil people are just we ourselves. Therefore, humanity can be saved only if everybody renounces violence. There exist differences between collective and individual aspects of human beings. From an individual aspect, evil exists in others; but from the aspect of all human beings, evil lies in everybody. It must be emphasized that only when one realizes this truth is one's mercy seen as true mercy. Also because of this, the power of forgiveness dawns when one perceives inner brightness instead of darkness. Darkness is always only darkness; neither eliminating nor criticizing it can lead to brightness.

That is why even such a great man as Lu Xun, who also bravely faced and fought darkness, could not attain brightness. The New Testament mentions, 'The truth will set you free' and similarly, we must gain freedom from brightness, not darkness. Specifically speaking, when we gain through revenge the justice once destroyed by others, we have already first destroyed forgiveness itself. When we realize that to give up revenge means to achieve more, then forgiveness turns into a real possibility. We must also avoid pride and self-congratulation. This attitude reminds us of the pure virtue of forgiveness that can be found in some religious people. For quite a long time, people despised this virtue and called it idealistic or vague, but it is their own evil that should be despised.

True forgiveness is a towering accomplishment. When we are hurt, there are two possible reactions. One is revenge, regardless of the cost; the other is to nurture the fruit of love and forgiveness. This attitude is like a trampled violet which still imparts its fragrance to the trampling foot. We have realized that only love confronts evil, and other methods such as 'fighting evil with evil' and 'fighting violence with violence' actually surrender to or emulate evil. Leacock, in his *Ten Letters for a*

Young Poet, mentions that a poet, like a bee, collects the pains and joys of humanity and brews them into honey for people to enjoy.

Now let us return to Anne Cleary's three brothers. They did not choose revenge, but forgiveness and love. Xin Lin once wrote an article named *The Story of the City of Love* in which he told us:

> The gun murder shocked the whole country. The Chinese students in this small town all felt fear, sorrow, and great panic. This murder case first reflected hatred, but according to Anne Cleary's brothers, forgiveness is far better than revenge.
>
> The day of Anne's memorial meeting and funeral arrived. Driven by feelings of guilt, most Chinese students and scholars took part in the funeral. Nobody talked, all were bathed in sorrow. However, there was no black curtain or white gauze at the funeral. The crucifix hung there high with solemnity; beautiful flowers adorned Anne's portrait; the sound of the organ penetrated the air with the hymn 'Amazing grace, how sweet the sound'. People all sent me their best wishes, 'God bless you'. The priest said, 'If we let hatred surround this meeting, Annie will not forgive us'.
>
> During the reception after the funeral, Anne's brothers came to the Chinese students. They knew the heavy burden they were carrying, so they tried to shake hands and talk with every Chinese student. Their gentle smiles and sincere love caused many girls to cry, and even one of my friends, a grown man, cried too. The stream of love ran from hands to hearts; smiles appeared on the tearful faces. Such a life, such a death, such happy music and such hope are just what I have looked forward to. Frank, the eldest brother, held my hand and told me, 'I was born in Shanghai and China is my home'. Tears filled my eyes, but warmth filled my heart. Suddenly, I found my previous fear and the heavy burden in my heart had all disappeared. A good, bright feeling entered my heart.

At the end of the article, the writer called the small town 'the city of love' and quoted the proverb, 'the river runs as usual, but I am no longer the person I was yesterday'. In fact, many people who had experienced this event and read the letters of Anne's brothers were no longer the same as they were the day before. Is that not a lofty achievement?

To love is to be willing to love. If you are simple, the world is simple too; whatever kind of person you are, then your world is that kind of world. Therefore the results of forgiveness may not be tangible, but everybody will see that forgiveness has aroused a great echo in people's hearts. This great echo has created our past, present and also the future. Maybe because of this, Archbishop Desmond Tutu, nominated by President Mandela as Chairman of the Truth and Reconciliation Commission, cried out, 'If there is no forgiveness, there will be no future'. Yes – how true that is!

Chapter 5

Latin American Perspectives on Peace Research

Úrsula Oswald Spring

Introduction

This chapter focuses on the Latin American Council for Peace Research (CLAIP), the leading peace studies organization in Latin America.[1] It offers an introduction, a section on peace studies in Latin America, and a reflection on the evolution of the concept of security, expanding from narrow military definitions in the region. It analyses also the new threats, challenges and vulnerability linked to the globalization process, cultural homogenization and climate change. In a special part, the chapter deepens the traditional concept of security, including human and environmental security and widening into my own concept of HUGE: Human, Gender and Environmental Security. This concept responds to current trends of violence in which vulnerable persons are targeted, and where their human suffering is frequently linked to structural injustices in the free market system, environmental destruction and violent conflict for control over natural resources.

After a detailed introduction I review CLAIP, the regional peace research organization established in 1977 during a period of social upheaval in the region. The evolution of peace research in Latin America is closely related to historical processes in the sub-continent during the past five hundred years, as well as to political events in the rest of the world. As is well known, the global positioning of the USA always has a profound impact on politics in Latin and South America. But it is also important to understand the profound historical divides between indigenous and non-indigenous peoples of the region; and to reflect on the new possibilities that Latin Americans have for international cooperation, for example with Asian countries.

1   This article was translated from Spanish by Ms Serena Eréndira Serrano Oswald. I am grateful also for her comments during its elaboration, as well as to Hans Günter Brauch for his constructive criticism.

Historical Legacy and Geopolitical Context of Latin America

The military and ideological conquest of Latin America by Spain, Portugal and the Roman Catholic Church led to the imposition of a colonial order, to economic underdevelopment and subordination. A plethora of natural resources – foodstuffs, gold, silver, minerals, medicinal and therapeutic plants – were systematically looted. Forced labour under the *encomienda* system, as well as new illnesses, decimated the native population, obliging Spanish conquerors to bring in African slaves to replace the indigenous workforce in mines and agriculture.[2]

Due to superior military technology, the Spanish destroyed the great Meso-American cultures and kingdoms: *Mexica* in Tenochtitlan (Mexico City); *Maya* in the Yucatan Peninsula; the *Incas* in Peru.[3] Ideological control was entrusted to the Roman Catholic missionaries who transformed both religious beliefs as well as productive and cultural systems. This geopolitical hegemony with its resulting dependency, as well as the systematic negation of autochthonous cultures, laid the foundation for the human, material and natural exploitation of Latin America.

A wave of independence movements in the nineteenth century *de facto* responded to Creole interests aiming at national self-control free from foreign dictates, disregarding any liberation or development of indigenous populations. Independence struggles led to the establishment of Creole and later *mestizo* élites, who despotically controlled all natural and cultural resources. Conflicts within ruling élite groups in various countries throughout the sub-continent were characterized by fratricidal struggles, which impeded attempts by indigenous groups to challenge the emergence of *encomenderos* (landlords) and *hacendados* (large cultivators of cash crops), local strongmen, ecclesiastic landlords, corrupt bureaucrats and authoritarian military or presidential regimes. Poverty increased as local communities were excluded from socio-political decision-making, rooting the current situation of extreme inequality inherent for all Latin American countries. Furthermore, the loss of half of Mexican territory to the USA inaugurated an increasingly dominant influence by the superpower, which has directly and subtly shaped the entire sub-continent since the nineteenth century.[4]

The twentieth century commenced with the Mexican Revolution, the first indigenous peasant movement, defying landlords and incipient transnational capital in the hands of sugar-cane industry owners. It was increasingly led by the middle classes, generals and commercial farmers, most of who originated from northern states. The Mexican Revolution (1910), followed by the October Revolution in Russia (1917), seeded a socialist utopia seeking to redistribute political power to workers and peasants. However, alliances between the armed forces and the rising

---

2   Jared Diamond, *Guns, Germs, and Steel* (New York, 1997).

3   I provide references in the Bibliography to classic and modern accounts of the conquest. See the works by Cortés, El Colegio de Mexico, Prescott and Thomas for Mexico and the Yucatan Peninsula; and works by Estete, Fuentes, Pizarro and Prescott for Peru.

4   Francisco Aravena Rojas, 'Repensando la Seguridad en América Latina' in Salinas and Oswald (eds), *Culturas de paz* (Mexico DF, 2003), pp. 161–82.

bourgeoisie soon imposed autocratic and repressive regimes through military coups throughout Latin America. The USA also participated in this rush towards militarization.

After the Second World War the Cold War divided the world into capitalist and communist blocs for some forty years. Latin America, like many parts of Asia and Africa, became a battleground for conflict by proxy. Both blocs struggled to expand their influence by promoting alliances and economic support, as well as imposing embargoes and exacerbating conflicts. The USA launched the Organization of American States parallel to the North Atlantic Treaty Organization in Europe and Association of South East Asian Nations in Asia as barriers to the spread of communism. Under the pretext of stopping a communist 'domino effect', that would allegedly lead to world communism, the USA justified internal repression, McCarthyism; and through agencies, like the notorious School of the Americas, they repeatedly instigated military coups, genocide and ethnic repression throughout Latin America – its so-called backyard.

Latin America also had phases of limited autonomous development. In 1958 the Cuban Revolution was won 'by the people' against Bautista's dictatorship. During the 1950s and 1960s independence movements flourished, as in different parts of Asia, Africa and the Caribbean. Independence was granted to formerly colonial states, although ethnic conflicts ripened, sometimes justified by clashes between so-called communists and liberals in at least thirty African countries. But essentially forty years of Latin American history were predominantly determined by Cold War activities and American–Soviet efforts to control the South. The colonial era was over, but decolonization paved the way for neo-colonialism, the expansion of the free market system and conflicts which have remained unresolved today. It is well known that the Middle East acquired an increasing geopolitical importance due to its enormous reserves of quality oil and gas, an importance that has made the region explosively vulnerable. The Latin American oil-producing countries (Venezuela, Mexico, Ecuador and Colombia) are the second largest source of oil to the USA. For this very reason the USA closely monitors and wishes to control its oil interests in the region.

Medical and pharmaceutical advances in recent decades led to the generalized use of antibiotics and vaccines against polio, smallpox and measles, resulting in some health improvements. But technology, investment and industrialization did not bring expected developments to the majority of the population. Facing repressive political scenarios and mounting poverty, guerrilla movements emerged throughout the sub-continent from the 1950s; while peasant, urban-popular and middle-class-led movements allied in order to voice their opposition. Since the 1960s dependency theory stemming from Latin America was transformed in Europe into the theory of 'structural imperialism'.[5]

Another strand of opposition came from committed Roman Catholics influenced by the new ideas that became known as 'liberation theology', whose radical priests and spokespersons believed that the Church should side actively with the dispossessed, rather than with the élites. In many states, military coups and authoritarian regimes brutally repressed these social movements.

In Mexico we find a more sophisticated system of selective repression: leaders were either corrupted or eliminated. Intellectuals were severely repressed under the pretext of their alleged communist affiliation. Starting with massacres of students in Tlatelolco, Mexico in 1968 and 1972, military coups ensued in Chile (1973), Argentina (1976) and in Central America. Poverty increased, and the 1980s and 1990s in Latin America are considered lost decades by official economists, for example the UN's Economic Commission for Latin America and the Caribbean.[6]

More recently, following decades of US-sponsored extra-judicial disappearances, torture and murders, often known as the Dirty War, the USA has been withdrawing part of its military aid to Latin American governments. It has even demanded respect for human rights in Latin America, as do many European agencies. Thus dictatorial governments have been forced to undergo a process of transition or a 'democratization wave'. During the 1980s and 1990s many Latin American countries returned to democratic political systems with elected governments. The electoral system empowers popular voters to have a say in national issues and to lobby for their interests. Nevertheless, the debts of the Dirty War are yet to be compensated, as thousands of young citizens have disappeared; the residual pain and anger is apparent in peaceful demonstrations by their mothers and other citizens.

Re-iterative economic crises and debt burdens hinder Latin American governments' scope to improve infrastructure and living conditions. The policies imposed by structural adjustment plans (promoted by the International Monetary Fund [IMF], World Bank and global capital) define economic policies, giving priority to debt repayments and the privatization of basic services. These policies have generally worsened the living conditions for the masses. At the same time, local and international élites are ever more closely tied, which means that some urban and recreational spaces are orchestrated into the concert of globalization.

The result is an increasing urban chaos with highly segmented space; sophisticated, developed areas back on to appalling slums. In rural areas, abandoned fields and empty communities are subsumed into transnational agribusiness migrant

---

5   Ruy Mauro Marini, *El secreto intercambio desigual* (Mexico DF, 1973); Ruy Mauro Marini, *Teoría de la Dependencia en América Latina* (Mexico DF, 1975); Johan Galtung, 'Violence, Peace and Peace Research' in Johan Galtung (ed.), *Peace: Research, Education, Action*, vol. 1, *Essays in Peace Research* (Copenhagen, 1975), pp. 109–34; Dieter Senghaas, *Der strukturelle Imperialismos* (Frankfurt, 1978).

6   CEPAL, *Balance preliminar de la economía en América Latina* (Santiago de Chile, 2004).

flows. Migration has become the sole alternative for peasants facing the loss of food sovereignty. Soil erosion, water pollution and scarcity result from unequal competition, given the indiscriminate agricultural subsidies for basic foodstuffs in developed countries. Inequality between social groups hinders development, yet IMF policies have increased the gap between rich and poor.[7]

Neither liberation struggles – whether against foreign conquerors, élites, the military or transnational capital – nor democratization in urban areas, increasingly incorporating rural regions, have brought justice to indigenous peoples who remain excluded politically, socially and culturally. Yet indigenous peoples represent the majority of the population in countries such as Guatemala, Ecuador, Bolivia and Peru. In other countries they are a significant minority. Nonetheless, their rights and resistance have been historically silenced by Creole and *mestizo* groups, and increasingly by transnational capital. Many of their traditional territories in Bolivia, Colombia, Ecuador and Central America are rich in bio-diversity, with copious resources including oil, gas, uranium and water. Struggle for control over these lands can seed ethnocide of local peoples.

Confronting new threats at the hands of transnational capital and paramilitaries, some indigenous peoples have actively allied with peasants, workers and diverse popular movements. They demand territorial sovereignty, absolute respect for their cultural traditions, use of the natural resources in their lands, food sovereignty, and an end to all forms of repression. Some examples are the struggles for water rights in Bolivia, and for oil in Mexico and Ecuador. The convergence of such multiple currents, with ethnic and ideological elements, gives Latin American social movements great flexibility, and ground them in a trajectory exceeding five hundred years.

To summarize, three important roots of dissent in recent decades have been:

1. guerrilla movements and ideals (Castro, Che Guevara, Cabañas, FARC, Shining Path);
2. Christian groups, strengthened by liberation theology and active grassroots nonviolence in practice, who directly oppose government-led neo-liberal policies;
3. indigenous groups which call on resistance and survival strategies developed over the past five hundred years.[8]

Following this convergence, peasants, workers, urban sectors and indigenous groups, allied with the middle classes and severely affected by two decades of lost

7 CEPAL, *Balance preliminar de la economía en América Latina* (Santiago de Chile, 2004).

8 Readers may consult a variety of recent papers and books, referenced in the Bibliography, by Latin American scholars. Especially Christian groups: Ameglio, Cadena, Calva, Cordera, Lópezllera, Martínez, Polensky and Saviñón; indigenous movements: Gaitán, Gil, Menchú, De la Rúa, Armendáriz, Rojas, García, Oswald and Ríos. Most are included

development, have created a broad scope of alternatives. In recent elections citizens have attempted to oust their neo-liberal governments that have been close to the 'Washington Consensus'. However, foreign debts, international agreements, IMF dictates and the interests of ruling élites who seek quick wealth at any price, through corruption or other means have hindered alternative attempts. But a mounting despair has been evident in marches, demonstrations and national strikes, forcing the resignation of presidents in Ecuador, Argentina, Bolivia, Brazil and Peru.

The globalization processes led by the US and multi-national enterprises have directly affected the sub-continent both in economic relations and in terms of migration. The new motors of development are world finance webs, international trade and technological improvements. Power has shifted from states and territories to global networks. The state, accountable for social, economic and political stability in the past, is now delegating these responsibilities to the market, where optimizing benefits is the core priority. Social security networks are increasingly becoming obsolete as economic disparities widen, increasing the socio-economic gap between North and South overall, and within both hemispheres also between rich and poor. The dismantling of the welfare state has internally created new conflict situations, frequently visible in massive demonstrations against privatization processes, for example in Cochabamba, Bolivia.[9]

In 1989 the euphoria of the demise of the Berlin wall and the vision of a settled *Pax Americana* outlined in Fukuyama's 'End of History' thesis quickly drowned in the resurgence of both old and new armed confrontations. Instead of employing financial resources to alleviate poverty, new conflicts and international terrorism gave birth to a new arms race, comprising weapons of mass destruction and a re-orientation towards small nuclear arms. Today at least eight countries (USA, Russia, UK, France, China, India, Pakistan, Israel) have nuclear weapons and a few others may be developing them (North Korea, Iran): most of them possess medium and long-range missile technology. Some countries and experts have claimed an increasing threat of deploying nuclear materials for terrorist attacks and dirty bombs. Latin America has, however, maintained a nuclear-free position.

The new threats after 1989, such as global warming, migration, extreme poverty, unemployment and environmental destruction, as well as the global North–South relations, stimulated a new scientific debate. The security concept deepened from a focus on nation-states to other reference objects, from the individual

---

in the two collections: Úrsula Oswald (ed.), *Soberanía y desarrollo regiona: El Mexico que queremos* (Mexico DF, 2003); and Úrsula Oswald (ed.), *Resolución noviolenta de conflictos en sociedades indígenas y minorías* (Mexico DF, 2004).

9　Ifigenia Martínez, 'Planeación del desarrollo regional y de los sectores estratégicos y prioritarios' in Úrsula Oswald (ed.), *Soberanía y desarrollo regional: El Mexico que queremos* (Mexico DF, 2003), pp. 233–46; and José Luis Calva, 'Balance de las políticas públicas: la economía mexicana bajo el consenso de Washington' in Úrsula Oswald (ed.), *Soberanía y desarrollo regional: El Mexico que queremos* (Mexico DF, 2003), pp. 143–72.

to the global level.[10] The concept was also sectorialized to deal with issues such as food, health, labour rights and water security: initiatives were often taken by multi-lateral organizations such as the Food and Agriculture Organization, the World Health Organization, the International Labour Organization and the United Nations Environmental Programme. The whole concept of security was widening from the narrow military dimension to additional societal, economic, humanitarian, environmental and gender perspectives.[11] In recent years, we have continued to witness growing poverty and inequality, resource scarcity, population growth, technological threats (genetics, cloning, nano-technology), and increasing vulnerabilities to natural disasters which are frequently human aggravated and particularly severe in the Gulf

---

10 See, for example, Ulrich Beck, *La sociedad de riesgo: Hacia una nueva modernidad* (Buenos Aires, 1998); Ulrich Beck, *Políticas ecológicas en la edad del riesgo* (Barcelona, 2001); Anthony Giddens, *Modernity and Self-Identity: Self and Society in the Late Modern Age* (London, 1991); Anthony Giddens, *Beyond Left and Right: The Future of Radical Politics* (Stanford, 1994); Jürgen Habermas, *Más allá del Estado nacional* (Mexico DF, 1998); Jürgen Habermas, *La constelación posnacional: ensayos políticos* (Barcelona, 2000); Jürgen Habermas, *Kommunikatives Handeln und detranszendentalisierte Vernunft* (Stuttgart, 2001).

11 Among recent publications on these issues, I recommend on social issues: A. Touraine, *Actores sociales y sistemas políticos en América Latina* (Santiago, 1987). On economic issues: José Luis Calva, 'Balance de las políticas públicas', pp. 143–72; Amartya Sen, *Inequality Reexamined* (Harvard, 1995); Joseph E. Stiglitz, *Globalization and Its Discontents* (New York, 2002).

The environmental dimensions are discussed in several publications by Hans Günter Brauch: 'Security and Environmental Linkages in the Mediterranean: Three Phases of Research on Human and Environmental Security and Peace' in Hans Günter Brauch, P.H. Liotta, A. Marquina, P.F. Rogers and M. El-Sayed Selim (eds), *Security and Environment in the Mediterranean: Conceptualising Security and Environmental Conflicts* (Berlin, 2003), pp. 35–143; 'Environment and Human Security: Towards Freedom from Hazard Impact', *InterSecTions*, 2 (Bonn, 2005); 'Threats, Challenges, Vulnerabilities and Risks in Environmental and Human Security', *Source*, 1 (Bonn, 2005). See also Thomas F. Homer-Dixon and Jessica Blitt (eds), *Ecoviolence: Links between Environment, Population, and Security* (Lanham, 1998); and Günther Baechler, 'Environmental Degradation and Violent Conflict: Hypotheses, Research Agendas and Theory-Building' in Mohamed Suliman (ed.), *Ecology, Politics and Violent Conflict* (London, 1999), pp. 76–112; Günther Baechler, K.R. Spillmann and M. Suliman (eds), *Transformation of Resource Conflicts: Approach and Instruments* (Berne, 2002).

Gender perspectives are found in Betty Reardon, *Sexism and the War System* (New York, 1996); Maria Mies, *Patriarchy and Accumulation on a World Scale* (Melbourne and London, 1998); Vandana Shiva, *Staying Alive: Women, Ecology and Development* (London, 1988); Úrsula Oswald, 'Sustainable development with Peace Building and Human Security' in M.K. Tolba (ed.), *Our Fragile World: Challenges and Opportunities for Sustainable Development*, forerunner of *The Encyclopedia of Life Support Systems* (2 vols, Oxford, 2001), vol. 1, pp. 873–916.

The United Nations Development Programme reports are also useful: UNDP, *Report on Human Development* (London, 1996–98).

of Mexico (for example the hurricane effects in Haiti, Mexico and southern USA). In an unstable environment, Latin American peace researchers face new challenges.

Peace Research in Latin America

Peace research, like peace movements, is closely linked to local and global conflicts. The Korean and the Vietnam wars; apartheid in South Africa; the Palestinian issue; military dictatorships in Latin America have all given impetus to systematic reflection on peace, conflict resolution and nonviolence. Worker movements, trade unionist, bourgeois and socialist peace movements in late nineteenth century, the Hague Conference in 1899 and the Red Cross constitution opened the public's eyes to the atrocity of war and injustice. Further impetus was given by institutions and individuals such as the International Court of Justice in The Hague, Lewis Frye Richardson's work in the UK in the1930s and 1940s and Quincy Wright's work *A Study of War*, which gathered together research conducted between 1926 and 1942. Discussions in Ann Arbor in the mid-1950s together with the foundation of the *Journal of Conflict Resolution* in 1957 analysed the crimes of two world wars and a cold war.

Johan Galtung founded the *Peace Research Institute in Oslo* (PRIO) in 1959 and the *Journal of Peace Research* in 1964. In 1962 WILPF established a Consultative Commission on peace research. Stimulated by the parallel efforts in North America and in Europe, an International Peace Research Newsletter appeared in 1963, a preliminary meeting was held in Switzerland, and in December 1964, and the International Peace Research Association (IPRA) was established in London. IPRA organized its first international meeting from 2–5 July 1965 in Groningen, The Netherlands that was attended by 73 scholars from 23 countries. Two of IPRA's founders, Elise and Kenneth Boulding, coming originally from Norway and the UK, assisted IPRA in co-ordinating research efforts in both hemispheres. The Bouldings together with other peace researchers founded the Consortium on Peace Research, Education and Development (COPRED) in May 1970 and soon after the Peace Studies Association was created by Walter Isard. Today the two have converged as the Peace and Justice Studies Association, the North American affiliate of IPRA.

In 1966, at the inspiration of Alva and Gunnar Myrdal, the Swedish Prime Minister Erlander established the Stockholm International Peace Research Institute (SIPRI) in commemoration of Sweden's 150th anniversary of permanent peace. In the 1960s and 1970s other peace research institutes were established: for example the Polemological Institute, founded by Bert Röling, operated in Groningen, The Netherlands, until its closure in 1990. In Denmark, a private Institute for Peace and Conflict Research was founded in 1967. It dissolved in the early 1970s, but in 1985 the Copenhagen Peace Research Institute was set up by the Danish Parliament, merging in 2003 with the Danish Institute for International Studies. In Finland in 1970 the Tampere Peace Research Institute was set up with the support of the Finnish

Parliament. In Germany a Working Group on Peace Research was founded in 1969. Subsequently in 1971 the Peace Research Institute in Frankfurt was set up, and in the mid 1970s the Institute for Security and Peace Research Hamburg was established. In 1987 AFES-PRESS evolved from an informal study group at Stuttgart University into an international scientific society that regularly met from 1981 to 1987.[12]

The constitution of the European Peace Research Association allowed IPRA to promote regional associations, although activities and theoretical thinking were still mostly based in the north. In 1972 IPRA organized its first congress in India, then known as a 'Third World' country, where much learning from active nonviolent movements took place. During the 1970s peace educators joined peace researchers in IPRA; and in the 1980s representatives of peace movements became the third pillar of the organization.

Given this general background, the specific history of peace research in Latin America can trace its roots as follows. In 1977 IPRA held its international congress in Mexico, which had been sheltering refugees expelled by, or fleeing from, repressive military dictatorships from almost all Latin American countries. With more than 180 Latinos present, the Latin American Council of Peace Research (CLAIP) was created. Its activities were linked to the ongoing democratization wave and the international denunciations of torture, human rights violations, massacres and disappearances of social and political leaders. Slowly, during the 1980s and 1990s, many of these researchers were able to return home to democratically governed countries, bringing peace research with them, and new ideas on how to improve popular participation in fragile democratization processes.

CLAIP showed the value of a broad range of links between universities, social movements and democratization processes inside governments. Its positive experience was echoed in other regional associations, stimulating the establishment of the Asia–Pacific Peace Research Association in 1980 in Yokohama, Japan. The highly conflictive situation in Africa induced the creation of an African Peace Research Association. In 1998 IPRA held the international congress in Durban, South Africa, in order to learn from the peaceful transition processes of the 'rainbow nation' led by Nelson Mandela. Mandela's leadership in Africa integrated multiple peace efforts and reconciliation processes between historically divided ethnic groups

---

12 For this history, see Hans Günter Brauch, *Entwicklungen und Ergebnisse de Friedensforschung (1969–1978): Eine Zwischenbilanz und konkrete Vorschläge für das zweite Jahrzehnt* (Frankfurt, 1979); and Egbert Jahn, 'Friedens- und Konflitkforschung' in Andreas Boeckh (ed.), *Internationale Beziehungen*, vol. 6 of Dieter Nohlen (ed.), *Lexikon der Politik* (7 vols, Munich, 1994), pp. 158–63.

In addition, most of the organizations mentioned in the text maintain websites, a selection of which is provided here: <http://www.afes-press.de/> and <http://afes-press-books.de/index. html>; <http://www.peacejusticestudies.org/index.php>; <http://www.diis.dk/sw152.asp>; <http://www.hsfk.de/>; <http://soc.kuleuven.be/pol/ipra/about_history.html>; <http://www. ifsh.de/>; <http://www.uta.fi/laitokset/tapri/>.

and struggling clans, involving African researchers, especially women, who are now promoting peace in their countries.[13]

Links with these 'southern' regional associations have enriched CLAIP and also IPRA with invaluable empirical peace and conflict resolution materials, opening the door for intercultural exchange and deepening theoretical reflections. Latin America with its contribution of dependency theory, Asia with *ahimsa* and nonviolence, the USA with Martin Luther King's racial liberation linked to black feminism, and Africa with the peaceful transition from the apartheid regime to an elected multiracial democratic government are all encouraging kernels of peace, both in theory and practice. Several universities are making them objects of systematic research (Harvard, Columbia, Northwestern, Coventry, Durban, Delhi, Buenos Aires), and they are transformed into peace education and nonviolence practices throughout the South (Salvador, Nicaragua and Guatemala). The reconciliation processes between victimizers and victims created models of multi-dimensional integration and 'Truth Commissions', promoting a deep democratization process with traditional grass-root practices such as *Gacaca*, a reconciliation instrument to overcome terror at village level in the Hutu–Tutsi conflict.

Latin Americans situate themselves in some way between Western and non-Western modes of understanding. For example, they have been able to question occidental models of law and justice, envisaging novel alternatives of integrating conflict prevention and nonviolent conflict resolution at the grassroots and indigenous levels. They have inculcated the values of their culture through education, myth, communitarian participation and social and family events. Contrary to the occidental punitive law establishment, which operates though the legal and police system, the emphasis in indigenous societies has been prevention. Nevertheless, when a transgression defies the social order, the community as a whole takes responsibility for the crime and takes the necessary measures to re-establish social harmony. The offence is conceived as a social disruption, a deviance that indicates a deeper root of imbalance, as the offender requires social support in order to be socially reintegrated. Punishments in this setting are complex; they must return equilibrium to the social collective. This procedure aims to restore the social tissue of the society affected by a crime.

Besides, there exist also several mechanisms of indigenous resistance, especially in regions where low-intensity warfare is taking place, such as in Colombia and Chiapas, where indigenous populations face multiple enemies. Overall, these processes suggest new avenues for conflict resolution and peace education, as well as leading to alliances to mitigate physical, structural and cultural violence. Peace activists have especially highlighted the local impact as civil populations are the prime victims that endure violence; primarily the most vulnerable groups have been women, children and elders.

CLAIP and IPRA have adapted to changing conflict scenarios. Several study groups have revised their initial research subjects, incorporating globalization

---

13 Nelson Mandela, *Long Walk to Freedom*, 9th edn (London, 1997).

processes, amongst others, as a threat to peace. For example, the 'Food Study Group' evolved into the 'Human Right to Food Group', and now it has developed into two commissions: one dedicated exclusively to the study of human rights with special emphasis on women and children; and the second group including environmental rights and the new threats of global warming, water scarcity and environmental pollution in war situations, and environmental security in post-conflict regions. These changes reflex the increasing complexity of a globalized world, and the widening, deepening and sectorialization of the narrow military security into a conceptualization able to deal with human, environmental, societal and gender security issues.

HUGE: Human, Gender and Environmental Security

The interaction of peace education with practical peace courses, including collaboration between peace researchers and peace activists have infused a new dynamism to the organization. Worth mentioning is increasing parity between regions, as well as gender sensitivity. Convinced of the importance of forging this equilibrium, CLAIP has made a strong commitment to promoting gender balance within the organization as well as in several universities and research projects. However, we ascribe a much more extended meaning to the term 'gender' than is conventional. For our purposes, gender is not solely related to women's issues. Rather, all vulnerable and excluded profiles have been incorporated, trying to give them visibility, a voice and direct empowerment. This concept of gender includes indigenous groups, children, elders, minority religious groups, ethnic or sexual minorities, disabled people and men living in poverty without decision-making capacities.

Theoretically, gender security should be linked to human and environmental security, promoting a security concept which brings to the fore different ways to deal with new and old threats: security threats in a world that changes at an unprecedented pace, transcending traditional Hobbesian and Machiavellian concepts of military security. Human security has been defined by the United Nations Development Programme as: 'Protection from the threat of disease, hunger, unemployment, crime, social conflict, political repression and environmental hazards'. On the governmental level, the concept of human security has emerged from several initiatives of the Canadian and Norwegian governments as 'freedom from fear', and from the Japanese government and the Human Security Commission as 'freedom from want'. The United Nations University has proposed a third pillar of human security as 'freedom from hazard impacts'.[14] The former Canadian Minister of Foreign Affairs Lloyd Axworthy has designated human security as a descriptor for a new foreign policy

---

14 Janos Bogardi and Hans Günter Brauch, 'Global Environmental Change: A Challenge for Human Security – Defining and Conceptualising the Environmental Dimension of Human Security' in Andreas Rechkemmer (ed.), *UNEO – Towards an International Environment Organization – Approaches to a Sustainable Reform of Global Environmental Governance* (Baden-Baden, 2005), pp. 85–109; Brauch, 'Environment and Human Security'; Brauch, 'Threats, Challenges, Vulnerabilities and Risks in Environmental and Human Security'.

Peace Studies in the Chinese Century

and worldview, as an alternative to arms races and military confrontation. Military ideologies are to be replaced by progressive attitudes such as respect for human rights, international humanitarian laws, refugee protection acts, and promotion of humanitarian aid in case of natural hazards, disasters and wars, development based on gender and social equity, and cultural diversity with religious freedom.

Increasing threats to environmental security are related to a cluster of at least six key factors of a survival hexagon representing the three elements of nature or supply factors: soil and water (degradation and scarcity), air (pollution, climate change, ozone layer depletion), as well as demand factors such as population growth, urban (urbanization, anthropogenic pollution and contamination) and rural factors (agriculture, food, fibre). These manifold environmentally-induced security threats, challenges, vulnerabilities and risks are negatively affected by post-war situations, by the arms trade and its facilities, and also by industrial and agricultural waste. These anthropogenic as well as natural variability factors have contributed to climate change, soil erosion, food scarcity and alteration of hydrological cycles. In what he calls a 'survival hexagon', Brauch has reviewed the long-term structural input factors; the medium and short term political processes; and the short, medium and long-term outcomes, where state, economy and society have to take decisions in order to prevent, mitigate or handle disasters, crises or conflicts (see Figure 5.1).[15]

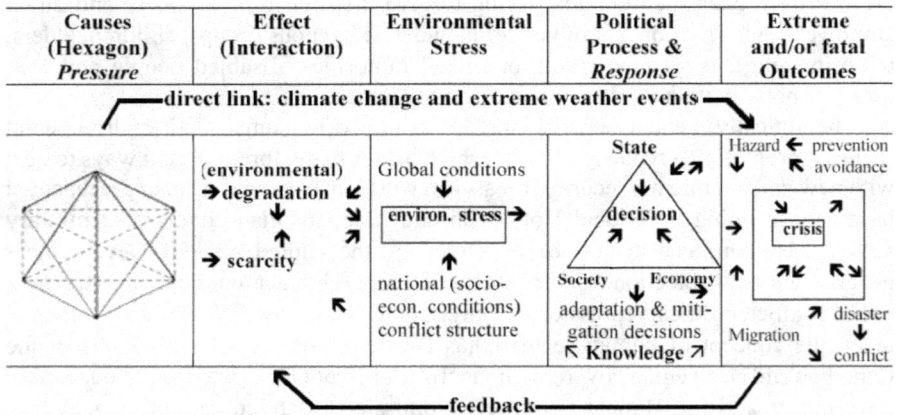

Figure 5.1   Causes and potential outcomes of environmental stress

15 Brauch, 'Security and Environmental Linkages in the Mediterranean', pp. 35–143. See p. 126 for a version of Figure 5.1, and also Brauch, 'Environment and Human Security', p. 16.

Bjørn Møller distinguishes the narrow state-focused concept of national security that is used in 'realist' security studies from three extended or widened security concepts. He labels societal security as 'incremental'; human security as 'radical'; and environmental security as 'ultra-radical'. Moving beyond the classical realist security definition provided by Wolfers,[16] Møller distinguishes these four concepts with regard to the different referent objects (state, nation, societal groups, individuals, humankind and ecosystem), the values at risk, and the sources of threat. This classification offers a specific heuristic contribution that has inspired many subsequent additions and modifications.[17]

In response to this analysis, an integral security concept is proposed, namely 'HUGE: Human, Gender and Environmental Security' that combines gender in a broad sense with the conceptual and political debates on environmental and human security.[18] Developing Møller's approach further, the HUGE paradigm deepens a 'trans-radical' approach that offers gender security guarantees (see Table 5.1). Relations including gender, indigenous and minority status are the referent objects; and equity and identity are the values at risk. The source of threat comes first from a patriarchal order, characterized by totalitarian institutions, such as authoritarian governments, churches and élites.[19]

Gender security is normally taken as given, socially identified and represented. The world has been organized for more than four thousand years in a patriarchal structure, where the male gender – the strong sex – dominates over the female one – the weak or second sex. The symbolic distribution assigns the male the public space: production, *res publica*, *homo sapiens*; and the women the private one: reproduction, home, *homo domesticus*. The distribution of power also acquires generic forms. Men exercise a hierarchical and vertical power of domination and superiority. Women live stripped of goods, subordinates, exercising their powers within the oppressive

16 Arnold Wolfers, 'National Security as an Ambiguous Symbol' in Arnold Wolfers, *Discord and Collaboration: Essays on International Politics* (Baltimore, 1962), pp. 147–65.

17 See Bjørn Møller, 'National, Societal and Human Security Discussion: A Case Study of the Israeli-Palestine Conflict' in Hans Günther Brauch, P.H. Liotta, Antonio Marquina, Paul F. Rogers and Mohammad El-Sayed Selim (eds), *Security and Environment in the Mediterranean: Conceptualising Security and Environmental Conflicts* (Berlin, 2003), pp. 277–88.

18 Úrsula Oswald, 'Sustainable development with Peace Building and Human Security', pp. 873–916; Úrsula Oswald and M. Lourdes Hernández, *El Valor del Agua: una Visión Socioeconómica de un Conflicto Ambiental* (Tlaxcala, Mexico, 2005).

19 Serena Eréndira Serrano Oswald, 'Exploring a Socio-cultural Social Psychology: A Potential for Regional Studies', paper presented at the 18th Pacific Regional Science Conference, Acapulco, Mexico, July 2003; Serena Eréndira Serrano Oswald, 'Changes of Women's Social Identity in Modern Mexico', unpublished Master's dissertation, Department of Social Psychology, London School of Economics and Political Sciences, 2003; Serena Eréndira Serrano Oswald, 'Género, migración y paz: incursiones a una problemática desde una perspectiva multidimensional e incluyente' in Úrsula Oswald (ed.), *Resolución noviolenta de conflictos en sociedades indígenas y minorías* (Mexico DF, 2004).

framework as maternal power (mother–wife, nuns), erotic power (lover or prostitute) or from outside it as 'crazed'. However, these processes are not only linear, and there exists an interdependence between patriarchy and female submission. Submission is converted into a social habit, as assigned female identity morally obliges women to be at the disposition of males, as a process of socialized self-identification.[20]

Table 5.1   Human, Gender and Environmental Security as a trans-radical concept[21]

Degree of expansion	Denomination	Reference objects (security of whom?)	Value at risk (security of what?)	Sources of threat (security from whom and for what?)
No expansion	National security (political, military)	The State	Sovereignty, territorial integrity	Other states, terrorism, sub-state actors
Incremental	Societal security	Nations, societal groups	National unity, identity	Nations, migrants, alien cultures
Radical	Human security	Individuals, humankind	Survival, quality of life	State, globalization, élites, terrorism
Ultra-radical	Environmental security	Ecosystem, humankind	Sustainability	Nature, humankind
Trans-radical	Gender security	Gender relations, indigenous minorities, children, elders	Equity, identity, solidarity, social representations	Patriarchy, totalitarian institutions (government, religions, élites), culture, intolerance

In a patriarchal system the values at risk are the identity and the social representations. Social identity is now lived in a world where the processes of unification and diversification are proceeding with giant steps, quicker than ever in the past. People have a basic necessity to simplify and to put order into the reality, where the categorization of the social environment is done through social comparison which improves self-esteem positively.[22]

---

20 Marcela Lagarde y de los Rios, 'Los cautiverios de las mujeres: madresposas, monjas, putas, presas y locas', unpublished doctoral thesis, National University of Mexico, 1990; and Marcela Lagarde y de los Rios, *Claves feministas para la autoestima de las mujeres* (Barcelona, 2000).

21 I here tabulate the ideas presented by Møller, 2003, p. 279.

22 Hogg, M.A. and D. Abrams, *Social Identification: A Social Psychology of Intergroup Relations and Group Processes* (London, 1988), p. 78.

Precisely, the social representations of gender are charged with stereotypes – women as weak, incapable, dependent and vulnerable. However they are social categories, rich and complex in a symbolic system, where they are socially and dialogically constructed. They form part of an inalienable collective life, enriched by ideologies, rites, beliefs and daily practices.[23]

Moscovici describes the social representations as 'systems of values, ideas and practices' which simultaneously create a system of order, able to offer a person the possibility to get familiarized to dispose of the social and material world. The communication within a community offers a code of social common interchange, where several aspects of life, personal and collective history are classified without ambiguity. For this reason, social representations originate in daily life, where society is the thinking system. The theory of social identity establishes a continuum between personal and social identity, giving the identity a *processual*, relational, multidimensional, contextual and essential character.[24]

In a social organization based on sexual differences, one is born as man or woman. This implies specific identity conditions, distinctive mechanisms of exercising power, and different processes of empowerment. The trans-radical level of expansion in gender security is related to the upcoming theories of eco-feminism, eco-indigenism, cultural resistance and the 'other world is possible hope' philosophy (raised at Porto Alegre, World Social Fora). In all these approaches the traditional social identity patterns are questioned in a holistic way, linking together social equality, environmental sustainability, cultural diversity and gender equity.

Security Concepts in the Post-Cold War Geopolitical Context

In this complex world situation, the end of the Cold War world apparently changed geopolitics. Germany reunified, the Soviet Union disintegrated, and several Eastern European countries joined the European Union. There was great hope for a stable period of international peace. However, a rapid process of political and economic democratization (*perestroika* and *glasnost*), obsolete productive systems, extensive bureaucracies, corruption, over-centralization of government, systematic repression of dissidents and independence wars in Afghanistan and Chechnya submerged the former USSR into a systemic crisis. The Soviet Union was divided into fifteen

---

23 These ideas are explored at length in the works of Jürgen Habermas referenced in note 10. Readers may also consult studies of early myths, such as Robert Graves, *The Greek Myths* (Harmondsworth, 1960).

24 See Serge Moscovici, *Social Influence and Social Change* (Cambridge, 1976), p. xiii. Social identity is *processual* because it is permanently changing, *relational* because its transformation is linked to interaction, and *multidimensional* because it is operating inside and between individuals, groups and ideologies, as discussed by W. Doise, *Levels of Explanation in Social Psychology* (Cambridge, 1986); it is *contextual* because it forges a relation in specific contexts, and it is *essential* because the diversity and complexity of the social interaction is sustained and transformed by identity processes (see Serrano, 'Género, migración y paz').

independent republics, although Russia still retains the biggest arms arsenal and controls natural resources. However, the reconstruction of its economy, linked to corruption in the process of privatization of oil and gas, has limited the future of the former superpower. The speed of its disintegration surprised political analysts and its impact extended to the formerly communist allies, North Korea, Cuba and Angola. China has re-oriented its economy to market forces and a kind of 'social capitalism' with high industrial growth rates, low agricultural ones, and increased disparities between rural and urban areas. Similar processes are occurring in India and the Mercosur association, with the Andean Pact reinforcing the Brazilian economy. Predictors show that the BRIC countries – Brazil, Russia, India and China – will soon become a dominant economic power.[25] The question is, what will happen with their geopolitical interests?

These tensions also reflect the global world order, where old conflicts (Palestinian–Israeli, Indian–Pakistani, Chinese–Taiwanese, North–South Korean, African ethnic confrontations) are linked to new threats: conflicts over natural resources – especially oil, gas and water – and the internal gap between rural and urban areas and between social classes. This quite complex situation is reinforced by structural violence such as poverty, street children, women and child trafficking, marginalization, women's discrimination, torture, extra-judicial executions, illegal judicial processes and human rights violations.

But we have also developed an expanded conceptualization of security in place of the narrow military one. How can a world, increasingly unsecured by threats, challenges, vulnerabilities and risks of natural and social disasters, create processes which increase HUGE security in such a way that all social classes, races, gender and age groups would find a place to live in harmony with nature and society in a plural, cultural diverse and peaceful world?

The 2005 conference in Nanjing was a step in exploring new possibilities for peace research, in a complex world scenario where China will be one of the main players. I hope that the modest reflections from Latin American and IPRA's experiences can help Chinese researchers to situate their country in the present geopolitical game, and to promote a less violent world through research, education and daily nonviolent practices. Conflicts can be positive motors of change and development; but when conflicts are tied to personal ambitions and geopolitical interests, mismanaged conflict and change dynamics can destroy the entire world.[26] Physical and structural violence is inherent in the highly competitive free-market system and its present laws of globalization. The Socialist utopia was destroyed by a repressive and bureaucratic communist regime in the USSR. Which utopia is left to develop ethical principles, communitarian responsibility and environmentally sustainable development, in order to induce a 'postmodern consensus democracy', with equity, real citizen representation and quality of life? The history of wars, domination and destruction brought poverty and death; will the emerging civilization guarantee diverse, just,

---

25 See predictors given by *The Economist* in *Pocket World in Figures* (London, 2004).
26 Max Gluckman, *Custom and Conflict in Africa* (Oxford, 1956).

equitable and sustainable coexistence, with care of the vulnerable? This is the challenge for peace researchers, educators and actors, and CLAIP has to resume its effort to find concrete answers to these new challenges.

We are left with many doubts, and possibly some useful experiences, to hand on to our Chinese colleagues, eager to see them guide their society on a route of peace and nonviolent conflict resolution processes. Cultures of peace, diverse, open to change and integrative, could channel potential tensions in a positive way, creating an ambience where all of us can live in a world of sustainable peace in harmony with natural and cultural diversity.[27] The challenge is colossal, and only by uniting forces can we initiate this noble task and collaborate with China and its people to forge this attainable utopia.

---

27 Elise Boulding, *Cultures of Peace: The Hidden Side of History* (New York, 2000).

Chapter 6

The Peace Process in South Africa

Paddy Meskin

There is an old Rabbinic teaching that just before a person dies, an angel comes to him or her and asks the vital question: 'Tell me, is the world a better place because of your life which is about to end? Is the world a better place because of the efforts you exerted? Is the world a better place because you were around?'

Introduction

Can religious leaders and religious communities be peace-makers? Does not the history of religion show that religious differences have all too often been used to promote war? So many contemporary conflicts are the tragic results of religious divides, where leaders on all sides misuse their religion to intensify the conflict for their own ends. Many people – all over the world – must feel that religions talk peace but actually fuel conflict. My own involvement in the peace process has been from a faith-based perspective, and I therefore report here on peace-work by faith-based organizations (FBOs) as well as non-governmental organizations (NGOs) and academic institutions, providing a review of the past decade and current trends and programmes. We certainly have had divisive issues in South Africa, but one thing I hope to show in this chapter is that religious communities can play a progressive and pro-peace role. South Africa has a high level of participation in religious life, with a strong church influence in both the black and white communities, and also important Hindu, Muslim and Jewish institutions. I start with a review of recent history, because the struggle against apartheid was the defining feature of our social and political movements in the twentieth century. Although we have had a non-racial, democratic system of government since 1994, much of our peace-work is still profoundly influenced by events and legacies of the apartheid era.

I am sure that most human beings would subscribe to the idea that their lives should make a difference to the world. Verses in all holy books extol the virtues of peace, prayers ask God to 'make me an instrument of peace', to 'grant us peace'. But generally peace is seen as a dream, a mirage. The desire for peace has perhaps existed since the beginning of time, but it has always been elusive: at no point in recorded history has there ever been peace throughout the world. There are many very different concepts or definitions of peace. Readers from a faith-based background may like to know that one of the anonymous definitions which we have used in

South Africa states: 'Peace is not just the absence of war, but also the presence of God'. This statement for some of course would have no meaning, but to those who do believe, God is peace.

The Anti-Apartheid Struggle

The peace process in South Africa is intimately linked to the struggle against apartheid. Peace and racism are like oil and water. Historians suggest that racial discrimination began with the arrival of Jan van Riebeck in the Cape in 1652. The concept of apartheid, separate status for different races, was to develop over the next three hundred years until apartheid as a formal system of government commenced in 1948 with the election of the Nationalist Party. The evils of apartheid reached new heights through the racist legislation introduced between 1950 and 1955. During this period compulsory discrimination against people on the basis of their race – for practical purposes, their skin-colour – became law.

The next four decades would see justice, democracy, freedom and peace in South Africa become a distant dream for millions of disenfranchised, marginalized people. The divide between black and white was so wide that there were many for whom it seemed unbridgeable. Fortunately there were those who were not daunted and who defied the laws of the time. In fact defiance was an early symbol for the struggle, when in 1951 the Defiance Campaign was initiated to reject the most hated aspect of the legislation, the 'Pass Laws' which denied fundamental human rights such as the right to travel or reside in certain zones, or to freely seek employment.

The people burned their passes, Nelson Mandela being one of the first.[1] Thousands were charged and sent to jail. The Freedom Charter, written and adopted at the Kliptown Congress of Delegates in 1955, was a milestone: the document was much later to become one of the pillars of the new constitution, ratified on 18 December 1996.[2] Political protests grew. On 9 August 1956 20,000 women from all walks of life marched to the Union Buildings in Pretoria to present a manifesto against the Pass Laws. Their slogan was 'You have struck the rock!', indicating that the white government was taking on not only a possibly superficial political struggle but that it was confronting African women, the bedrock of the continent. This defiance came at a price, as it escalated the violence. Armed police used attack dogs to break up the 9 August demonstration, leaving dead and wounded women on the streets.

One cannot overstate the role that women played in the struggle: women like Lilian Ngoyi, Ruth First, Helen Joseph, Helen Suzman, Albertina Sisulu and Ela Gandhi to name but a few. Their strength was vital to the civic movements, in the political arena, and in the external and underground structures. They fought hard to overthrow traditional male domination as well as apartheid. As a result, today there are many instruments safeguarding women's rights, and South Africa has one of the

---

1   Charlene Smith, *Mandela* (Cape Town, 1999), p. 9.
2   See <http://www.gpg.gov.za/publications/freedomcharter.html>.

greatest numbers of women in government. There is currently a move to make it mandatory to have 50 per cent of the Members of Parliament women.

1960 was a watershed year. On 21 March 1960 the Sharpeville Massacre took place: 69 people were killed and 186 wounded when the police opened fire on a crowd demonstrating against the Pass Laws. The government declared a state of emergency, more than 11,000 people around the country were arrested, and the African National Congress (ANC) and the Pan African Congress (PAC) were banned. One of the proscribed individuals, who served his third banning order, was the remarkable Chief Albert Lutuli, chief of his tribe, President-General of the ANC and leader of ten million black Africans in their nonviolent campaign for civil rights in South Africa. Intolerant of hatred and adamant in his demands for equality and peace, Lutuli forged a philosophical compatibility between two cultures, the Zulu culture of his native Africa and the Christian–democratic culture of Europe. In 1960 he became the first South African to be awarded the Nobel Peace Prize. The following sentences from his acceptance speech illustrate the spirit of the South African movement:[3]

> This year, as in the years before it, mankind has paid for the maintenance of peace the price of many lives. I recognize ... that in my country, South Africa, the spirit of peace is subject to some of the severest tensions known to men. Yes, it is idle to speak of our country as being in peace, because there can be no peace in any part of the world where there are people oppressed. ... I therefore regard this award as recognition of the sacrifice made by many of all races, particularly the African people, who have endured and suffered so much for so long.

While some activists remained committed to a completely nonviolent process, the level of oppression tipped the majority of the population into active or at least passive support for armed struggle. In 1961 the *Umkhonto We Sizwe* (Spear of the Nation) military wing was formed: Nelson Mandela went to Algeria for training, accepting that the ANC could no longer rely on nonviolence as a way to change the thinking of the government.[4] Initial actions were unsuccessful, and in 1963 Nelson Mandela, Walter Sisulu, Denis Goldberg and others were sentenced under the Suppression of Communism Act. Mandela, together with the other accused, was imprisoned on Robben Island. He remained a prisoner for twenty-seven years.

16 June 1976 was another watershed, the day of the Soweto Uprising when black youths rebelled against the imposition of Afrikaans as the medium of instruction in schools. The police attacked, wounded and killed scores of black children who were demonstrating in a peaceful protest. The protest spread nationwide after police killed thirteen-year-old Hector Peterson during a demonstration. By the following February 575 people, a quarter of them children, had been killed in the unrest. The following years saw tens of thousands of young blacks virtually deprived of formal education: they became known as the lost generation because of their belief in 'liberation before education'. The photo of young Hector which went round the world contributed to

---

3 See <www.anc.org.za/ancdocs/history/lutuli>.

4 Smith, p. 10.

changing international attitudes to South Africa, and intensified the boycott which had been started in the 1960s by the Reverend Trevor Huddlestone and like-minded people. The late 1970s saw the rise of trade unions and student groups. In 1977 a brilliant young man, Steve Biko, a black consciousness-movement leader who had promoted nonviolence, became the forty-sixth person to die in detention. This led to an outcry from many anti-apartheid activists living overseas and hardened the determination of those activists within South Africa. International isolation increased. Sports, culture and business boycotts all helped the struggle for peace and democracy; but at the same time they brought increasing hardship and violence to the very people that the boycotts were intended to help. As the ANC, PAC and other liberation groups escalated the level of violence in the struggle, so the violence of the Special Forces in government became more indiscriminate. Detention without trial was common practice. Age was no protection and thousands of young boys and girls disappeared without trace. Families were torn apart, brother fought brother, sons and daughters spied on parents. For young people living in townships, violence was the norm.

Despite all this ugliness, there were organizations and courageous individuals who promoted nonviolence: two that stand out are the End Conscription Campaign (ECC) and the Free Mandela Campaign, both of which received support from the outside world. Conscription was compulsory for all white men over the age of eighteen. Young men who did not wish to comply had two options: either to leave South Africa and not return, or face a jail term of up to six years. Religious communities and organizations like Diakonia and Black Sash were important supporters of the ECC. The late Archbishop Denis Hurley, vociferous in his opposition to apartheid, was a strong advocate for the ECC and extremely active in assisting the many people in detention and their families.

In 1984 another son of South Africa received a Nobel Peace prize: Archbishop Desmond Tutu.[5] In 1978 Tutu became the first black General Secretary of the South African Council of Churches (SACC), a contact organization for the South African churches which functions as a national committee for the World Council of Churches. It was in this position, which he held until 1985, that Tutu became a national and international figure. The Afrikaans churches disassociated themselves from the organization as a result of SACC's unambiguous stand against apartheid. Around 80 per cent of its members are black and they now dominate the leading positions. SACC was committed to fulfilling the social responsibility of the church, and Tutu as its chairperson led a formidable crusade for justice and racial reconciliation in South Africa. Tutu formulated his objective as 'a democratic and just society without racial divisions', and set forward the following points as minimum demands:

---

5   See <http://www.tutu.org/main.htm> for more information.

1. equal civil rights for all;
2. the abolition of South Africa's Pass Laws;
3. a common system of education;
4. the cessation of forced deportation from South Africa to the so-called 'homelands'.

Also in 1984 Tutu, together with religious leaders from the different faith communities, launched the South African chapter of the World Conference on Religion and Peace (WCRP), which I discuss later. During the second half of the 1980s tensions escalated on different fronts, including between the ANC and the Inkatha Freedom Party (IFP), which represented sectors of the KwaZulu–Natal population. Antagonism between the leaders resulted in the followers of both committing acts of violence in their communities, including the horrific practice of 'necklacing'. Subsequently peace monitors and mediation programmes were set up in most parts of South Africa, especially in KwaZulu–Natal, the province with one of the worst records of violence. Religious leaders from the different faith communities played vital roles in attempting to bring peace to the areas in which they lived.

New South Africa

In 1986 Mandela offered to begin talks with the state president, P.W. Botha, and a negotiated settlement slowly began to emerge. In 1990 President de Klerk removed the ban on the ANC and other organizations, and on 2 February 1990 Nelson Mandela was released from Pollsmoor Prison, a free man after 27 years imprisonment. In 1990 negotiations began for the creation of an Interim Constitution, based on the Freedom Charter and a Bill of Rights; in January 1991 Mandela met IFP leaders to discuss ways to bring peace to Kwazulu–Natal. Democratic elections were held on 27 April 1994. This day is, and will remain, a highly significant date, not just in South African history, but in world history. Democratic elections were held for the first time in South Africa, with a vote for every citizen over the age of eighteen. Some saw it as a modern miracle, and indeed it was, for there was concern that the process would be marred by the kind of violence that had been seen in so many other countries: but the elections were free, peaceful and fair. On 10 May 1994 Mandela was installed as the first nationally elected President of South Africa.

The democratic South Africa was born with the aspiration to create a new nation, a 'rainbow nation'. A major task was to redress the imbalances of the past for the millions who had been marginalized, yet at the same time to ensure the commitment to the new process of the former élites. One attempt at popular participation was the formulation of the new Constitution. Every sector of society was invited to provide input. The faith communities, lawyers, business people, rural and urban citizens, and even school-children: thousands of men, women and children made history by contributing their ideas and being a part of that historic document. On 18 December

1996, when the new Constitution was ratified, the true peace process in South Africa began.

At a peace lecture in 1994 President Mandela had stated: 'I wish to emphasize the role of the religious community in the struggle and in the reconstruction and development. ... Your prophetic voice is crucial in reinforcing the moral fibre of the new democratic state – be it in the application of human rights or the integrity of ... other practices'. Archbishop Tutu became a key mediator and conciliator in the difficult transition toward democracy. In 1996 he was appointed by President Nelson Mandela to chair the seventeen-member Truth and Reconciliation Commission (TRC), the body set up in 1995 to probe gross human rights violations during the apartheid era between 1960 and 1994. Many of the commissioners, including Tutu, were religious figures and members of WCRP.[6]

There were those in the country who thought the TRC, although intended as a means of working towards reconciliation through clarifying the truth, would only create more hatred, anger and violence. Equally there were many who believed in the maxim 'the Truth will set you free': by learning about and finding closure on many of the horrific events that had occurred during the apartheid era, we could go forward to build a nation of which we could be proud. The TRC held public hearings throughout South Africa at which former victims of human rights abuses told their stories. The commission's amnesty committee processed more than 7,124 applications by perpetrators of such violations. A reparation and rehabilitation committee was established to recommend appropriate forms of compensation for human rights victims. The commission's report was presented to President Mandela in October 1998.

In 1997 new opportunities for interfaith solidarity emerged. President Nelson Mandela and Vice-President Thabo Mbeki met for three days with religious leaders from all the faith communities in the country, and out of this meeting the National Religious Leaders Forum (NRLF) was born. The euphoria of the first election had worn off, giving way to concerns about divisions and escalating violence: poverty, housing, unemployment, discrimination, moral values, education and redressing the imbalances of the past. The meeting sought the active participation of FBOs to deal with the many problems facing the new democracy. The NRLF was to be an organization of top religious leaders to serve in a consultative capacity to the President. They also produced a document entitled the *Ubuntu Pledge* which is still used in schools and communities.[7]

---

6   See the official website at <http://www.doj.gov.za/trc/>.

7   See report on the first signing of the Ubuntu Pledge at <http://bahai-library.com/newspapers/PR100398.html>.

Peace Activities in South Africa

This section reports on peace studies, conflict transformation and similar areas of work. I have divided it into academic, NGO and FBO groupings, although there are naturally many overlaps. Following the demise of apartheid, priorities for peace-workers in South Africa have evolved into the following:

* implementing the recognition that every human being is entitled to equal opportunity and basic human rights, regardless of race, creed or colour;
* eradicating racism and discrimination;
* establishing the right of all people to freedom of speech, religion, language and association;
* seeking nonviolent solutions to social and political conflicts;
* seeking the truth and redressing the inequalities of the past;
* addressing the HIV/AIDS pandemic and gender violence;
* demonstrating concern for conflicts in neighbouring states and other parts of Africa.

Peace Research and Academic Institutions

No actual peace studies chairs or departments have been established at tertiary institutions, but many university teaching and research programmes are linked to peace studies. It is not surprising that internal conflict has been the primary concern of peace research in South Africa. Conflict resolution continues to be a central area, as do human rights, violence and the sources of violence. Such programmes are affiliated to various faculties: political studies and law especially, but also media, psychology, economics, social development, gender studies and adult education.

From the 1960s, discourse at state universities was split mainly along linguistic lines, with the English-speaking universities of Cape Town, Natal (Durban and Pietermaritzburg) and Witwatersrand (Johannesburg) providing increasingly radical alternatives to the apartheid political system. Programmes were often formulated by Marxist-influenced social-sciences faculties that contrasted sharply with the traditionally conservative Afrikaans-speaking universities of Stellenbosch and Pretoria, although critical views were expressed by staff at Afrikaans theological faculties, among them the late Reverend Dr Beyers Naude and Reverend Dr Gerrie Lubbe, both of whom became founder members of the WCRP.

In the apartheid era most research on South Africa was conducted overseas and not published internally. Conversely, I believe that only parts of South Africa's varied research output are known internationally. The lack of a peace studies umbrella organization also made it difficult to gain an overview of the institutional situation of peace and conflict researchers within the university sphere, although South Africans as Conflict Resource to Africa aimed to create a network of individuals in the conflict-research sphere. Many of the programmes became part of the South

African Political Studies Association whose publications regularly deal with conflict research. The following is a list of some of the most important institutions.

Founded in 1992, the African Centre for the Constructive Resolution of Disputes (ACCORD), under the direction of Vasu Gounden, has played an important role in the political transformation of South Africa. It was first located on the campus of the University of Durban–Westville in the troubled province of KwaZulu–Natal. The first four years of its existence was spent training peace monitors and election observers, as part of the National Peace Accords, and providing training to police and legal services, assisting staff to deal with local conflicts. With its yearly African Peace Award, ACCORD also honours individuals who have rendered outstanding services to peace in Africa. In order to pass on South African conflict-resolution experiences to other countries, ACCORD has compiled a comprehensive data-bank on Africa and has sent teams to places such as Somalia, Burundi, Nicaragua and Sri Lanka. ACCORD's other activities include the Preventive Diplomacy Forum, a kind of rapid response force for the peaceful resolution of conflicts; publishing the *African Journal of Peace Research*, the *ACCORD Occasional Papers* and a *Preventive Diplomacy* series; and maintaining a documentation centre. ACCORD aims to set up a permanent Conflict Prevention Centre as a research and training centre for the continent.

The Centre for Conflict Resolution (CCR) at the University of Cape Town functions in a similar way to ACCORD. Founded in 1968 under the name Centre for Intergroup Studies, it works at the regional, national and continental levels, providing training for mediators, facilitators and police officers in South Africa and Zimbabwe. The CCR has also monitored the reform of the South African armed forces. On the international front their focus is on disarmament, peacekeeping and regional security. CCR mediators have been active in Mozambique, Zimbabwe and the Great Lakes region. *Track Two*, a quarterly periodical published jointly with the Media Peace Centre, provides information on 'constructive approaches to community and political conflict'.

The Institute of Security Studies is not formally affiliated to a university, but it does aim to produce high-quality research. Founded in 1990 as the Institute for Defence Policy in Johannesburg, it is financed through membership fees and subsidies from private and public donors. In contrast to ACCORD and CCR, the Institute's main expertise falls within a narrower definition of security: many staff are former military working on three focal areas: regional security, small-arms control and criminality. The Centre for the Study of Violence and Reconciliation, Johannesburg, is likewise not attached to any academic institution. It focuses on the field of trauma research, offers advice to victims of violence, organizes seminars and conferences, and produces training materials, videos and study programmes for political education within the field of democracy and reconciliation. Outstanding research has also been produced by the South African Institute of Race Relations, founded as early as the 1920s, the Institute for a Democratic South Africa and the Institute for Multi-party Democracy. These privately financed research institutes are not academic in the narrower sense, but they have all made, and continue to make, important contributions to the understanding of racial conflicts. Most of the above mentioned organizations and institutions were closely associated with the liberal middle classes and supported the idea of political power-sharing for the majority coloured population.

Relatively few universities offer peace studies as part of their standard programmes. The University of Port Elizabeth is the only university in South Africa offering courses at both under-graduate and post-graduate levels. In 1997 its Institute for the Study and Resolution of Conflict launched an interdisciplinary award 'Masters in Conflict and Conflict Resolution'. It is also worth noting individual programmes in this area. The University of South Africa offers similar courses by distance-learning, deliberately aimed at a broad audience. At the University of Stellenbosch, Du Toit works chiefly on theoretical conflict-research, and Breytenbach studies conflicts in Africa. The University of KwaZuluNatal offers some modules, mostly at post-graduate level within the politics faculty. Finally, Malan offers an interdisciplinary post-graduate course in 'Conflict Studies' at ACCORD's regional offices in the University of the Western Cape in Cape Town. South African peace research remains a rich and varied part of the international research landscape, recognized by the 17th International Peace Research Association Conference being hosted in Durban in June 1998.

NGOs

South Africa has a rich heritage of NGO activity, a substantial part of which is engaged in peace work. A common problem for newly emerging democracies is a belief that appears to be held by donors and funders: now your country is a democracy we can move our funding elsewhere. The truth is that democracy and peace building only start after the first election takes place. Building peace and democracy is an ongoing process that never ends, and one that can so easily slip away if the people who own it do not guard and protect it. Whereas previously political emancipation occupied centre-stage, the main concern now is to overcome the economic divide between the races. The renewed outbreak of conflict in KwaZulu–Natal and a series of brutal murders of white farmers have added fuel to the fire, and the deteriorating economic and unemployment situation has led to a dramatic increase in crime. We are fortunate that several organizations, despite funding difficulties, are managing to maintain a momentum. ACCORD, the Centre for Peace Action, the Independent Mediation Service of South Africa (IMSSA), Black Sash, Women for Peaceful Change, Peace Now, Gandhi Development Trust and Satyagraha have all played an important role, both during the struggle and in the post-apartheid era. A good example of this aspect of peace work is provided by IMSSA. With 43 permanent employees and over 400 freelance workers engaged in mediation, arbitration and training, IMSSA is one of the largest independent institutions in conflict resolution. It provides services to companies, mediating between employees and management and also in conflicts between companies. IMSSA offers training programmes in mediation and publishes the *IMSSA Review*. In the same field, Community Conflict Management and

Resolution in Johannesburg runs training courses for local mediators/facilitators, as does the Community Dispute Resolution Trust. Similar work is done by Future Links in Cape Town and the Human Rights Trust in Port Elizabeth. Another innovative group, founded in 1990, the Independent Projects Trust is a facilitation, training and research consultancy which seeks to help organizations, both public and private, that are undergoing transformations owing to political, social and economic changes. All the above organizations were active during the struggle to make the first election process peaceful and fair.

I cannot report on the whole range of NGO activities, but should give a few illustrations. Many arts institutions and organizations were involved in the anti-apartheid struggle: the process drew in music and arts communities, especially protest theatre and protest literature. For example, the poems of Mongane Wally Serote touched the hearts of the people; Athol Fugard politicized the theatre, going public not only in South Africa, but throughout the world; Miriam Makeba warmed her people with her beautiful voice; and Nadine Gordimer, a Nobel prize-winner, authored thought-provoking stories. The Children's Rights Centre and the Children's Rights Alliance were established in the 1990s specifically to cater for the rights of children and ensure training and information given to teachers and carers and, in particular, all aspects of HIV/AIDS. In South Africa the huge pandemic has become a major issue for activists. Discrimination and violence is rife against and among those affected by HIV/AIDS. Finally, FBOs, which had contributed greatly to the peaceful struggle against apartheid, were to play significant roles during the transition to democracy, for example providing most of the mediators, monitors, observers and organizers for the election process. It was also mainly from FBOs that the Truth and Reconciliation Commission would draw their commissioners, counsellors, interviewers and researchers.

Case Study: The WCRP

One aspect of apartheid was strict segregation of communities not only on racial lines, but also religiously, according to the provisions of the 1950 Group Areas Act. Hindus, Muslims, Christians and African traditionalists, forced to live and work separately, could barely speak to each other, let alone understand each others' faiths. Yet we saw growing cooperation and solidarity of faith communities and leaders, particularly during the 1980s as the various communities escalated their opposition to the apartheid regime. Much of this was channelled through the WCRP, an international interfaith organization committed to the realization of each religious tradition's potential for peace-building. WCRP served as a forum to deepen the solidarity of these groups and to explore positively religious diversity within organizations working for peaceful and nonviolent change. WCRP symbolized a determination to transcend religious barriers and reached out to those within the interfaith community who were committed to peaceful struggle against apartheid, through dialogue around practical matters and by sharing the conviction that 'doctrines divide but humanity unites'.[8] WCRP did not view itself as 'an exercise in abstract interfaith dialogue focussing merely on the analysis of concepts or customs … but proceeds from joint commitment to the struggle for justice and peace in South Africa'.[9] The WCRP, together with a number of mainstream religious organizations, was extremely active both during the struggle and post-1994.

While many people of faith supported the idea of a free and democratic South Africa, the issue of violence was inevitably divisive. Some felt that violence was justified and indeed necessary; others, particularly within the faith communities, felt very strongly that peace and democracy do not come through the barrel of a gun.

WCRP mobilized religious leaders and grassroots members from organizations such as SACC, Diakonia, the Roman Catholic Church, Muslim Youth Movement of South Africa, the Hindu Youth Association, Jews for Social Justice and numerous other FBOs in a unified, prophetic, defiant stand against the gross injustices and cruelties of apartheid. Sadly this stand rarely received the wholehearted support of leadership structures. As was later revealed in TRC interviews, not only did some religious leaders fail to denounce apartheid, they actually gave it active support. Fortunately there were great religious leaders among all the faiths who stood up to be counted, among them people like Reverend Gerrie Lubbe, Ayusaf Akhalwaya, Ms Yamin Sooka, Ms Ela Gandhi and of course the patron of WCRP, Archbishop Desmond Tutu. WCRP became the target of state harassment by the apartheid regime, some of its members banned and others detained. Even the very first lecture to honour Tutu's Nobel Peace prize was banned! This interfaith action was to be the forerunner of many where faith communities worked together to oppose the government, and also of constructive activities in the post-apartheid regime.

In 1987, under the leadership of Desmond Tutu, WCRP took a delegation of local and international religious leaders to Lusaka to meet with the ANC in exile expressly to discuss 'Religious Communities in Post-Apartheid South Africa'. In 1988 a national consultation was held with religious leaders and activists to obtain their support for the 'journey into the new South Africa'. The next few years saw much consultation and discussion to articulate the hopes and concerns of the religious communities. In June 1992 a WCRP workshop produced a draft document based on feedback from interfaith and single faith conferences. In November 1992, at the National Interfaith Conference in Pretoria, after three days of debate 150 representatives of diverse religious communities adopted the 'Declaration on Religious Rights and Responsibilities'. Its Preamble acknowledged the diversity of the faith communities and expressed regret that 'religion had been used to contribute to the oppression, exploitation and suffering of people'. It also affirmed freedom of conscience, including the freedom of accepting or changing religious affiliation, the equality of all religious communities before the law, the right to religious education,

---

8   Gerrie Lubbe, *Believers in the Struggle for Justice and Peace* (Johannesburg, 1988), p. 16.
9   Klippies Kritzinger, 'Introduction' in Gerrie Lubbe, *Believers in the Struggle for Justice and Peace* (Johannesburg, 1988) pp. 1–2.

access to public media, recognition of systems of customary law and the propagation of teachings and the observance of holy days.

Current and Future Focus

Although the promotion of peace is on the government agenda and we have one of the most enlightened constitutions in the world, there are still alarming problems in South African society which contribute to a very high level of violence. For example:

- one of the worst records of rape in the world: 44,000 reported in 2004, and doubtless tens of thousands unreported;
- an increasing level of gender violence and child abuse;
- the largest number of people living with HIV/AIDS in a single country (recent estimates indicate 6.4 million) in a pandemic which devastates rape victims and families;
- the families of those affected and infected by HIV/AIDS are subjected to horrifying levels of discrimination which many call the 'new apartheid';
- almost half our population live below the poverty line;
- crime, especially violent crime, is extremely prevalent;
- numerous wars and armed conflicts in neighbouring states;
- millions of our citizens do not have access to the most basic of human rights, such as shelter, health care, education and potable water.

Without addressing these problems, we cannot hope to achieve a peaceful society. Peace cannot grow with such oppression and denial of basic human rights. It is no use talking about peace to people who have no home, no place to rest at night, no safe space for their children, no access to water, education or health care, or whose stomachs are aching because they have had no food for days and they are not sure when their next meal will come. Talking to them of promoting peace, nonviolence, democracy and freedom is more likely to make them angry. It is essential that basic needs are addressed in the path to promoting a world of peace and nonviolence. The peace activist, I believe, should also be involved in addressing the problems that contribute to violence. Poverty, corruption, human-rights abuses, ethical and religious conflicts, HIV/AIDS must be tackled, their causes addressed and solutions implemented before we even begin to see signs of peace, justice, freedom and opportunity for all. Academic research is important, but only when it is linked to realities and to a positive way forward. Yet notwithstanding the need to focus on basic rights, South Africans are continuing to come up with new initiatives directly connected to the promotion of peace. Some examples are:

- *Living museums.* A number of major new museums have recently opened and others soon will be, a wonderful way to educate citizens of the new South

Africa about different aspects of the freedom struggle. They include the Apartheid Museum in Johannesburg, The Robben Island Museum close to Cape Town, the Holocaust Museum in Cape Town and a Gandhi Museum of Peace planned in Durban.

- A new *life skills curriculum* has been incorporated into the education syllabus. It provides for every student to study issues such as human rights, the Holocaust, apartheid, the religions and cultures of the communities of South Africa, the making of choices, and what happens when racism and prejudice become law.

- The *empowerment of women* is of great importance not only to all stakeholders in civil society, but also to government. This is witnessed by the fact that South Africa has one of the highest numbers of women in parliament, and a decision has been taken to increase the level to 50 per cent.

- *Peace education programmes* in communities, schools and youth groups. Examples are those created by organizations such as WCRP: the Youth Peace Forum, Teaching Tolerance for teachers, travelling exhibitions, workshops for teachers and peer educators. They also promote commemorative events like International Peace days. The Children's Rights Centre and the Children's Rights Alliance cater specifically for the rights of children, in particular all aspects of peace, nonviolence and HIV/AIDS.

- Continuing investment in academic programmes. For example, discussions are taking place to set up a *Chair of Peace Studies* in Durban.

- *The Desmond Tutu Peace Centre* is a landmark institution primarily aimed at using the experience of the South African people and the example of Desmond Tutu to inspire a new generation of visionary peace builders. Its focus is to teach the extraordinary principles – practised by ordinary people – that were able to guide South Africa from violence to a cooperative peace.

- With South African government support, the *Human Rights Commission*, the *Gender Commission* and the *Commission for Religion, Language and Culture* have been established.

We are in the sixth year of the UN decade to promote a culture of peace and nonviolence. We have a very long way to go. Indeed there are possibly more wars, more conflict and more poverty than when we began the decade five and a half years ago. We have experienced 9/11, the second Iraq invasion, suicide bombing both in the Middle East and other parts of the world, terrorist attacks in supposedly peaceful countries. Every day we are bombarded with images of war from Darfur and the Democratic Republic of Congo, destruction by hurricanes and tornados, and the heartbreaking stories of millions of children who exist in the most appalling conditions. The effects of poverty, famine, disease and unemployment in some parts of Africa seem to be worse than ever. Despite the dire problems, South Africa still has immense advantages, and thus responsibilities, compared to many neighbouring countries. Consequently, since 1994 the South African government has tried to play a role in promoting peace and tolerance internationally. For example, South

African politicians have been invited to offer support to peace processes in Burundi, Liberia, Sierra Leone and Mozambique to name but a few. President Mbeki, together with President Obasanjo of Nigeria, launched the African Union and the African Renaissance. Former President Mandela, President Mbeki and Deputy President Zuma have all invested considerable effort in peace initiatives around the region.

From the Mahatma to Mandela

Finally, it would be remiss not to mention Mohandas Karamchand Gandhi, perhaps the greatest advocate of peaceful political change, who spent twenty years in South Africa. Because of his vast spiritual and political achievements Gandhi was often known by the honorific title Mahatma or Great Soul; and Gandhiji as an affectionate name. Gandhi arrived in South Africa in 1894, a young man of 24 who until then had led a rather sheltered life in India and in the UK, where he had studied law. Within a few days of his arrival he experienced a number of violent racist incidents which were to change his whole way of life. He was ejected from a court for refusing to take off his turban, and soon afterwards thrown off a first-class train for refusing to obey a white person who, unwilling to share the compartment with a 'coolie', had told him to leave. Gandhi was also assaulted when he refused to sit on the footboard of a carriage on his way to Pretoria, and he was insulted in hotels in the Transvaal. Such experiences shocked him into a strong desire to confront this ugly racism, and marked the genesis of a transformation as he began to reconsider his role as a lawyer, his middle-class life, and his responsibilities to the community.

Gandhi was so touched by the plight of the poor that he urged the Indian community to protest against the many discriminatory laws, and himself started a newspaper, *The Indian Opinion*, to publicize atrocities and to raise awareness. He also worked to improve living conditions for the Indian minority. This activity, which was especially directed against increasingly racist legislation, deepened his religious commitment and will to self-sacrifice. In the struggle for basic human rights for the Indian community, Gandhi formulated a method of nonviolent political action that was to have world-wide repercussions. The method, known by its Sanskrit name *satyagraha* (sometimes translated as soul-power or truth-force) was formally born on 11 September 1906. Gandhi spent the next four decades developing and implementing *satyagraha* in South Africa and in India, where it became one of the key strategies leading to the peaceful removal of Britain as colonial ruler. *Satyagraha* implied steadfast but peaceful opposition to oppression. Its practitioners should resolutely oppose injustice, but in a highly idealistic, spiritual way: they should act against the oppression itself, while forgiving and building good relationships with their oppressors, recognizing that in the process they would suffer persecution and punishment. Gandhi advised that the rule of law as a principle should be respected, but particular laws should be opposed by civil disobedience where necessary. In the particular context of South Africa, he advocated that Indians should break those laws which were unreasonable or suppressive, accepting that each individual would have to accept punishment for having violated the law. This would lead eventually, he reasoned, to white South Africans being willing to change their outlook and abandon, or at least modify, the oppressive legislation.

Gandhi believed implicitly that political movement should go hand-in-hand with humanitarian and spiritual efforts. Whilst living in Durban, he visited the Mariannhill Monastery and became deeply affected by the work being done by the nuns and the priest. He offered free services to St Aidan's Hospital and launched the Phoenix Settlement in order to create a self-sufficient community. He made contact with John Dube, who owned adjacent land, and together they began a school. He also met Reverend Isaiah Shembe of the Nazareth Baptist Zionist Church in Inanda, a neighbourhood close to Phoenix, and was deeply impressed by the strong beliefs and faith shown by the followers of his church. Their simplicity and adherence to peace and nonviolence appealed to Gandhiji. Gandhi refined his ideas of education at an initiative known as Tolstoy Farm, established in 1910 and built by Gandhi's great friend Hermann Kallenbach. Teams of students and inmates all took turns to do the chores. In an idealistic environment Gandhiji personally educated the children here as they walked through the farm on nature trails, learning history through discussions, and mathematics through carpentry and leather work. In 1913 the activities were moved to Phoenix Settlement in Durban.

Gandhi left an indelible impression on the life of South Africa, its freedom movement and its peace workers. Naturally the large Hindu community in and around Durban reveres his legacy, but his life's work also inspires people of all faiths with its commitment to political freedom, social welfare, reconciliation and creative education: hallmarks of the best of South African activism. For example, the peaceful transition from apartheid was largely due to inclusivity during the process, conscious effort to keep radical forces on both sides at the negotiating table, and continuous dialogue between all parties. We have seen how the remarkable commitment of great individuals has blossomed to touch the lives of millions. Gandhiji, Albert Lutuli, Nelson Mandela, Desmond Tutu and many others were inspired by influences from various cultures, taking the best from their own faith and heritage, as well as from the example of foreign freedom movements, even from the history and literature of their oppressors. They have forged a vision of humanity that can encompass all peoples and that sets a precedent for the rest of the world. In 1993 the Nobel Committee declared that it had decided to give the Peace Prize to Mandela and then President De Klerk for their 'looking ahead to South African reconciliation instead of back at the deep wounds of the past'. South Africa had been the very symbol of racial suppression, and the peaceful termination of the apartheid regime accordingly 'points the way to the peaceful resolution of similar deep-rooted conflicts elsewhere in the world'.

The African continent is characterized not only by an endless series of wars and humanitarian catastrophes, but also by the ability to overcome them. One of South Africa's four Nobel Peace Laureates, Archbishop Tutu, has stated, 'Africa has this thing called *Ubuntu*: it is about the essence of being human, it is part of the gift that Africa will give the world. We believe a person is a person through another person. When I dehumanize you, I dehumanize myself'.[10] Similarly, in his Nobel lecture, Nelson Mandela referred to an organic world-view, calling himself a mere representative of the millions of people across the globe who 'recognized that an injury to one is an injury to all'. This statement is the essence of *ubuntu* philosophy universally applied. I hope it is a message for all people. I conclude with two quotes used by former President Mandela, the first an ancient Bantu adage: '*umuntu ngumuntu ngabantu*' (we are people through other people). Second: 'the common ground is greater and more enduring than the differences that divide'. Inevitably, there is mutual interdependence in the human condition. In South Africa the concept of the African renaissance is linked with that of a peaceful society where all people have equal opportunity and where no-one is denied basic human rights.

---

10 Tutu cited in *Pan African Education: A Newsletter of the Umtapo Centre*, 2 (1998):14.

Chapter 7

Japanese Peace Museums:
Education and Reconciliation

Kazuyo Yamane

I first learned of the terrible atrocities that the Japanese military committed against Chinese people during the Second World War through reading Iris Chang's *The Rape of Nanking*.[1] Having read the book I began to feel very ashamed of being Japanese. In 1998 I went to Changde City in Hunan Province to investigate the biological warfare conducted by the Japanese Army during the Second World War. My second visit to China was to Nanjing itself, in 2005. I was deeply shocked to discover the historical facts, and to learn about the victims who have been suffering from the effects of biological warfare. I had never had a chance to learn these facts at school, nor from the Japanese media. As a Japanese citizen I wanted to apologize sincerely to the Chinese people for Japan's aggression during the war, so with other people at a peace museum called Grassroots House in Kochi, Japan, I began to support the Chinese victims who demanded an apology and compensation from the Japanese state.

This chapter first introduces peace studies in Japan, defining its mainstream agenda and institutions, with an emphasis on the issue of Japan's responsibility for the aggression. Secondly, I provide an overview of peace museums in Japan, together with some original research on such museums internationally to contextualize the efforts in Japan. I go on to discuss exhibitions of Japan's aggression at various Japanese peace museums. Japan has the highest number of peace museums of any country in the world, but the scope of exhibits is problematic because Japan's aggression is not exhibited at many public peace museums. However, it is encouraging that this aggression is acknowledged at private peace museums, and that citizens are active in peace-making processes. I hope that readers can gain some insights into the kind of issues that peace educators engage with in Japan today.

Peace Studies in Japan

The Peace Studies Association of Japan (PSAJ) was co-founded in 1973 by a Peace Research Group that had been set up in 1964, and by the Japanese branch of the International Peace Science Society. A statement of purpose defines its mission: 'The true intention of establishing PSAJ is to promote and develop a genuinely scientific

---

1   Iris Chang, *The Rape of Nanking: The Forgotten Holocaust of World War II* (London, 1998).

and objective science of war and peace through integrating various research methods and thus to consolidate the conditions for lasting peace'. There were about eight hundred registered individual members and 12 corporate members as of November 2004. The PSAJ is a member of the International Peace Research Association (IPRA), and it was a host organization, with the Science Council of Japan, of the 1992 IPRA Conference in Kyoto, at which some five hundred peace researchers from 40 countries participated.

The purpose of the PSAJ is to focus on conflicts between nations, to carry out scientific research on the causes of conflicts and conditions for peace, and to contribute to academic progress in related fields of study. The Association holds local conferences in different regions to disseminate research results and to promote mutual exchanges of the members and citizens. It also holds general conferences twice a year, and smaller *ad hoc* research meetings on peace studies, peace education and so on. The PSAJ has an active publication programme including research by its members, a Japanese-language journal *Peace Studies*, and an English-language newsletter. It also promotes exchange among Japanese and foreign researchers and sponsors various activities.

The main theme of the PSAJ general conference in November 2004 was 'The International Movement to Ban Depleted Uranium and the Role of Civil Society'. Uranium weapons, often called 'depleted uranium' (DU) weapons, are manufactured from radioactive waste materials produced during the nuclear fuel chain. They cause widespread and long-lasting radioactive contamination of the environment. In areas such as southern Iraq, where uranium munitions were used by the USA and the UK, there have been reports of increases in cancers, leukemia and birth defects. There have been activities by citizens to prohibit its use, such as the 'International Petition to Ban Uranium Weapons' which calls for an immediate end to the use of uranium weapons by the Coalition to Ban Uranium Weapons.[2]

Peace studies at universities and peace institutions in Japan are summarized in a report by the National Committee for Peace Research of the Science Council of Japan, an advisory committee to the Japanese government. The report, published on 26 November 2002, states that 'peace does not only mean the "absence of war" but it means economic/political stability, respect for fundamental human rights, political freedom and participation in political process, benign and safe environment, improvement of welfare, and a life of economic satisfaction'. This concept of peace is important in order to understand the following important topics found in academic peace studies at present.

1. Research and education on military, conventional and nuclear war, the arms race, militarization, prevention of war, nuclear testing, ethnic conflicts, war crimes, terrorism, militarism, peace keeping, arbitration, mediation, cooperation, crisis management, disarmament, nonviolence, international law and the United Nations.

---

2   Further information about the PSAJ may be found on its website <http://wwwsoc.nii. ac.jp/psaj/>.

2. Research and education on political, economic, cultural, religious and racial liberation such as North–South problems, neo-colonialism, illiteracy, minority issues, child-labour, sexism, racism, revolution and violations of human rights.
3. Research and education on studies and developments of matters such as energy issues, over-population, ecology, nuclear power plants and harmony with nature.
4. Research and education on learning process and attitude formation such as fascism, nationalism, bullying, conflict resolution and tolerance.
5. Research and education on philosophical, ethical, theological and religious peace thinking such as examinations of peace concepts, pacifist world view, philosophy of peace, ethics of peace and theology of peace.

I believe that the first course in peace studies in a Japanese University was started in 1976 by Professor Mitsuo Okamoto. According to a 2005 survey, 42 Japanese universities offer a course entitled 'Peace Studies', and nine universities offer 'Peace Research'. Related topics like 'Theory of Peace', 'Theory of International Peace', 'Theory of Peace and Conflict' and 'Research on Human Rights and Peace' are found at other universities. They deal with similar issues although their titles are different. Furthermore, there are 168 universities (out of 565) where peace related courses are offered under such titles as 'Theory of International Conflict', 'War and Peace', 'Peace and Human Rights', 'Dealing with Nuclear Issues' and so on. It means that some sort of peace studies/peace research in a broad sense is being offered at about 30 per cent of Japanese universities. However, there is no department of peace studies at any Japanese university, and many Japanese students who are interested in peace studies tend to study abroad. In this context the National Committee for Peace Research published a report arguing for the creation of peace studies departments at Japanese universities.

In addition to university-level teaching, there are ten peace research institutes in Japan, and also several institutes that approach peace studies in a more general sense, such as the Institute for International Relations at Sophia University, the Institute for International Understanding at Teizukayama University and so on. The Kyoto Museum for World Peace at Ritsumeikan University, recognized internationally as a valuable asset to peace research, stands out as a unique peace studies/peace research institute annexed to the university.

The introduction of peace studies/peace research into the curriculum of higher education has had three major benefits, according to the 2002 report. Firstly, it has facilitated research and teaching of topics which were difficult to deal with within the traditional curriculum. Secondly, it has enabled an analysis of issues from the viewpoint of 'common values which recognize the unity and diversity of humanity' (Professor Akira Iriye of Harvard University). Thirdly, it has facilitated an approach to new problems arising from rapid globalization and the emerging new world order, which is characterized by rapid movements of goods, information and services across international borders.

What are the main issues in current academic studies of peace? A report titled 'Challenges of peace research in the period of globalization' was submitted to the government in autumn 2004. The report points out that human interest should now be emphasized more than national interest. Peace studies is defined as the 'ultimate science for human survival' because it addresses the following crucial issues:

1. Abolition of nuclear weapons
2. Disarmament (small arms)
3. Defence using information technology
4. National security and human security
5. Humanitarian intervention (not military intervention)
6. Conflict resolution/transformation without the use of force
7. Increasing poverty
8. Terrorism
9. US unilateralism
10. Environmental issues
11. Infectious diseases such as HIV
12. Religion, race and ethnic issues
13. Gender issues
14. Coexistence of multi-ethnicity and multi-culture
15. Peace education
16. Peace movements.

Taken together with the five areas of study mentioned earlier, these topics delineate the mainstream of peace studies in Japan today.

As for Japan's war responsibility, there is an important organization which deals with Japan's aggression in terms of peace research and also supporting the victims of Japan's aggression. The organization's background dates to 1992 when a historian, Professor Yoshiaki Yoshimi, discovered evidence in the Defence Research Library that Japanese military was involved with a sexual slavery system, which refuted the claim of the Japanese government that the women worked for private dealers. Since it became clear that such study was much needed, the Center for Research and Documentation on Japan's War Responsibility (JWRC) was established in April 1993. Its purpose is dedicated to fulfilling Japan's responsibility to Asians victimized by Japan during the Second World War. Since the JWRC was established it has published a quarterly journal *Kikan Senso Sekinin Kenkyu* [Study on War Responsibility], in which research findings are made public. One remarkable achievement of JWRC was its investigation of the sex slave issue. 'This was submitted to the Japanese Government in 1993, and as a direct consequence the government was forced to admit for the first time that these women, who suffered at Japanese military Comfort Stations, were coerced into sexual slavery'.[3]

---

3   Center for Research and Documentation on Japan's War Responsibility (JWRC), 'Membership of the Center for Research and Documentation on Japan's War Responsibility', <http://www.jca.apc.org/JWRC/center/english/Center.htm>.

The JWRC is supported by peace researchers, historians, legal experts, writers and conscientious citizens and it is impressive that the emphasis is put on not only research but also action to support Asian victims of Japan's aggression.

International and Japanese Peace Museums

Van den Dungen's article 'Peace Education: Peace Museum'[4] lists 34 main peace museums, founded between 1946 and 1995. I have since identified several others, totalling 48 peace museums in many countries, but not including Japan. I include brief comments about each in the Appendix to this chapter.[5] There is a fairly efficient network of information about peace museums. The International Network of Peace Museums was created when the first International Conference of Peace Museums was held at the University of Bradford in the UK, and the Japanese Network of Museums for Peace was created in 1998 when the third International Conference of Peace Museums was held in Osaka and Kyoto. The *Muse* newsletter, edited by the author, was first published at the Grassroots House and sent to peace museums, universities, peace institutes and peace groups in 60 countries. The *Muse* office was moved to the Kyoto Museum for World Peace in 2001, from where the newsletter has been published both in Japanese and English.[6] For Japan, I have compiled a table of 53 peace museums listed by date of opening (see Table 7.1).

Table 7.1   Peace museums in Japan

Prefecture	Peace museum	Year founded
Hiroshima	Hiroshima Peace Memorial Museum	1955
Nagasaki	Nagasaki Atomic Bomb Museum	1955
Saitama	Maruki Gallery	1967
Okinawa	Okinawa Prefectural Peace Memorial Museum	1975
Tokyo	Display House of the Fifth Lucky Dragon	1976
Fukuoka	Peace Museum for the People	1979
Kanagawa	Soka Gakkai Toda Peace Memorial Hall	1979
Miyagi	Sendai Hukkou Memorial	1981
Okinawa	Life is Treasure House	1984

---

4   Peter van den Dungen, 'Peace Education: Peace Museums' in Lester R. Kurtz (ed.), *Encyclopedia of Violence, Peace and Conflict* (3 vols, San Diego, 1999), vol. 2, pp. 691–703.

5   The author would like to thank Dr Peter van den Dungen, the general-coordinator of the International Network of Museums for Peace, for giving her information and advice on, and assistance in visiting, peace museums in Europe.

6   See <http://www.museumforpeace.org>.

Table 7.1   Continued

Prefecture	Peace Museum	Year Founded
Osaka	Liberty Osaka	1985
Hiroshima	Okunoshima Poison Gas Museum	1988
Wakayama	Teranaka Art Museum	1988
Kochi	Grassroots House	1989
Okinawa	Himeyuri Peace Museum	1989
Kyoto	Tanba Manganese Memorial Hall	1989
Nagasaki	Shoukokumin Museum	1990
Kochi	Kochi Liberty and People's Rights Museum	1990
Osaka	Osaka International Peace Centre	1991
Wakayama	Ishigaki Memorial	1991
Hiroshima	Mirasaka Peace Museum of Art	1991
Osaka	Suita Peace Centre	1992
Kyoto	Kyoto Museum for World Peace	1992
Kanagawa	Kawasaki Peace Museum	1992
Hokkaido	No More Hibakusha Hall	1992
Tokushima	German Museum	1993
Saitama	Peace Museum of Saitama	1993
Okinawa	Sakima Art Museum	1993
Shizuoka	Shizuoka Peace Centre	1993
Hiroshima	Fukuyama City Human Rights and Peace Museum	1994
Osaka	Sakai City Peace and Human Rights Museum	1994
Nagasaki	Oka Masaharu Memorial Nagasaki Peace Museum	1995
Kagawa	Takamatsu Civic Culture Centre: Peace Museum	1995
Hiroshima	Holocaust Education Centre	1995
Iwate	Pacific War History Museum	1995
Hyogo	Historical Himeji Peace Centre	1996
Saitama	Ou Kounichi Anti-War Art Museum	1996
Osaka	The Peace, Human Rights and Children Centre	1997
Nagano	Mugonkan Art Museum for Peace	1997
Oita	Yawaragi: Peace Memorial in Saiki	1997
Kanagawa	Kanagawa Plaza for Global Citizenship	1998
Tokyo	Tokyo Holocaust Education Resource Centre	1998
Nagasaki	Art Museum of Picture Books	1999
Gifu	Chiune Sugihara Memorial: Gifu	2000
Fukui	Yukinoshita Peace Culture Museum	2001
Tokyo	Kourai Museum	2001

Table 7.1   Continued

Prefecture	Peace Museum	Year Founded
Tokyo	Tokyo Document Centre on Air Raids	2002
Gifu	Gifu Peace Museum	2002
Hiroshima	Hiroshima National Peace Memorial Hall	2002
Nagasaki	Nagasaki Peace Museum	2003
Nagasaki	Nagasaki National Peace Memorial Hall	2003
Okinawa	Tsushima-maru Memorial	2004
Okayama	Peace Museum of Air-raids on Okayama	2005
Tokyo	Women's Active Museum on War and Peace	2005

In Japan, the majority (52 per cent) of these peace museums were created in the 1990s. It seems that the establishment of peace museums in the 1990s was influenced by the Japanese and international peace movements of the 1980s. Further details on Japanese peace museums are available from *Muse: Newsletter of Japanese Network of Museums for Peace*, which is published at the Kyoto Museum for World Peace, Ritsumeikan University.[7]

One can see the relatively large number of peace museums in Japan from the handbook *Worldwide Peace Museums*, first published by the United Nations in 1995, with a second edition in 1998.[8] Unfortunately only two peace museums in China were included, possibly because there was little Chinese contact with the International Network of Peace Museums at that time, and there may be other inaccuracies since museums elsewhere were perhaps not known to the compilers. I hope that more Chinese museums for peace will be included in the UN handbook in the future. The international distribution in 1998 was as follows: out of 100 peace museums world-wide, 52 were in Japan and 10 in Germany. In other countries, there were six in the USA; four in Austria; three in India, the Netherlands and Switzerland; two in Belgium, China, France, South Korea, Spain, the UK and Uzbekistan; and one in Italy, Kenya, South Africa, Tanzania, and Vietnam. For further information please see the Appendix to this chapter.

---

7   The newsletter *Muse* is published by Kyoto Museum for World Peace thanks to its director, Ikurou Anzai, and Masahiko Yamabe, a curator. The website of the peace museum is <http://www.ritsumei.ac.jp/mng/er/wp-museum/e/eng.html>. The newsletter is available at the website of the Grassroots House both in Japanese and English: <http://ha1.seikyou.ne.jp/home/Shigeo.Nishimori/>.

8   United Nations, *Peace Museums Worldwide*, Archives of the League of Nations, Geneva, United Nations Publications on Peace Series, first edition (Geneva, 1995); second edition, in association with the Department of Peace Studies, University of Bradford (Geneva, 1998).

Problematic Issues in Japanese Peace and War Museums

The issues surrounding peace and war museums in Japan are highly problematic. To take an example, Japan has the largest number of peace museums in the world, but what about their quality and content? Which also raises the question, what are the differences between a war museum and a peace museum? To gain some insight, we can contrast the Yushukan Museum – which is sited within the precincts of the controversial Yasukuni Shrine in Tokyo – with the Kyoto Museum for World Peace at Ritsumeikan University in Kyoto. The Yushukan is a war museum, founded in 1882 as the first museum in Japan, rebuilt in 1932, and renovated in 2002. An official Yushukan Museum leaflet explains:

> The renovation process extends to the exhibits, many of which are new. We are especially pleased to have the opportunity to display a carrier-borne Mitsubishi Zero fighter aircraft. From the Yushukan's collection, which encompasses over 100,000 items, we have selected those that shed a new light on modern Japanese history.

The Zero fighter aircraft was one of the main combat planes of the Japanese navy during the Second World War. Such a display is characteristic of war museums' positive portrayal of weaponry. For example, the author visited the Musée de l'Armée in Paris in 1993 and grew tired of seeing so many weapons. (There were no exhibits on the atomic bombing of Hiroshima and Nagasaki, probably because of the French policy of conducting nuclear tests in the Pacific Ocean at that time: the effects of nuclear weapons were perhaps deliberately downplayed). To give another example, the National Army Museum in Chelsea, London shows British soldiers through five centuries with their medals, weapons from the longbow to the mass-produced weapons of today, military costumes and so forth.

It should be noted that the Yushukan Museum leaflet puts an emphasis on 'a new light on modern Japanese history'. Is the concept of history really new? The exhibits at Yushukan museum did not seem to be new at all when the author visited after its 2002 renovation. Reminiscences and histories of combats are exhibited to glorify war and there are, for instance, no exhibits on Chinese people's suffering, as the following example shows.

The Marco Polo Bridge [*lukouqiao* in Chinese] Incident on 7 July 1937 was a flashpoint of Japan's aggression against China. But an article in the *Tokyo Nichinichi Shinbun*, a pro-government newspaper, dated 7 July 1937 is exhibited without any criticism of Japan's aggression and the incident is explained as follows:

> On 7 July 1937, while Japanese troops were conducting night manoeuvres near the Marco Polo Bridge on the outskirts of Beiping [modern Beijing], shots were fired at them. Shots were also fired at Japanese reinforcements who arrived the next morning. A battle was subsequently fought against the Chinese at Wanping … (Noted by the author during her visit in 2002).

There is no perspective that this incident marked the start of Japan's all-out invasion of China. It implies there was a good reason for Japanese troops' attacks on the Chinese. There has been a debate among historians about the origin of these 'shots'; but even if some shots were fired by the Chinese, the context was Japanese aggression in China that had started at least a decade earlier.

Another example from the same museum is an exhibit on the Nanjing massacre. When the author visited the Yushukan museum there was the following explanation of the 'Nanking Operation':

> The purpose of the Nanking Operation was to surround the capital, thus discouraging the Chinese from waging war against the Japanese. Tang Shengzhi, commander-in-chief of the Nanking Defense Corps, ignored the Japanese warning to open the gates of the city. He ordered his troops to defend Nanking to the death and then escaped. Therefore, when the hostilities commenced, the leaderless Chinese troops either deserted or surrendered. Nanking fell on December 13.

There is no reflection on Japan's aggression in this explanation. It should be noticed also that the harmless and politically neutral word of 'operation' is used, although the rest of the world calls it a 'massacre'. It is generally known that there was a mass slaughter in Nanjing in December 1937 and according to Iris Chang's definitive study, 'more than 300,000 Chinese civilians and soldiers were systematically raped, tortured, and murdered – a death toll exceeding that of the atomic blasts of Hiroshima and Nagasaki combined'.[9] In fact, at Yushukan museum there are no exhibits at all on the result of the assault on Nanjing. The exhibition is used to glorify war by exhibiting photos of Japanese 'successes' and in remembrance of Japanese soldiers who were killed in action in China.

The two examples above show Japan only as a successful military power, but there are no exhibits on the nature and consequences of Japan's aggression.

What were visitors' impressions? Visitors are asked to write comments in a notebook at the end of the exhibition. There are generally two types of opinion: one tends to praise the museum and the other criticizes the content of the exhibits. A 24-year-old man wrote, 'I felt that I touched the spirit that modern Japanese tend to lose'. On the other hand, a 15-year-old non-Japanese wrote, 'There really was a Nanking massacre!! Japan is telling a lie. She should reflect on the war. Down with Japanese Imperialism!!' An anonymous person criticized this comment and wrote, 'Are you Chinese? You, the Chinese, are brainwashed by the Chinese government. Wake up! The more China and Korea fuss about the past, the more the USA and Europe would be happy. Try to look at the world more openly, Chinese!' These visitors were all born after the Second World War and hence did not know its reality, but a 71-year-old man, reflecting on the war, wrote:

---

9 Iris Chang, *The Rape of Nanking: The Forgotten Holocaust of World War II* (Harmondsworth, 1998), back cover.

We should not forget that three million Japanese and twenty million foreigners were killed. Japan should not try to justify the aggressive war. I was forced to be a suicide bomber and was taught to die for the emperor. I thought Japan would fall even if the emperor was protected. Though the emperor system remained after World War II, people suffered terribly from the lack of food. War means murder and there is no just war.

This old man is very critical of the museum, while young people who do not really know about the war tend to be influenced by the Yushukan. The exhibits glorify war and fail to show any exhibitions on Chinese suffering. As a result the historical truth of Japan's aggression is not revealed.

How could Japan's aggression be exhibited at a peace museum? The Kyoto Museum for World Peace is a good example of how Japanese aggression can be shown objectively. The Kyoto Museum for World Peace was founded on the campus of Ritsumeikan University in Kyoto in 1992. It is perhaps the only peace museum in the world that exists at a university. The aim of the museum is written in an inscription in six languages near its entrance:

> The Kyoto Museum for World Peace, Ritsumeikan University, was built with the hope of contributing to the realization of world peace. Through these exhibits, we hope to convey the tragic reality of war, to illustrate the efforts of those who oppose war, and to provide an understanding of the importance of establishing peace.[10]

To show 'the tragic reality of war' means not only to show Japan as the victim, for example of the atomic bombing, but also to show the horrific consequences of Japan's brutality. In contrast to the Yushukan museum, Japan's aggression and its results are clearly exhibited in a section on 'The Indiscriminate Bombing and Massacre of People', with an explanation that 'The Japanese army killed people indiscriminately in China and other parts of Asia'. For example, the peace museum displays a photo showing Chinese people who were burnt to death in Nanjing.[11] The Marco Polo Bridge Incident, referred to above, is explained as follows:

> Japan gained control of north-eastern China as a result of the 'Manchurian Incident'. Japan then aimed at occupying the northern part of China. She started total war against China using the military conflict at the Marco Polo Bridge in July, 1937.[12]

This explanation is much more accurate and honest than that given at the Yushukan museum. The results of Japan's aggression are also revealed: ten million Chinese were killed; many Chinese and Korean men were drafted into military service and

---

10 Kyoto Museum for World Peace at Ritsumeikan University, 'Inscription', *Academeia*, 21 (1999): 1.

11 The Kyoto Museum for World Peace was renovated in April 2005 and Japan's aggression is well exhibited. The author would like to thank Ms Kyoko Kawamoto for sending the author new information on the exhibition.

12 Kyoto Museum for World Peace at Ritsumeikan University, *Jousetsu Tenji Shousai Kaisetsu* [Detailed Manual on Permanent Exhibition] (Kyoto, 1997), p. 48.

often sent to the front lines; countless Chinese and Korean women (the so-called comfort women) were forced into sexual slavery for Japanese military personnel.

In the 1990s other Japanese peace museums also started putting exhibits of Japan's aggression on display. These peace museums were discussed in an article entitled 'Japan: Fresh Look at Aggression' in *The International Herald Tribune* dated 15 August 1994:

War museums recently built in Osaka, Kyoto, Kawasaki, Saitama and Okinawa all deal forthrightly with Japan's aggressive strategy, its harsh and often murderous treatment of conquered Asian peoples and its refusal to surrender until the United States unleashed nuclear weapons.[13]

It is strange that this article introduces all these peace museums as 'war museums', even though each museum's full name is given: Osaka International Peace Centre, Kyoto Museum for World Peace, Kawasaki Peace Museum, Peace Museum of Saitama and Okinawa Prefectual Peace Memorial Museum. This may be because the American journalist who wrote the article did not know anything about peace museums, although there were peace museums in the United States at that time such as 'The Peace Museum, Chicago' and 'Swords into Plowshares Peace Centre and Gallery, Detroit'. Or he might have known the concept of war museum but never understood that of peace museum. But even if 'peace museums' are called 'war museums' by mistake, I welcome such a report on Japanese peace museums where the historical truth is exhibited.

I tried to clarify further some characteristics and problems of peace museums in Japan by conducting a survey in 2001: a questionnaire was sent to 48 peace museums, of which 44 responded. In particular I wanted to gain some understanding of the purpose of each museum, its choice of exhibits and the context in which they were presented. I present this information in three sub-sections.

The Purpose of Peace Museums in Japan

According to the responses (see Figures 7.1 and 7.2), the primary purpose of a peace museum is peace education that takes place not only at school but also in the community (82 per cent). It is possible to educate children at school; while a museum reaches not only children but also adults. Twenty-one peace museums (48 per cent) put their main emphasis on school education while 24 (55 per cent) focused on education for the community. Thirteen peace museums (30 per cent) also stressed other activities such as the publication of teaching materials for peace education. This shows that peace education both at school and in the community are regarded as important.

---

13 Kyoto Museum, *Jousetsu Tenji Shousai Kaisetsu*, p. 27.

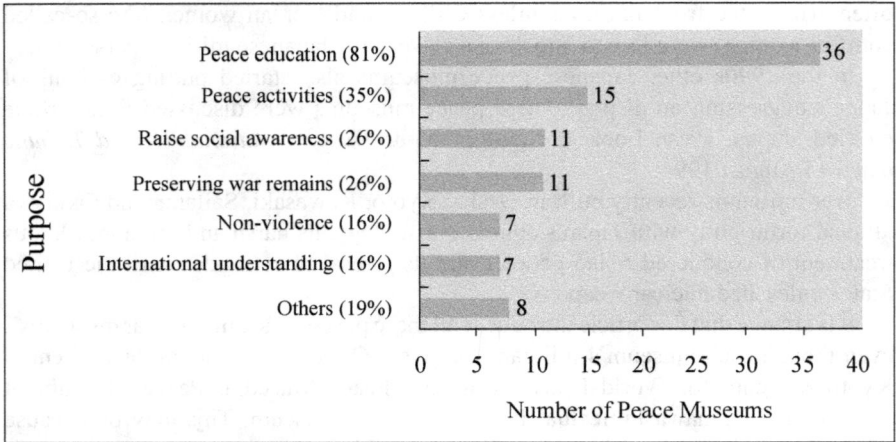

Figure 7.1   The purpose of peace museums

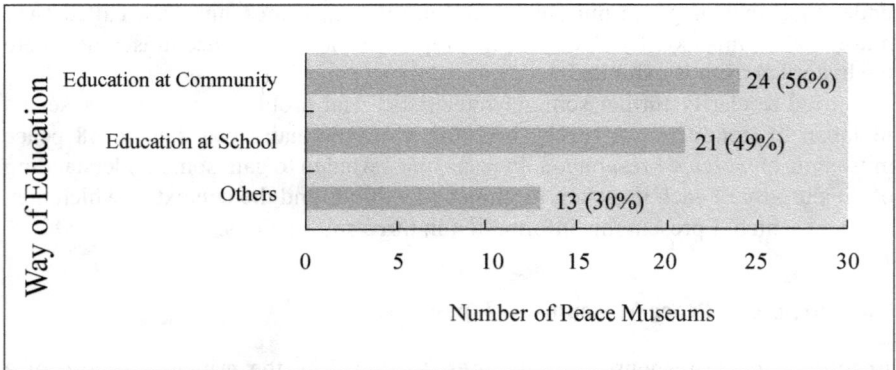

Figure 7.2   Methods of peace education provided by peace museums

The second highest-rated purpose of peace museums (given by 34 per cent of the respondents) was to 'encourage people to work for peace more actively'. It is important to raise public awareness, to promote activities for peace in order to prevent war in the future. Twenty-five per cent of peace museums responded that the purpose of establishing a peace museum is 'to raise citizens' awareness of various issues'. The same number (25 per cent) chose 'Preserving war remains, etc.' as one of their purposes. War remains seem to be regarded as useful tools to teach the horror of war and the preciousness of peace to the next generation. Japan has a National Association of Preserving War Remains which, with some related NGOs, has been trying to establish a peace museum.

On the other hand, only 16 per cent of peace museums answered that their purpose is to 'spread ideas of nonviolence'; and only 9 per cent mentioned 'training conflict resolution skills'. These ideas of nonviolence and conflict resolution seem to gain more emphasis at peace museums in Western countries. For example, an emphasis is put on Gandhian nonviolence and conflict resolution skills at Peace Galleries in Bradford and the European Museum for Peace in Stadtschlaining, Austria.

Another purpose, given by 16 per cent of peace museums, is 'to promote international understanding'. Although there have been exchanges of exhibits between Japanese and overseas peace museums, it is often not easy to communicate with one another because there are major differences of opinion, for example on atomic bombing. Most Japanese think that nuclear weapons should never have been used, while some Americans think that it was right to drop the atomic bombs. There is also a language barrier because English is the only compulsory second language at high school in Japan. As a result, it is not easy for the Japanese to communicate with, for example, the Chinese unless they study Chinese at college; while few non-Japanese can communicate well in our language.

The Themes of Exhibits: Fewer Exhibits on Japan's Aggression

One can easily gain the impression that Japan's suffering as victim in the Second World War is emphasized more than its aggression. I formulated the following brief questionnaire to explore the themes of exhibits, to see how they may reflect this attitude:

What are the main themes of the exhibitions?

1. World peace
   – Atomic bombing, US air raids and war experiences
     (Japan's victim sied of the Second World War)
   – Japan's aggression of other countries
   – Anti-war activities and pacifists
2. The protection of the environment
3. Human rights
4. Sustainable development
5. Others

A summary of answers appears in Figure 7.3.

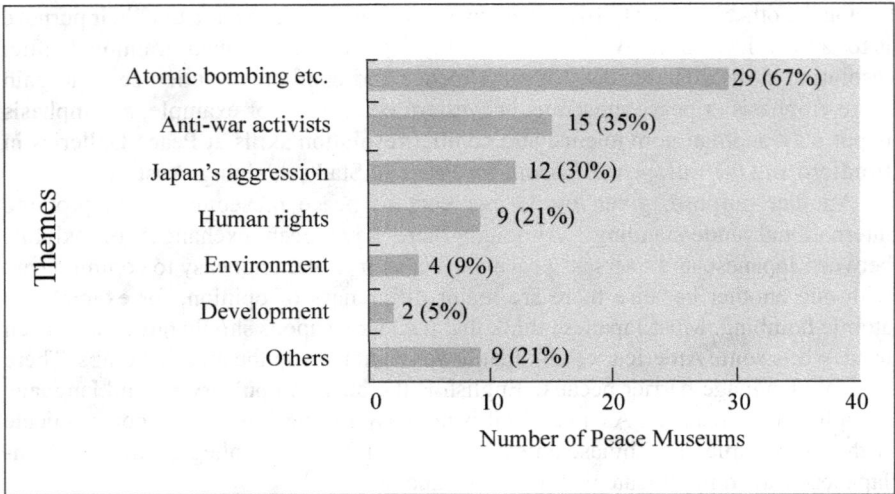

Figure 7.3   Themes of exhibits at peace museums

There are many themes showing Japan's victim status during the war, especially the atomic bombing and other US air raids (66 per cent). On the other hand, the number of peace museums showing Japanese aggression is much lower (27 per cent). The number of exhibits on Japan's aggression did increase in the 1990s, but attacks on them by nationalists hindered museum directors. Some important peace museums that show Japan's aggression honestly are Osaka International Peace Centre, Kyoto Museum for World Peace, Oka Masaharu Memorial Nagasaki Peace Museum, Children's Centre for Peace and Human Rights in Sakai City, Osaka and the Grassroots House in Kochi City. (It should be noted that the Osaka International Peace Centre is the only public peace museum). It is important for young people to visit such peace museums because Japan's aggression is not sufficiently explained in school textbooks. It is also important for pupils to learn about anti-war activists and pacifists, because they are not described in textbooks either. Only 34 per cent of peace museums recognize anti-war activists, which is not a large enough number to educate people, including children, adequately.

Peace is not possible if human rights are not respected. Peace museums with an emphasis on human rights are Osaka International Peace Centre, Sakai City Peace and Human Rights Museum (Osaka), Children's Centre for Peace and Human Rights (Sakai City, Osaka), Osaka Human Rights Museum, Kochi Liberty and People's Rights Museum (Kochi City, Kochi) and Fukuyama City Human Rights and Peace Museum (Hiroshima). Exhibits are explained in English and Hangul at Osaka International Peace Centre, which is important for non-Japanese visitors. The reason why there are several peace museums with an emphasis on human rights in Osaka is that many Koreans were forced to go to Japan and work there during the Second

World War. In 2004, of about 630,000 Koreans in Japan, some 170,000 lived in Osaka Prefecture.[14]

The Context of the Exhibits

Why is Japan's victimhood emphasized more than Japan's aggression? Why is Japan's historical aggression not written into school textbooks in Japan? One reason offered, in comparison with Germany, states:

> Ironically, one reason Japanese are stalemated over how to remember the recent past is that post-war occupation policies permitted far more continuity of personnel and rules in Japan than in Germany. The Allied victors demanded that the post-war German government eliminate Nazi leadership, yet they kept the Japanese emperor and many of his advisers in power to ensure stability. Cold War priorities were another reason the United States protected Japan from Asian demands for reparations and punishment during and after the occupation. In some ways, Japan avoided overseas pressure until the post-Cold War era to rethink its wartime actions; Germany faced and responded to similar pressures earlier.[15]

Why did post-war occupation policies permit this continuity? It seems that there were perceived strategic advantages for the USA in hiding Japan's aggression and co-opting the establishment. For example, documents on experiments on human beings conducted by Unit 731 in China were given to the United States, while Japanese doctors who were war criminals were exempted from responsibility. Yuki Tanaka explains:

> Ishii and other senior staff of Unit 731 approached Sanders (an American intelligence officer) through Naito and proposed that they would share all of their knowledge of biological warfare in return for immunity from prosecution for war crimes. Sanders conveyed the proposed arrangement to MacArthur (the leader of the US Army in the Pacific area and Commander in chief of the Occupational Allied Forces), who instantly agreed to it.[16]

The USA used biological warfare data accumulated by Japanese doctors in the Korean War.[17] That is the main reason why Japan's aggression has not been taught in

---

14 There are about 630,000 Koreans who live in Japan. About 450,000 Koreans were those who were forced to go to Japan to work during the Second World War. 180,000 Koreans went to Japan after the war.

15 Laura Hein and Mark Selden (eds), *Censoring History: Citizenship and Memory in Japan, Germany, and the United States* (Armonk, NY, 2000), p. 11.

16 Yuki Tanaka, *Hidden Horrors: Japanese War Crimes in World War II* (Boulder, 1996), p. 159.

17 Association to Expose American Germ Warfare in Korea (Tokyo), 'America Waged Germ Warfare in Korean War', <http://www1.ocn.ne.jp/~sinryaku/beigunsaikinsenzittai. htm> (accessed 28 June 2004).

schools, and why Japan's victim status during the war is emphasized at public peace museums more than Japan's military aggressions. The Japanese people, who have not been informed of Japan's aggression, and other Asian people who suffered at the hands of the Japanese army in the Second World War, hold very different views. I hope that Japan's aggression may be taught not only in schools but also at peace museums, to increase mutual understanding among people in the world, especially Asian people, and also to create a more peaceful future. But how is it possible to make exhibitions on Japan's actions during the war?

There are many anti-war museums that show the horror of war and the importance of peace in Japan. One may wonder if they can really be called peace museums, because it is easy for visitors to feel horrified on seeing exhibits that show the cruelty of war. It would be important to consider children in making such exhibitions, because it would be disconcerting for small children to see only the cruelty of war during the course of a visit. It would also be important to show positive aspects of history, such as pacifists and their efforts for peace: it is encouraging to learn about them, for example in the Peace Museum in Hindelang, Germany.

Is it sufficient to focus only on showing the past? I believe it could be significant for visitors to learn also about various issues on peace, human rights, environment and sustainable development at a peace museum. Still more desirable, visitors should not only learn about such issues but also discuss them with others and try to contribute to the solution of various problems in which they are interested. In this spirit, dialogues are emphasized in the Peace Museum in Wolfsegg, Austria; and an emphasis is put on conflict resolution at the Peace Gallery in Bradford, England.

At our small private museum, the Grassroots House in Kochi in south-western Japan, we have tried to assist various groups to come together. We hold Peace Concerts, Peace Art Exhibitions, Peace Film Festivals and so forth. The museum is small, but community-based and active in international exchanges. Thanks to a young Korean researcher, not only Japanese but also Chinese and Korean young people have started to convene there. Young musicians held a peace concert to protest against US attacks on Afghanistan and Iraq, and young people held vigils in downtown Kochi City against the US-led invasion of Iraq, thereafter continuing to meet every Friday to discuss various issues such as the question of sending Self Defence Forces to Iraq. Furthermore, Grassroots House members supported Chinese lawsuits against Japan which sought apologies and compensation. Grassroots House also prepares flyers on various issues, which we call 'peace education on the street'.

Thus conflict resolution, dialogues, reconciliation activities and an honest depiction of the Second World War aggression seem more possible at a small, private or community-based peace museum than in the public peace museums which tend only to exhibit Japan's victim side of the war.

Peace Studies and Peace Museums

In this final section I present observations about peace studies and museums in the light of recent developments in Japan. Members of Grassroots House made a series of visits to China to investigate the role of army units from Kochi in the occupation of China. Six visits were made between 1991 and 1998 and the findings were published as booklets. They have been used as teaching materials, playing an important role in educating students because Japan's wartime behaviour has not been written clearly in standard school textbooks. It was significant that not only peace researchers and historians but also ordinary citizens joined the investigation. This is because citizens who learned of Japan's aggression and Chinese suffering had become active in creating a huge peace monument in Kochi City. The monument, which reads 'Japan will never fight against China', was funded by citizens' donations and opened on 18 September 1992.

In 1997, 180 Chinese survivors of the massacre launched a law suit against the Japanese government. They demanded that Japan admit it had used biological weapons, apologize, and pay each of them ten million yen in compensation. The Tokyo district court, in its ruling in August 2002, acknowledged that Unit 731's activities had caused 'immense' suffering and were 'clearly inhumane'. But the court turned down their other demands, saying that all compensation issues had been settled when Japan and China normalized diplomatic relations in 1972.

Three members of the Grassroots House, including the author, travelled to Tokyo to listen to the ruling at Tokyo district court in August 2002. After the unjust and disappointing ruling we participated in a protest march. The ruling and the ensuing protest by the Chinese and some Japanese were reported in the Grassroots House newsletter. They were also reported in newspapers in Japan, but it is necessary that information on the trial should be more widely reported in the Japanese media. In autumn 2004 representatives of the plaintiffs started giving evidence in their appeal at the Tokyo high court. It is strange that even after 7 December, when two Chinese victims and one Chinese scholar gave testimony on Japan's use of germ warfare, information about the case was not available in Japanese newspapers. On the other hand, an article titled 'Japan's sins of the past' had already appeared in the UK *Guardian* newspaper on 28 October 2004. A ruling was given at the Tokyo high court on 19 April 2005. Ten plaintiffs had their appeal unjustly dismissed. They had suffered from human experiments by Unit 731, they were victims of the Nanjing Massacre and victims of indiscriminate bombing who were demanding the Japanese government compensate them for terrible damages. In this situation the Japanese judicial system seems to be hopeless, but it is encouraging that Japanese citizens continue to support Chinese victims at a grassroots level, including through private peace museums.

In 1987 a course called 'Peace and Disarmament' was started at Kochi University, where the author is a lecturer. About 150 students of the Department of Humanity, Science, Education and Agriculture are enrolled. The theme of 2001 was 'Peace in Asia and Japan' and focused on Japanese relations with China and Korea. Many students were shocked to discover Japan's wartime activities. When I gave a lecture on Japan's aggression to students studying international issues at Kochi University, they were also shocked. When I asked them to write about it, a Chinese student who had lived in China until she was 13 wrote that she began to understand Japan's germ warfare by watching a TV drama when she lived in China. She wrote:

> Most young Japanese people don't know about the germ warfare because the Japanese government has not made it public and it has not been reported in media or taught in history education at school. It is important to teach the historical facts so that students will learn the horror of war and the preciousness of life and this will lead to the prevention of war.

Japanese students knew nothing about the germ warfare; one of them wrote:

> I didn't know anything at all about the germ warfare and I was very shocked to know the historical facts. I think that Japan should apologize to the Chinese and compensate them for the terrible damages. I also think that it should be taught in history education at school and peace museums, and also should be reported in the media. The fact that the Japanese don't know what really occurred makes it hard for the Japanese to have normal relations with other Asian people.

In our experience in Kochi, the peace research of a peace museum combined with the publication of its results paved the way for promoting peace education in the local university. Peace museums may thus play an important role in peace research and education, as well as reconciliation between conflicting parties. A peace museum can also play an important role in community education. For example, a more truthful presentation about wartime aggression, and also about anti-war and pacifist activities, can be provided, especially in Japan, by smaller private peace museums. It is encouraging that there are three other private peace museums that deal with Japan's aggression: the Peace, Human Rights and Children Centre in Sakai City, Osaka, Oka Masaharu Memorial Nagasaki Peace Museum in Nagasaki and Women's Active Museum on War and Peace that focuses on women who were forced to work as sex slaves.

My hope is that improved communication among peace researchers, peace educators at museums and the public will improve through the internet and other means so that people will be able to promote peace research, peace education and peace-making.

Appendix: Notes on Peace Museums outside Japan

I have identified 48 peace museums outside Japan, listed here. Incidentally my research shows that 16 of them (33 per cent) were created in the 1980s, the decade that produced the most.

Table 7.2   Peace museums outside Japan

Peace Museum	Location	Country	Year
The International Museum of War and Peace	Lucerne	Switzerland	1902
Peace Palace and Library	The Hague	Netherlands	1913
Imperial War Museum	London	UK	1917
Peace Memorial Museum	Zanzibar	Tanzania	1925
International Esperanto Museum	Vienna	Austria	1927
The IJzer Tower	Diksmuide	Belgium	1930
League of Nations Museum	Geneva	Switzerland	1946
Gandhi Memorial Museum	Madurai	India	1959
International Museum of The Red Cross	Mantova	Italy	1959
National Gandhi Museum and Library	New Delhi	India	1960
Anne Frank House	Amsterdam	Netherlands	1960
Berlin Wall Museum	Berlin	Germany	1963
Gandhi Smarak Sangrahalaya	Ahmedabad	India	1963
War Remnants Museum	Ho Chin Minh	Vietnam	1975
Peace Museum	Lindau	Germany	1980
Bridge at Remagen Peace Museum	Remagen	Germany	1980
Anti-War House Peace Centre	Sievershausen	Germany	1981
The Peace Museum	Chicago	USA	1981
Anti-War Museum	Berlin	Germany	1982
Peace Museum	Meeder	Germany	1982
Peace Library and Anti-War Museum	Berlin	Germany	1984
Memorial Hall of the Victims in the Nanjing Massacre	Nanjing	China	1985
Swords into Plowshares Peace Center and Gallery	Detroit	USA	1986
International Museum of Peace and Solidarity	Samarkand	Uzbekistan	1986
Käthe Kollwitz Museum	Berlin	Germany	1986
The Independence Hall of Korea	Seoul	South Korea	1987
Museum of the War of the Chinese People's Resistance	Beijing	China	1987
Caen Memorial	Caen	France	1988

Table 7.2   Continued

Peace Museum	Location	Country	Year
International Red Cross and Red Crescent Museum	Geneva	Switzerland	1988
Children's Friendship Museum	Tashkent	Uzbekistan	1989
Museum of Compassion	New York	USA	1990
National Civil Rights Museum	Memphis	USA	1991
The House of Sharing	Kwangju	South Korea	1992
Franz Jägerstätter House	Ostermiething	Austria	1993
Austrian Peace Museum	Wolfsegg	Austria	1993
The World Centre for Peace, Freedom and Human Rights	Verdun	France	1994
Prairie Peace Park	Lincoln	USA	1994
Peace Museum	Nürnberg	Germany	1995
Yi Jun Peace Museum	The Hague	Netherlands	1995
Peace Gallery	Bradford	UK	1996
Robben Island Museum	Bellville	South Africa	1997
'In Flanders Fields' Museum	Ieper	Belgium	1998
Gernika Peace Museum	Gernika	Spain	1998
Peace History Museum	Hindelang	Germany	1999
Peace Museum	La Vall d'Uixó	Spain	2000
European Museum for Peace	Stadtschlaining	Austria	2001
African Peace Museum	Nairobi	Kenya	2001
Dayton International Peace Museum	Dayton	USA	2004

In the preparation of these notes, the author has drawn on the invaluable guide *Peace Museums Worldwide*.[18] Quotations from this source are indicated by the abbreviation *PMW*.

1. The International Museum of War and Peace (Lucerne, Switzerland)
The International Museum of War and Peace was established in 1902 by Jan Bloch (1836–1902) to warn people of the danger of world war, but it was closed in 1918 because of the First World War. The author took the opportunity to visit the building that once housed the museum when she attended an international symposium marking the centenary of the museum's opening, held in Lucerne, 6–8 June 2002. It was impressive to learn of Bloch's efforts for peace education using exhibits.

---

18 United Nations, *Peace Museums Worldwide* (Geneva, 1998).

2. Peace Palace and Library (The Hague, Netherlands)
The Peace Palace was opened in 1913 by the Carnegie Foundation. It is 'home to the International Court of Justice, the Permanent Court of Arbitration, the Hague Academy of International Law, and the Carnegie Library. The Palace displays many peace artefacts and symbols' (*PMW*, p. 60).

3. Imperial War Museum (London, UK)
The Imperial War Museum was founded in 1917. Its aim is to 'record all conflicts in which Britain and Commonwealth countries have been involved from 1914 to the present day' (*PMW*, p. 69). The author visited the museum in August 1993. Interestingly, cassette tapes on pacifists are available for peace education even though it is called a 'war museum'.

4. Peace Memorial Museum (Zanzibar, Tanzania)
The Peace Memorial Museum is 'an informative look at Zanzibar's history. It has sections on archaeology, early trade, slavery, palaces, mosques, sultans, explorers (includes Dr Livingstone's medical chest), missionaries, colonial administrators, traditional crafts and household items, stamps, coins, fishing, and clove cultivation', according to the Ivory website.[19]

5. International Esperanto Museum (Vienna, Austria)
The International Esperanto Museum, Vienna, was founded in 1927. The Esperanto language was invented in 1887 by L.L. Zamenhof so that people from different countries of the world would be able to speak to one another. The author visited the museum on 10 November 1993, leading her to consider that the world-wide adoption of Esperanto could lead to world peace.

6. The IJzer Tower (Diksmuide, Belgium)
Founded in 1930 in Diksmuide, West Flanders, to commemorate 'the soldiers who died in World War I, and all victims of war and violence' (*PMW*, p. 24). The author visited the monument twice, on 11 May 1999, at the time of the Hague Peace Conference, and on 9 May 2003 when the 4th International Conference of Peace Museums was held. It was moving to pass through a First World War trench.

7. League of Nations Museum (Geneva, Switzerland)
The League of Nations Museum was founded in Geneva in 1946. Its aims are as follows: 'With the permanent display of documents and other visual material the League of Nations Archives wants to share its rich heritage of relatively unknown material with a larger public. The exhibition illustrates and reflects the history and work of the League of Nations' (*PMW*, p. 67). The author visited the museum on

---

19 <http://www.ivorynet.com/plan-zanzibar.htm>.

5 November 1993. The most noteworthy exhibits included '100 years international peace movement' and '*Lay Down Your Arms*, Bertha von Suttner and Other Women in Pursuit of Peace'.

8. Gandhi Memorial Museum (Madurai, India)

The Gandhi Memorial Museum was founded by the All India Gandhi Memorial Fund in 1951 in Madurai, India. One of its aims is 'to preserve and enshrine Gandhi's message in its original form' (*PMW*, p. 37).

9. International Museum of the Red Cross (Mantova, Italy)

Its aims are to inform people of 'international activities of the International Red Cross, history of the birth and development of the movement and international humanitarian law' (*PMW*, p. 39).

10. National Gandhi Museum and Library (New Delhi, India)

The National Gandhi Museum and Library was founded in New Delhi in 1960. Its aims are to promote and propagate the life, work and philosophy of Mahatma Gandhi, the Father of the Nation (*PMW*, p. 38).

11. Anne Frank House (Amsterdam, Netherlands)

The author visited the Anne Frank House in Amsterdam on 4 August 1993. Anne Frank's Diary is well known in Japan, and a play based on her life has been performed in several places in Japan. The preservation of the house is remarkable because it encourages visitors from all over the world to imagine vividly Anne Frank's experiences in the Second World War.

12. Berlin Wall Museum (Berlin, Germany)

The Berlin Wall Museum (Museum House at Checkpoint Charlie: Museum of the Worldwide Non-violent Struggle for Human Rights) was founded in Berlin in 1963. Its aim is to offer 'information about and documentation of violations of human rights, especially in the former GDR (Berlin Wall) and in eastern European countries and the fight against it' (*PMW*, p. 29). The author visited the house on 31 July 1993 and was inspired to see young people eager to view exhibits on nonviolent struggle for human rights.

13. Gandhi Smarak Sangrahalaya (Ahmedabad, India)

Gandhi Smarak Sangrahalaya was founded in Ahmedabad in 1963 to 'keep alive the message of Gandhi's life and work ... maintaining contact with the youth and student community and providing facilities to them for the study of Gandhian thought' (*PMW*, p. 36).

14. War Remnants Museum (Ho Chin Minh, Vietnam)

The War Remnants Museum was founded in Ho Chi Minh City in 1975. Its aim is 'to document war crimes committed by the United States during the war in Viet Nam

... and to learn lessons from history for the benefit of people everywhere' (*PMW*, p. 79). The author talked with the museum's director, Mr Nguyen Kha Lan, at the International Symposium of 'Exchange of Experiences and Future Cooperation of Asian Peace Museums' held at Kyoto Museum for World Peace on 19 June 2004. He gave a lecture entitled 'How to hand down the memories of the Vietnam War to posterity for making future peace'. Japanese peace museums have the same aim of handing down recollections of war to the next generation.

15. Peace Museum (Lindau, Germany)
The Peace Museum, Lindau, was founded in 1980. 'The Museum especially wants to create a greater public awareness of the life and work of famous and unknown pioneers of peace, and of conciliation grounded in Justice. In this way it also aims to contribute to peace education' (*PMW*, p. 31). The author visited the museum on 6 November 1993. There were no exhibits that displayed photos of the cruel results of the atomic bombs, but there was a *kokeshi* doll as a symbol of peace.

16. Bridge at Remagen Peace Museum (Remagen, Germany)
The Bridge at Remagen Peace Museum was founded in 1980. The bridge was built for war from 1916 to 1918; it was conquered on 7 March 1945 and collapsed on 17 March 1945. The museum has documentation on the history of the bridge and exhibits on the Nobel Peace Prize. The author visited the museum on 9 August 1993. Dr Regine Mehl, the acting director of the Peace Research Information Unit Bonn, called the museum 'not a peace museum but a war museum', an indication of the difficulty of defining a peace museum.

17. Anti-War House Peace Centre (Sievershausen, Germany)
The Anti-War House Peace Centre was founded in Sievershausen in 1981. Its aims are 'to gather and display documentation about war in order not to forget, and to display the work of peace activists in order to encourage involvement in practical peace work' (*PMW*, p.35).

18. The Peace Museum (Chicago, USA)
The Peace Museum, Chicago was founded in 1981. Its aims are 'to motivate children, teenagers and adults to achieve creative solutions to the problem of violence ... through on-site, travelling exhibitions and community-based programmes' (*PMW*, p. 70).

19. Anti-War Museum (Berlin, Germany)
The Anti-War Museum (Anti-Kriegs-Museum) was founded in 1982. It was originally founded by Ernst Friedrich in 1925 in Berlin, but it was destroyed by the Nazis in 1933. He opened the second Anti-War Museum in Brussels in 1936, but again it was destroyed. The third one was founded by a group of teachers headed by his grandson, Tommy Spree, in 1982. The museum shows historical materials on the First and

Second World Wars. The author visited the museum in July 1993 where she saw photos of the atomic bomb victims. The museum showed the cruel reality of war.

20. Peace Museum (Meeder, Germany)
The Peace Museum, Meeder was founded in 1982. It 'aims to promote the peace tradition (which emerged in the area in 1651, at the end of the Thirty Years War) and keep it alive in the consciousness of the population' (*PMW*, p. 32). The history of the annual celebration (since 1651) for the coming of peace (i.e. Peace of Westphalia, 1648) is exhibited as well as the life and work of pacifists such as Anna B. Eckstein (1868–1947), who promoted the Hague Peace Conferences and the League of Nations idea.

21. Peace Library and Anti-War Museum (Berlin, Germany)
The Peace Library and Anti-War Museum was founded in 1984. Its aim is 'to work against war and to advance understanding of other peoples and cultures' (*PMW*, p. 30). The author visited the museum in July 1993. The exhibition on the German invasion of Poland and the Soviet Union was memorable as well as the exhibition on pacifists such as the White Rose, German students who resisted the war.

22. Memorial Hall of the Victims in the Nanjing Massacre (Nanjing, China)
The Memorial Hall of the Victims in the Nanjing Massacre was founded in 1985 to exhibit the Nanjing Massacre of 1937. Mr Zhou, the director, presented a paper entitled 'China–Japan Difference in Recognition of Nanjing Massacre and Future Prospect for Resolution' at the International Symposium of 'Exchange of Experiences and Future Cooperation of Asian Peace Museums', held at Ritsumeikan University, Kyoto on 19 June 2004. He criticized the lack of explanation of the Nanjing Massacre at the Hiroshima Peace Memorial Museum, a natural reaction since the exhibit showed some Japanese who celebrated Japan's attack on Nanjing. The author visited the museum in March 2005 and was shocked to see the exhibition, and perceived large discrepancies between the China and Japan exhibits. Japan's aggression should be exhibited much more at peace museums in Japan so that ordinary citizens will come to know the historical facts.

23. Swords into Plowshares Peace Center and Gallery (Detroit, USA)
The Swords into Plowshares Peace Center and Gallery was founded in 1986. Its aim is 'to use the creativity, power and persuasiveness of the arts to educate and sensitise people and groups to the need for peace in the world, and that all conflicts can be resolved in non-violent ways' (*PMW*, p. 71). Art is used for peace, and artwork warning of the dangers of war was sent to Grassroots House in 1998 in exchange for photos of the atomic bomb victims that Grassroots House had sent in 1995.

24. International Museum of Peace and Solidarity (Samarkand, Uzbekistan)
The International Museum of Peace and Solidarity was founded by the International Friendship Club Esperanto in 1986 in Samarkand. Its aims are 'promotion of peace

through citizen diplomacy, culture and the arts; development of public awareness of, concern over, and a sense of personal responsibility for, the global challenges humanity faces today' (*PMW*, p. 77). The author exchanged children's paintings from Grassroots House in Kochi with children in Samarkand. The Japanese paintings were widely reported in the media while paintings from Samarkand were also exhibited in Japan, proving that citizens and children can play important roles in promoting peace.

25. Käthe Kollwitz Museum (Berlin, Germany)
The Käthe Kollwitz Museum was founded in 1986. Its aim is to exhibit the works of Käthe Kollwitz (1867–1945), the theme of whose art is the suffering caused by poverty, starvation and death in war. The author visited the museum in July 1993 and was particularly struck by a painting depicting a mother who, suffering a shortage of food during the war, could not feed her children.

26. The Independence Hall of Korea (Seoul, South Korea)
The Independence Hall was opened in Chungcheongnamdo, South Korea in 1987. The objectives are described in a souvenir book issued by the museum: 'Independence Hall collects, studies and exhibits historic artefacts and materials related to the Korean national resistance to aggression, the fight for independence, the search for a national identity and the record of development and progress. It is intended to awaken the Korean national consciousness and promote patriotism'. The author visited the museum on 6 July 2002. One of the seven exhibition halls illustrates Japan's aggression, and it was shocking to see how cruel the Japanese military had been towards the people of Korea.

27. Museum of the Chinese People's Anti-Japanese War (Beijing, China)
The museum was established in Wanping City, beside Marco Polo Bridge (Lukouqiao), in the southwest suburb of Beijing in 1987. According to an article by Luo Cunkang, a researcher at the museum, its aims are to illustrate the course of China's revolution, in particular the Lukouqiao incident which sparked the national war of resistance against Japan.[20] The museum was established to 'strike back [at] some reactionary groups in Japan that do not acknowledge the war of aggression'. This statement refers to the fact that some Japanese politicians have not recognized Japan's military aggression and have glorified the Second World War.

28. Caen Memorial (Caen, France)
The Caen Memorial was founded by the city of Caen in 1988. Its aims are to bring 'to the fore, in the international context of the twentieth century, the stakes, the development and the significance of the Second World War, encouraging the visitor to ponder upon the plague of war and upon the stability of peace, and observation

---

20 Luo Cunkang, 'The Anti-Japanese War Museum in Beijing', *Muse: Newsletter of the Japanese Network of Museums for Peace*, 11 (June 2004).

of the world today'. The author visited the museum in August 1993. Films on Normandy were particularly powerful and impressive. The memorial was the only one in Europe that provided a nursery.

29. International Red Cross and Red Crescent Museum (Geneva, Switzerland)
The museum was founded in 1988 with the aim 'to tell and illustrate the story of those who, in the course of the major events of our era, have given part of their lives in the service of victims of wars or disasters, and to explain how the Red Cross and Red Crescent Movement acts' (*PMW*, p. 65). The author visited the museum on 5 November 1993. A film was screened about Henri Dunant (1828–1910), the founder of the Red Cross: despite being silent, it was not difficult to understand.

30. Children's Friendship Museum (Tashkent, Uzbekistan)
The 'Children of the Planet for Peace' Museum was founded by the Uzbekistan Ministry of Education in 1989. Its aim is 'to promote the cause of peace and to bring together children from all over the world in their search for a better future' (*PMW*, p. 78).

31. Museum of Compassion (New York, USA)
The Museum of Compassion was founded by the Poverty Awareness Coalition, Inc. in New York in 1990. Its aims are to 'develop compassionate people to help and remember the poor and to advance homeless and formerly homeless artists through their own artistic expression' (*PMW*, p. 75). Of particular interest is the fact that arts educational programmes are emphasized.

32. National Civil Rights Museum (Memphis, USA)
The National Civil Rights Museum was founded by the Lorraine Civil Rights Museum Foundation in 1991. 'The National Civil Rights Museum is the first and only comprehensive overview of the Civil Rights Movement in exhibit form in the world ... The Museum exhibits place the events in historical perspective, and provide a focus of national remembrance' (*PMW*, p. 73).

33. The House of Sharing (Kwangju, South Korea)
The House of Sharing was founded to provide a residential community for Korean women who had been forced to work as sex slaves for the Japanese military during the Second World War. The author visited the History Museum that had been founded there in 1998, and was heartbroken to learn how cruelly the Japanese soldiers had acted towards young Korean girls.

34. Franz Jägerstätter House (Ostermiething, Austria)
The Franz Jägerstätter House was founded in 1993. Its aim is to be a 'memorial to Franz Jägerstätter, sentenced to death as a conscientious objector and killed on 9 August 1943' (*PMW*, p. 20).

35. Austrian Peace Museum (Wolfsegg, Austria)
The First Austrian Peace Museum is a 'meeting place and communication centre for peace education' (*PMW*, p. 22). The author visited the museum on 8 November 1993 and was pleased to discover that the emphasis is put on citizens' dialogue and peace making. A Bosnian family of refugees was well taken care of in the basement of the peace museum, which illustrates the importance of direct action for peace.

36. The World Centre for Peace, Freedom and Human Rights (Verdun, France)
The World Centre for Peace, Freedom and Human Rights aims to 'give the general public a greater insight into the history and practicalities of peace, freedom and human rights; to develop an awareness of the importance and difficulties involved in such an undertaking; and to encourage discussion and research on an international level with a view to building peace' (*PMW*, p. 27).

37. Prairie Peace Park (Lincoln, Nebraska, USA)
Prairie Peace Park aims to establish 'an exhibition centre easily accessible to travellers that contains exhibits demonstrating new visions and humane ideas and practices about living together in unity and peace, and that disseminates this information to the public' (*PMW*, p. 72).

38. Peace Museum (Nürnberg, Germany)
The Peace museum at Nürnberg 'documents the history of the German peace movement of the last 100 years, and the development of pacifism' (*PMW*, p. 33).

39. Yi Jun Peace Museum (The Hague, Netherlands)
Yi Jun is 'one of the most honoured figures in Korea's struggle for independence, who died in the Museum building in 1907, when the Second Hague Peace Conference was held. He went to The Hague as a member of the Korean delegation which failed, however, to gain admittance to the Conference due to Japanese objections. Japan at this time was consolidating its occupation of Korea. The Museum aims to (1) preserve the historic site of the Korean national hero's death; (2) promote a spirit fostering the love of independence, justice, and peace; (3) advance peace education in the world' (*PMW*, p. 61). The author visited the museum in May 1999 at the time of the Hague Peace Conference. She realized that the history of Yi Jun is not taught in history education in Japan and that it is important to disseminate this history at peace museums.

40. Peace Gallery (Bradford, UK)
The Peace Gallery was founded in 1996. The author visited the gallery on 4 February 2001. The emphasis on pacifists and peace movements was striking as well as the training of conflict resolution skills in the community. It was very different from Japanese peace museums where history education tends to be emphasized.

41. Robben Island Museum (Bellville, South Africa)
Founded in 1997, Robben Island Museum (RIM), on the site of Nelson Mandela's imprisonment, 'aims to develop the island as a national and international heritage and conservation project for the new millennium. In managing its resources and activities, RIM strives to maintain the unique symbolism of the island, nurture creativity and innovation, and contribute to socio-economic development, the transformation of South African society and the enrichment of humanity'.[21]

42. 'In Flanders Fields' Museum (Ieper, Belgium)
'In Flanders Fields' Museum aims to 'give visitors the opportunity to experience the First World War in all its aspects by using eyewitness accounts and modern technology' (*PMW*, p. 25). The author visited the museum in May 1999 and again in May 2003. The museum is similar to many peace museums in its emphasis on the history of war for peace education.

43. Gernika Peace Museum (Gernika, Spain)
The Gernika Peace Museum was created 'to give visitors the chance to learn something of Gernika's history, and how it was completely destroyed during the Spanish Civil War', according to the leaflet produced for the 5th International Peace Museum Conference. The author visited the museum in May 2005 when the International Conference of Peace Museums was held and was impressed by the museum's emphasis on nonviolence in conflict resolution.

44. Peace History Museum (Hindelang, Germany)
The Peace History Museum in Hindelang aims to 'honour and commemorate individuals from ancient times until today whose efforts on behalf of peace and reconciliation have been exemplary'.[22]

45. Peace Museum (La Vall d'Uixó, Spain)
The author visited the Peace Museum at La Vall d'Uixó on 11 March 2003. Of particular note is the fact that the museum is subsidized by the city to the tune of approx. US$9,000 per year and a bank offered the building in which it is housed. Memorable exhibits included those on Sadako Sasaki who was killed in the atomic bombing.

46. European Museum for Peace (Stadtschlaining, Austria)
The author visited the European Museum for Peace in Stadtschlaining on 9 July 2004. The exhibits on conflict resolution at both international level and personal level (such as bullying) were especially noteworthy. Besides exhibits on peace, environmental issues were dealt with using old cars and photos.

---

21 <http://www.robben-island.org.za/vision.asp>.
22 International Network of Peace Museums, *Newsletter of the International Network of Peace Museums*, 12 (February 2000): 17.

47. African Peace Museum (Nairobi, Kenya)
One of the aims of the African Peace Museum is to 'collect, document and preserve all material on African peace-making processes in the past and present' (*PMW*, p. 58).

48. Dayton International Peace Museum (Dayton, Ohio, USA)
Among the many goals and objectives listed on the Dayton International Peace Museum website, the museum declares its intention to contribute to the prevention of wars and to foster a culture of peace.[23]

---

23 <http://www.daytonpeacemuseum.org>.

Chapter 8

The Development of Peace Studies in the United States

Carol Rank

The Emergence of the Peace Studies Field in the United States

Although the origins of peace studies can in large part be traced to European peace research, much of the development of the field, in terms of teaching programmes, has taken place in North America, particularly in the USA. In this chapter I examine how Peace Studies emerged as a new field of study in the USA, its core concerns and distinguishing characteristics, and some of the challenges to its development. I also examine different models and types of programme development, and the contribution that Peace Studies can make to the creation of a culture of peace.

The first peace studies programme was established in 1948 by one of the historic peace churches, the Church of the Brethren, at Manchester College, a small, religious-based university in Indiana.[1] Their pacifism informs the curriculum as it does in other similarly religious-based universities such as Earlham, which was established by the Society of Friends (Quakers). Values of peace and justice are an inherent part of these traditions, so peace studies finds a natural home in such settings. However, the majority of peace studies programmes in the USA are found in secular universities (liberal arts colleges and private and public universities).

Peace studies programmes were few in number until the late 1960s and early 1970s, when students and professors began initiating courses and teaching programmes in response to the Vietnam War.[2] Students and faculty came together to discuss their opposition to the war and the personal dilemmas they faced in terms of conscription, pacifism and protest. Some of these programmes were short-lived,

---

1 Interestingly, in the past several years there has been dynamic new growth in peace studies in that state, with a new consortium having received generous funding, the Plowshares Peace Studies Collaboration of Earlham, Goshen and Manchester Colleges. The state is also home to another of the most long-standing Peace Studies programmes, at Notre Dame University.

2 For example, as a response to the Vietnam War, Manhattan College in New York City began its Peace Studies programme in 1968, while Colgate University's Peace Studies programme began in 1969. Kent State University in Ohio established their Center for Peaceful Change as a 'living memorial' to the four students who were shot and killed by National Guardsmen in an anti-Vietnam War demonstration.

while others evolved into well-established peace studies programmes. Nonviolence was a key area of study in many of these programmes.

Another surge in programme development took place in the 1980s in response to the dangers of an escalating nuclear arms race. By the mid-1980s many peace studies programmes in the USA were focused on international conflict and the threat of nuclear war.[3] Thus in different historical periods peace studies has responded to the crises of the time, seeking out and putting forth nonviolent alternatives in the face of violent conflict and the nuclear threat.

With the end of the Cold War the emphasis of peace studies courses shifted somewhat away from international politics, giving more attention to structural, domestic and civil violence.[4] After the dissolution of the Soviet Union, when the conflict between the superpowers no longer dominated international politics, scholars turned their attention instead to intrastate conflicts – civil wars, ethnic conflicts and power struggles within countries, which had come to the fore.[5] The feminist critique from the 1980s was taken on board, that peace research and peace studies should be about more than 'weapons counting', and that such topics as the relationship between gender and militarism needed to be explored. Furthermore, the feminist axiom that the 'personal is political' when related to peace studies meant that such issues as domestic violence (particularly violence against women in the home) became a part of the remit of peace studies.[6]

The concept of 'security' became broadened from 'national security' to collective, environmental and comprehensive security, which acknowledged the relationship between international and individual security.[7] This expanded definition of security reflects a shift from a focus on 'negative peace' – the cessation of direct violence – to 'positive peace' – the conditions that eliminate the causes of direct violence such as social, economic and political justice.

Johan Galtung coined the terms 'negative and positive peace' in his writings on direct and structural violence, which have helped to lay the foundations for the field. A milestone in the development of the field was Galtung's establishment of the International Peace Research Institute in Oslo, Norway (PRIO) in 1959 and the founding of the *Journal of Peace Research* in 1964, which has been published continuously since then. Much of the peace studies programme development in

---

3   Barbara J. Wien (ed.), *Peace and World Order Studies: A Curriculum Guide*, 4th edn (New York, 1984).

4   Ian M. Harris, 'Peace Studies in the United States at the University and College Levels' in Ake Bjerstedt (ed.), *Peace Education: Global Perspectives* (Stockholm, 1993), pp. 49–67.

5   Hugh Mial, Oliver Ramsbotham and Tom Woodhouse, *Contemporary Conflict Resolution* (Cambridge, 1999), p. 2.

6   For a discussion of gender issues in peace studies see, for example, Birgit Brock-Utne, *Educating for Peace: A Feminist Perspective* (New York, 1985).

7   Carolyn M. Stephenson, 'New Approaches to International Peacemaking in the post-Cold War World' in Michael Klare (ed.), *Peace and World Security Studies: A Curriculum Guide* (Boulder, 1994), pp. 14–28.

the USA has taken place on an *ad hoc* basis without being linked necessarily to European peace research, but the insights from Galtung and other peace researchers have shaped the field and continue to do so.

Another thread of peace studies development is the area of conflict resolution, which has been a part of the field since its inception. Some would argue that conflict resolution is a 'sister field' of peace studies, but in fact all peace studies programmes address conflict in some way. One of the first journals in the peace studies field was the *Journal of Conflict Resolution*, established by one of the founders of the field in the USA, Kenneth Boulding, and his colleagues at the University of Michigan. Boulding argued for a more narrow definition of peace in the negative sense, as he felt that the broader definition was too broad to be manageable as a field of study. In this he differed from Galtung and their 'twelve friendly quarrels' are a part of the literature of the field.[8] The study and teaching of conflict resolution has shifted over time in response to critiques of it being oriented to 'pacification' rather than needed social change. Hence the term 'conflict transformation' was coined and is in much use today.

The diversity of approaches to peace studies was reflected in a 1994 curriculum guide which listed the following headings for courses: war, conflict and peace in the post-Cold War era; the new nuclear agenda; North–South relations; conflict resolution; international law; psychology and peace; the economics of peace and security; development, debt and global poverty; the environment, population growth and resource scarcity; human rights; race, ethnicity and conflict; feminist perspectives on peace, militarism and political violence; nonviolence, peace movements and social activism.[9] An earlier 1991 study by the United States Institute of Peace had come up with an 'intellectual map' of the field which also reflected the diversity of the field. Their headings included: traditional approaches (collective security and deterrence); international law approaches (international law, interstate organizations, third-party dispute settlement); new approaches (transnationalism, behavioural approaches, conflict resolution); and political systems approaches (internal systems and systemic theories/world systems).[10]

The growth of the peace studies field has been documented in the succession of curriculum guides and directories published by the Consortium on Peace Research Education and Development (COPRED). In 1981, 36 universities and colleges were listed as having peace studies courses and programmes. In 1986 the number had grown to 106, and by 1995 to 288 universities in 30 countries offering peace studies in one form or another. The most recent (2000) edition lists 381 colleges

---

8 Kenneth Boulding, 'Twelve Friendly Quarrels with Johan Galtung', *Journal of Peace Research*, 14/1 (1977): 75–86.

9 Michael Klare (ed.), *Peace and World Security Studies: A Curriculum Guide* (Boulder, 1994).

10 W. Scott Thompson and Kenneth Jensen (eds), *Approaches to Peace: An Intellectual Map* (Washington, DC, 1991).

and universities in 42 countries, with the USA having by far the greatest number of programmes.[11]

Peace studies in the new millennium in some ways has the same agenda as in previous decades – to study how to move the global community away from violence toward nonviolence or, as stated by Galtung, to study how to promote 'peace through peaceful means'. In the world of the first decade of the twenty-first century peace studies must address the most pressing issues of the time, such as terrorism, globalization, civil wars and environmental destruction. Two interrelated topics, forgiveness and reconciliation, have also now come to the fore in peace studies, and they are central to our research and teaching at Coventry University in the UK. The themes may shift, but the core remains the same: to explore and promote nonviolent alternatives, to turn our societies away from violence, and to build a culture of peace.

Distinguishing Characteristics of Peace Studies

As described above, peace studies is clearly about more than just international relations. In fact, peace studies arose as a revolt against traditional approaches to the study of international politics. In his essay, 'Could We Study International Relations as if People Mattered?', Roy Preiswerk argued that the study of international relations was state-centric and focused on 'national interests' and the dealings of political élites (power balances, sovereignty, diplomacy and strategic policy-making). Other 'actors' in the global community (individuals, groups, movements, non-governmental organizations) were not being considered. Furthermore values that were implicit in the international-relations field, including that the use of violence and coercive force by states is 'legitimate', needed to be made explicit and critiqued.[12]

The starting point for peace studies was thus to question this 'legitimacy' and to make its own values explicit: that 'peace', like 'health', is a desirable condition toward which we should aim. Our research and teaching are thus value-based, and are aimed at constructive change. The scope of peace studies is also broader than international relations as it includes the study of interpersonal, intergroup and intersocietal relations. Peace studies goes beyond the nation–state and attempts to be global in its considerations, and it also looks *within* the nation–state at different levels of interaction. As described by Nigel Young, 'Peace research is an emancipation from ideas which are oppressive and ultimately supportive of a system which is destructive and potentially lethal. One has to critique the language, assumptions, and

---

11 Consortium on Peace Research, Education and Development (COPRED), *Global Directory of Peace Studies and Conflict Resolution Programs*, 2000 edition (Fairfax, VA, 2001).

12 Roy Preiswerk, 'Could We Study International Relations as if People Mattered?' in Gordon Feller, Sherle Schwenninger and Diane Singerman (eds), *Peace and World Order Studies: A Curriculum Guide* (New York, 1981), pp. 2–23.

strategies of that system, and that cannot be done within a traditional international relations framework'.[13]

In summary, some of the distinguishing characteristics of peace studies are that it is global rather than state-centric in its concerns; it looks at all levels of interaction, from the interpersonal to the international; it is value-based and action-oriented, and prescriptive in terms of alternatives to violence. Peace studies also encompasses a broader time frame than international relations, going further back in history than the period of the creation of the nation–state system and also further 'forward' in its consideration of desired futures.[14] Another important characteristic of peace studies is that it is broadly interdisciplinary, drawing on a wide range of perspectives from different fields in the social and natural sciences. As described by Alan Geyer, former director of the Colgate Peace Studies programme, peace studies should have a 'wide range of vantage points from which to engage any and all disciplines at the points of their neglect and potential ... Every branch of learning has its own contributions to make to the intellectual and practical struggle for peace'.[15]

As the field of peace studies continues to expand it is useful to look back to some of these core formulations as guidelines for programme development. A consultative group within the Consortium on Peace Research Education and Development (COPRED), who were asked in 1986 to define and, where necessary, delimit peace studies, came up with the following description of basic characteristics:

- *Central propositions.* 1) The traditional belief in the inevitability of war and injustice is questioned, based on data and insights from peace research and movements for social change; 2) The pedagogical purpose of peace studies is to provide students with appropriate intellectual tools with which to examine this traditional belief and inquire into possible alternatives to war and oppression.

- *Fundamental core.* 1) The central questions Peace Studies asks are: What is the nature of peace? What are the conditions that make peace possible? How are these conditions achieved? 2) The minimum areas of concern are: organized lethal violence among social groups at all levels of organization (war) and structural violence (systemic discrimination, deprivation, and oppression). 3) The basic values of Peace Studies are a world-wide human perspective,

---

13 Interview of Professor Nigel Young by Carol Rank at Colgate University Peace Studies Program, Hamilton, NY, 1987. Cited in Carol Rank, *Peace Studies in American Higher Education: The Emergence of a New Field* (PhD dissertation, University of California, Berkeley, 1988).

14 Carolyn Stephenson, 'The Evolution of Peace Studies' in Daniel Thomas and Michael Klare, *Peace and World Order Studies: A Curriculum Guide*, 5th edn (Boulder, 1989), pp. 9–19, at p. 12.

15 A. Geyer, 'Doing Peace Studies in Universities and Seminaries', *Manchester College Bulletin of the Peace Studies Program*, 7/1 (1977).

desirability of achieving peace and justice, and recognition of the possibility of their achievement.[16]

The notion of 'delimiting the field' might imply that programmes which stray too far from these central propositions and core characteristics might be losing direction in terms of what peace studies is all about. For some there might be a temptation to gravitate back to more traditional approaches to international relations and national security, as these might be seen as more 'legitimate' and 'objective' in academia.

Infrastructure of the Field

Peace studies in higher education has emerged as a recognized field of study with all the characteristics of established disciplines: a significant body of theory and literature, professional associations and journals, and numerous teaching programmes in the subject. Approaches to peace studies vary, as do the names of the programmes. The field is kaleidoscopic, yet underlying the diversity is a unity of assumptions and aims, as described above. The administrative structures of peace studies programmes also vary, from clusters of courses to full degree-granting programmes (under-graduate and post-graduate) and departments and schools of peace studies.

Along with administrative support provided by universities, professional associations and journals are essential elements of the field's 'infrastructure' and are indications of its acceptance in the academic community. Peace studies programmes and peace research institutes share a common professional association: the International Peace Research Association, founded in 1964. The North American affiliate of IPRA is the Peace and Justice Studies Association (PJSA). The PJSA was formed in 2001 as a merger of two previous organizations: the Consortium on Peace Research, Education and Development (COPRED) and the Peace Studies Association (PSA). The merger was significant in that it re-connected peace studies academics with teachers and activists. The older of the two preceding organizations, COPRED was formed, like many Peace Studies programmes, during the turbulent days of the early 1970s. As described by Chad Alger, the Vietnam War and 'turmoil on the streets and campuses at home' led to the founding of COPRED as an organization that could 'confront the irrelevance of peace research to peace activists, and the gap between our educational practice and the competencies required of citizens who would act effectively for peace'.[17]

In contrast, the Peace Studies Association (PSA) was formed mainly to strengthen peace studies as an academic field. One of the tensions inherent in the field, between activism and academia, came to a head in the mid-1980s with the splitting off of the PSA from COPRED. Some of the founders of the PSA were concerned that the

---

16 'The Juniata Consultation on the Future of Peace Studies', *COPRED Peace Chronicle* (December 1986): 3–4.

17 C. Alger, 'Peace Studies at the Crossroads: Where Else?', unpublished paper presented at the Sixteenth Annual Conference of COPRED, Milwaukee, WI, November, 1987.

legitimacy of peace studies was called into question by activism, and that the remit of COPED, which also involved teachers in schools as well as peace movement activists and practitioners, was too broad to support the field in the ways that were needed. The new Peace and Justice Studies Association (PJSA) has managed to bridge that gap once again and bring practitioners and peace movement activists together with peace studies academics. This has infused new life into the field, particularly in the USA and Canada.

Challenges to the Development of the Field

Throughout its history the peace studies field has faced a number of challenges to its further development. These include problems in the definition of peace; lack of administrative support for interdisciplinary innovation; and, most important, criticisms of political bias.

The Definition of Peace

A common criticism of peace studies is that 'peace' is too vague a term to form the basis for a field. It can mean everything from a transcendental spiritual awareness to a 'Pax Romana' or 'Pax Americana' of enforced law and order. Peace has taken on a wide range of meanings in different cultural contexts throughout history. To some it conjures notions of 'appeasement' or pacification. In Hebrew, peace is 'shalom' – a sense of wholeness. Peace is a highly emotive yet abstract concept.

Some definitions of peace research (and peace studies) are so broad that the criticism of lack of definition does not seem unjustified. As described by the peace researcher Marek Thee, 'Peace research has expanded to encompass the study of armed conflict and conflict resolution, armaments and disarmament, underdevelopment and development, human deprivation and the realization of social justice, repressive violence and the realization of human rights … It has taken an aggressive interest in almost everything concerning the human condition and its betterment'.[18]

Being concerned with 'almost everything concerning the human condition and its betterment' can present problems in defining a coherent field of study. The scope of inquiry can become so broad that the boundaries are unclear. Critics from outside the field might thus see it as vague and 'soft' because of its normative approach. Some academics in the early days of the development of the field advocated a narrow definition of 'peace as the absence of war' in order to make the field more manageable. However, doing so severely limits the inquiry and ignores other forms of violence which themselves lead to war.

As described by Adam Curle, the definition of peace as the absence of war is insufficient so long as violence continues to exist within or between societies. Peace is a condition in which there is freedom from overt violence and from the conditions

---

18 Marek Thee, 'The Scope and Priorities of Peace Research', paper presented at Consultation on Peace Research, United Nations University, Tokyo, December 1980.

out of which violence grows. Thus 'peace' means freedom from political, economic or other restraints that limit the realization of human potential. Social change then becomes synonymous with peace-making, as it means altering political and economic structures or whatever else is a source of violence, removing the causes of oppression and injustice that prevent peace.[19]

Part of the problem of defining 'peace' is cultural – while we are taught about war, and see it every day in our media, learning what peace means and how to obtain it, is rarer. As peace studies and peace education become more broadly accepted there will be less of a problem in defining peace. In any case, the very complexity and diversity of elements that relate to peace and peace-making adds richness to the field, enabling it to engage with many different disciplines. While clearly defining what 'peace' means in terms of peace studies' conceptual core, the field can also 'infuse' a peace perspective into other disciplines. That can be a strength rather than a weakness.

Administrative Support for Interdisciplinary Innovation

The strongest peace studies programmes in the USA are those that have carved out a niche specifically defined as peace studies, while some of the weaker programmes remain a loose association of faculty members coming together from different fields. The Colgate Peace Studies programme, for example, had from its inception in 1969 an endowed chair for the head of the department and a clear identity that has been maintained ever since. For many in the peace studies field, however, their involvement in teaching peace studies is voluntary and is taken on in addition to their commitments in another field, such as in history, economics, psychology. Unless a university makes a commitment to fund and maintain an established peace studies programme, courses remain vulnerable to closure.

As described earlier, the interdisciplinary nature of peace studies can be a strength, but it can also be a weakness unless programmes are given adequate administrative support. The norm in the USA has been for peace studies programmes to be established by faculty and students who take it upon themselves to create and maintain their new interdisciplinary programmes. Rather than being rewarded for their innovations, many have in fact put their academic careers in jeopardy.

Professional advancement in academia depends on the extent to which faculty prove themselves in established fields, and rewards are not generally meted out to those who break new ground between disciplines. Faculty members who engage in interdisciplinary innovation (such as peace studies) often do so at the expense of their standing in their home departments. One way to avoid this problem is for universities to appoint lecturers and professors specifically in the field of peace studies, and to give professional and financial encouragement and rewards to those from a variety of fields who can contribute to the field. Until these administrative

---

19 For a further discussion of Adam Curle's definition of peace and peace-making see his book, *Making Peace* (London, 1971).

barriers are overcome the theoretical development of the field in North America, and as a whole, will be impeded.

As stated by one American peace studies lecturer, 'Our particular weaknesses have been lack of administrative time and lack of resources to encourage faculty interaction, growth and support. Similar to other non-traditional programmes, our faculty maintain their scholarship and employment base in separate disciplines. This creates dispersion and lack of curricular cohesion ... The organizational work of creating and sustaining Peace Studies has been done without reimbursement ... We have innovated, and have paid the price for extension into multiple discipline areas'.[20]

By supporting research and teaching on peace, colleges and universities can, in the liberal arts tradition, educate people to take on responsible roles in society. If peace studies can indeed help find solutions to some of our most pressing problems, and help reduce or eliminate violence in all its forms, it can be argued that universities have a moral responsibility to support those who are trying to contribute to the development of the field.

Political Bias and Censorship

In the 1980s peace education in schools was highly criticized in the USA by the Reagan administration, which claimed that it was politically biased and as such a form of 'indoctrination'. Likewise peace studies programmes at universities were highly criticized in the USA and the UK, with calls from some quarters to shut them down.[21] In the 1990s political debate on the nature of peace studies lessened, but now in the world of post 9/11, the field is once again meeting with opposition. In the current political climate of the USA, with tighter limits being imposed on civil liberties, some peace studies academics are experiencing what they consider to be censorship and attacks on their freedom of speech.

The conservative author, commentator and strategist David Horowitz, for example, recently authored an article for his on-line journal, said to reach 1.7 million visitors a month, attacking peace studies as 'pro-terrorist'. He wrote that peace studies programmes 'teach students to identify with America's terrorist enemies and to identify America as a Great Satan oppressing the world's poor and causing them to go hungry', and concluded that peace studies academics are 'political activists with fraudulent academic credentials conducting indoctrinations'.[22] In a divided nation,

---

20 D. Campbell, 'Peace Studies and Civic Responsibility in Higher Education', Sacramento: California State University War/Peace Studies (undated document).

21 See, for example, Caroline Cox and Roger Scruton, *Peace Studies: A Critical Survey* (New York, 1984).

22 Horowitz's on-line journal is entitled Front Page Magazine <http://www.frontpagemag. com>. See Seth Slabaugh, 'Peace Studies under Siege' <http://www.frontpagemag.com/ Articles/ReadArticle.asp?ID=16183>, 1 December 2004. Also 'Professor Says Terrorist Charges "Shameful" and "Absurd"', *The Star Press*, Muncie, IN, 30 November 2004 (no author given).

which the USA is today, such criticism is not necessarily accepted by the majority of the population. However, it has resulted in a wave of critical attacks on peace studies academics. This is only one example of the kind of censorship that is taking place in the post-9/11 USA.

Because the field of peace studies calls into question the use of war as a political strategy, such as that waged by the USA in Iraq, it is not surprising that it has met with a backlash. As Johan Galtung has said, peace studies is 'biased' against war and seeks its abolition, and there is 'nothing arcane or inane about that; it is the same as the abolition of slavery and colonialism … The abolition of war as a social institution means to deprive the state of its prerogative to wage wars, and the state doesn't like that'.[23]

Peace studies is no more 'biased' than any of the professional schools. Schools of public health and social welfare aim to contribute to the public good. Schools of business promote profitable enterprise and schools of engineering are 'biased' toward the building of safe highways and bridges. All of these subject areas assume certain goals or values (health, welfare and so on), and organize their teaching accordingly. Such a value-based orientation, while accepted without question in other fields, is problematic for peace studies.

The more that peace studies programmes encourage students to actively work for peace and justice, the more likely they are to be criticized as 'biased'. The action–orientation of peace studies is seen as a form of advocacy that pollutes the academic purity of detached scholarship. Nevertheless, most peace studies faculty and students would agree that their aim is not only to teach *about* peace, but *for* peace.

Building a Culture of Peace

Given the hegemony of the USA in the world today, it is increasingly important to maintain the critical edge of peace studies, helping students in the USA to see their country from a more global perspective; the kind of learning that is needed is engaged scholarship, which is not afraid to question or to take the kinds of actions that are needed to bring about a more peaceful society and world. With research and teaching aimed at peace rather than war, justice rather than oppression, peace studies can help bring about changes in political and economic policies and foster the kinds of long-term attitudinal changes that are needed to build a culture of peace.

---

23 Johan Galtung, interview by Carol Rank at Institute on Global Conflict and Cooperation conference, Los Angeles, March 1987.

Chapter 9

Peace Studies in the UK:
A Personal Reflection

Andrew Rigby

Introduction

In this chapter it is not my aim to present an authoritative history of the development of the field of peace studies within the UK. Rather, to present a set of reflections upon the development of the field based on my own involvement in the overall project since the 1960s. In the chapter I use the term peace studies to cover all academic activities, including research and teaching, relating directly to the study of how to avert the threat of war and achieve a peaceful world.

My main arguments are three-fold:

1. Peace studies as a field of academic enquiry emerged out of the concerns and the initiatives of the wider peace movement, and the changing agenda of peace studies has to some degree been driven by the issues raised by peace movements.
2. The broad peace movement can be portrayed as a general social movement concerned with promoting peace and combating war. Within this general movement there have been and are a wide range of more specific movements with different priorities, programmes and projects. These different 'tendencies' within the overall peace movement have been reflected within the general field of peace studies.
3. The vitality and health of the overall peace movement has depended in part upon the creative tension generated by the different stances, priorities and commitments of the different specific movements and groupings within the general movement. In similar vein the vitality of peace studies as a field depends crucially upon the tensions generated by a plurality of approaches to the overall project of studying how to bring about a more peaceful world. The field becomes impoverished to the extent to which one particular approach or 'school' asserts its hegemony over others.

I shall try to illustrate these points by means of an outline of my own experiences of the development of the peace studies field in the UK since the 1960s.

Peace Studies in the UK in the 1960s and 1970s

The first peace research institute to be created in the UK was at the University of Lancaster in 1959. One of its founding members was Paul Smoker, who was also an active member of Lancaster's Campaign for Nuclear Disarmament (CND). The institute became known as the Richardson Institute, honouring the memory of the Quaker scientist Lewis Richardson who was one of the early pioneers from before the Second World War in the UK who devoted his intellect to the dilemma of how to avert the incidence of war.

Like the better-known Peace Research Institute of Oslo (PRIO), established by Johan Galtung in that same year of 1959, the Lancaster initiative reflected the need felt by young scientists who were also involved in the burgeoning anti-nuclear movement of that time to apply their knowledge and expertise to avert the risk of nuclear holocaust as the Cold War deepened.

In 1968 I was a post-graduate sociology student at the University of Essex. Johan Galtung was one of our professors and it was there that I first heard about peace research – from Johan but also from someone who had been involved with the institute at Lancaster. I was excited by the project – using ones expertise in social science to study and promote the cause of peace and avert the risk of war. Although I had to admit that I felt a little out of my depth, as most of the young scholars that I came to know seemed to be very adept at mathematical modelling and other quantitative methods and approaches.

By this time the threat of nuclear war had eased somewhat with the ban on atmospheric testing in 1963 and the subsequent Non-Proliferation Treaty. Some of the more radical peace researchers had begun to shift the focus of their concern from the East–West axis to that of North–South global inequality. This was a period when the anti-Vietnam war movement was at its height, and peace researchers who were caught up in this movement began to question the over-riding concern of peace studies with averting war. Could it not be the case that some forms of armed struggle were justifiable as wars of liberation against oppression? It was during this period that Johan Galtung introduced the notion of structural violence, and I – like others of my generation no doubt – remember being greatly influenced by the arguments of a Swedish researcher Herman Schmid who criticized main stream peace researchers for failing to engage with the implications of the axiom that there can be no true peace without justice.[1]

Here for the first time I witnessed the tensions within the peace studies field between what might be considered the 'minimalist' project of those concerned primarily with the prevention of outbreaks of overt interpersonal violence in the guise of war and the 'maximalist' project of those who extended the concept of violence to cover any aspect of exploitation and domination and sought to use their intellectual and organizational resources to bring about a secular 'heaven on earth'.

1　Herman Schmid, 'Politics and Peace Research', *Journal of Peace Research*, 3 (1968): 217–32.

I identified very much with the maximalists, although as a pacifist I was at odds with some of their number who seemed to believe the false rhetoric about the liberatory wonders of 'revolutionary violence'. At one twenty-four-hour vigil outside the premises of a company based in London that was involved in supporting the American war effort in Vietnam I got talking with an older protester who told me about a company called Rowen Industries that employed people with disabilities. Its name came from Robert Owen, the utopian socialist of the nineteenth century. This set me thinking about the importance of creating alternative institutions and structures as a nonviolent and non-coercive mode of social transformation, the power of exemplary action by individuals and collectives to bring about change at a far deeper level than could be achieved by getting involved in electoral party politics or even engaging in the demonstration politics of the anti-Vietnam war movement. This in turn led me to the topic of my doctoral research – the commune movement in Britain during the 1970s.

In 1969 and 1970 I used as my base the premises of the Richardson Institute, which had moved from Lancaster to London. It was there that I first met Adam Curle who, a few years later in 1973, became the first professor of peace studies at the University of Bradford. At that time Adam was working on his book *Making Peace* and its companion volume *Mystics and Militants* in which he explored different approaches to the struggle for peace and justice – the inner and the outer. To some degree this focus reflected the concerns within the British pacifist movement, as expressed within the pages of the weekly paper *Peace News*, to develop an approach to peace-making that would combine personal change at the level of the individual with wider institutional change. This grew out of unease with 'demonstration politics' that had been the hallmark of much of the peace and anti-war movement through the 1960s. There was a felt need to widen the field of analysis beyond foreign policy issues and weapons systems to encompass the whole socio-economic and political structures that gave rise to nuclear states, the arms race and international war. In the pages of *Peace News* contributors began to explore the relationship between people's sense of powerlessness in everyday life and the burgeoning power of the warfare state. We also emphasized the importance of balancing the struggle *against* war with a vision of the social order we hoped to create. As important as campaigning and demonstrating against particular wars was the creative and constructive task of articulating a vision of a non-exploitative and nonviolent social order and embodying such a vision in our forms of organizing and working for change. I identified wholeheartedly with this standpoint.[2]

This broadening of concern was also reflected within peace studies. In 1973 the editors of the *Journal of Conflict Resolution*, which had been established at the University of Michigan in 1957, wrote:

---

2   For an overview of this orientation as developed within *Peace News* see Andrew Rigby, 'Peace News, 1936–1986' in Gail Chester and Andrew Rigby, (eds), *Articles of Peace: Celebrating Fifty Years of Peace News*, (Bridport, 1986) pp. 7–26.

The threat of nuclear holocaust remains with us, and may well continue to do so for centuries, but other problems are competing with deterrence and disarmament studies for our attention. The journal must also attend to international conflict over justice, equality, and human dignity; problems of conflict resolution for ecological balance and control are within our proper scope and especially suited for interdisciplinary attention.[3]

Peace Studies in the 1980s

With the resurgence of the nuclear disarmament movement in the 1980s, driven by a new and heightened fear of nuclear annihilation through a clash of the super-powers, I found my old concerns returning – how to achieve a balance between resisting the threat of war and sowing the seeds of a peaceful world? I had joined the School of Peace Studies at the University of Bradford in the late 1970s, and by the early 1980s we had become a major resource for the new disarmament movement. Much of the important research emanating from the School focused on the nature and threat of the new generation of nuclear weapons and the changes in strategic thinking that had accompanied their development. I needed no convincing of the crucial significance of this work, but I became a little concerned that in concentrating to such a degree upon the immediate threat of nuclear weapons, we were in danger of losing touch with more positive aspects of peace-thinking and peace-making. Of course I was familiar with the counter-argument that the threat of nuclear holocaust was so immediate that we could not afford the time to reflect upon less pressing matters. The implication was that it was self-indulgent to engage with the deeper questions, such as 'What would a nonviolent society look like? What would it require to achieve a world without war? What changes in personal and collective life would be necessary to eliminate the seeds of war?' However, I remained unconvinced by such an admittedly powerful argument. It seemed to me that unless we did make time to move beyond reacting to current crises in order to reflect upon such topics, however remote they might seem from immediate threats and issues, we were in danger of becoming mere technocrats of the nuclear disarmament movement, unrivalled in our expertise about the threat we were struggling *against*, but lacking the vision to give any positive content to the notion of the peace *for* which we were supposedly striving.

The professor of peace studies at Bradford at that time in a review of the field suggested that two of the main dangers confronting peace studies were 'marginalization and utopianism', claiming that 'those ... who cannot tolerate political negotiation or compromise without sullying their consciences, set themselves apart from the main decision-making structures of society and render themselves thereby ineffective'.[4]

---

3 Quoted in Paul Rogers and Oliver Ramsbotham, 'Then and Now: Peace Research – Past and Future', *Political Studies*, 47 (1999): 740–54, at pp. 745–6.

4 James O'Connell, 'Approaches to the Study of Peace in Higher Education: The Tensions of Scholarship' in Tom Woodhouse (ed.), *Peacemaking in a Troubled World* (Oxford, 1991), pp. 107–21, at p. 119.

His vision was of peace studies academics engaging in active dialogue with politicians and other decision-makers, acting as humanitarian leavening agents within the overall policy-making process. This tension within the field reflected the historic differences in emphasis and orientation within the British peace movement.[5]

Types of Peace Movements and Types of Peace Studies

Within the British peace movement there has been a tension between what we might term in ideal–typical fashion the minimalist approach of the war-resister and the maximalist project of the pacifists.[6] The 'resisters' are those who advocate the need to campaign actively against particular wars or particular aspects of war such as the use of nuclear weapons. The pacifists are those who place greater emphasis upon the longer-term task of working to eradicate the ultimate causes of war, wherever these might be located. In setting up this binary classification I am not trying to claim that all peace activists necessarily belong to one type or the other and that the two are mutually exclusive. Rather I am identifying for analytical purposes two types of peace activism, and the tension between them is something that individual peace activists can experience within themselves. For example, Gandhi experienced periods of grave doubt concerning the appropriate balance to draw between the political struggle for national independence and his constructive work to transform community life in India.

Whilst both resisters and pacifists, minimalists and maximalists, might seek to pursue their ends by means of influencing publics, resisters tend to be far more concerned with exercising a measurable impact on decision-makers by the conventional means available within pluralist democracies: the lobby and the mobilization of public pressure. Traditionally their prime target has been élite decision-makers. The pacifists, pursuing the far broader and longer term project of abolishing war itself, have also sought to influence and raise awareness amongst different constituencies, but rather than lobbying political élites about particular issues they have been more likely to engage in different forms of nonviolent direct action, especially in relation to their own lifestyle.

It is also possible to distinguish between these two ideal–typical approaches in terms of the dominant ethical system guiding their peace action. In his essay 'Politics as a vocation' the German sociologist Max Weber distinguished between two ideal types of ethical systems in the sphere of politics.[7] There is the ethic of responsibility, which acknowledges a need to be guided in political conduct by a sense of what is realistically possible within the parameters of existing conditions. Those guided

---

5   I am restricting my observations to the British peace movement, but my own sense is that the tensions I describe can be found within many national peace movements.

6   By pacifist I mean those people who would refuse to support or participate in any kind of war.

7   Max Weber, 'Politics as a Vocation' in Hans Gerth and C. Wright Mills (eds), *From Max Weber* (London, 1967), pp. 77–128.

by the ethic of responsibility accept the need for compromise with the realities of the world-as-it-is, recognize the necessity for pragmatism, bargaining and choosing between lesser evils if one is to operate effectively in the profane world of politics. In contrast to this ethic, Weber identified the ethic of ultimate ends (or conviction), characterized by an uncompromising commitment to a set of values and ideals. I have tried to summarize these observations in Table 9.1.

Table 9.1   War resisters and pacifists

	War resisters	Pacifists
Goal	'Minimalist'	'Maximalist'
	Stop particular wars or ban particular aspects of war	Abolish war as an institution
Time frame	Short to medium term	Long-term
Target groups	Decision-makers and publics	Self and publics
Prime means	Lobbying and mass pressure	Nonviolent direct action (including lifestyle politics), public education
Dominant ethic	Responsibility	Conviction

It was Weber's pessimistic conclusion that neither of these two modes could act as infallible guides to political action for change. Thus, with regard to the ethics of conviction, either it can lead to the belief that the good end justifies morally dubious means, a path that can lead to the concentration camps and genocide, or it can lead to the rejection of all but the purest of means, with a consequent failure to resist immediate evils in any effective manner. The pathway directed by the ethic of responsibility also has its dangers and its pitfalls. Guided by the need to exercise an influence in the here-and-now, people can experience the imperative to compromise, to recognize the realities of power and seek to bring about what change they can. But you compromise once, and then a second time – and in the process the vision has disappeared, the dream has been lost in a morass of technical problems involved in making the present system work.[8]

Similar dilemmas confronted the peace studies professionals in Britain in the 1980s who were guided by one or other of the two ethical systems and their associated projects. For example, a significant effort was made to influence the thinking of senior figures in the Labour Party that was in opposition in those Thatcher-years. However, those of my colleagues who were primarily involved in this project were required to accept and work within the basic paradigms held by the decision-making networks, sharing their parameters and their basic working assumptions.

---

8   These dilemmas of the 'slippery slope' have been explored with great insight by Arthur Koestler. See the title essay in Arthur Koestler, *The Yogi and the Commissar* (London, 1946).

One consequence of this was that over time their 'critical edge' was eroded, they became virtually indistinguishable from the other 'experts' consulted and co-opted by governments. An illustration comes to mind. One of my colleagues at Bradford in the late 1980s was researching how the number of NATO tanks at battle stations in Central Europe might be reduced, without undermining their deterrent threat vis-à-vis the tanks stationed in Eastern Europe under the command of the Warsaw Pact. For him this was an entirely legitimate and worthwhile project to undertake as a peace researcher, whilst for me it was a far cry from my understanding of peace studies as the study of how to achieve peace by peaceful means. But it has to be acknowledged that subsequently my colleague and his associates succeeded in obtaining significant government research and consultancy contracts. By acting 'responsibly' they were embraced by government networks, and their research income continued to rise.

But I was left pondering just what was distinctive about peace studies as a field once that commitment to the vision of a world-without-war was lost. I became more convinced than ever that once peace studies as a collective endeavour lost that guiding vision it forfeited one of its key functions – to be continuously pressing and testing the boundaries of what is possible in the pursuit of peace. As Gandhi remarked about his dream of India as an 'oceanic circle' of self-reliant villages, 'Let India live for this true picture, though never realizable in its completeness. We must have a proper picture of what we want, before we can have something approaching it'.[9]

Peace Studies in the 1990s

With the ending of the Cold War, at a time when state boundaries were becoming increasingly porous due to the increasing power of global communications, culture, commerce and other manifestations of global capitalism, there was an outbreak of brutal civil wars around the world fuelled by rival nationalisms, greed and political manipulation. In seeking to address this new world order, the report of Boutros Boutros-Ghali presented to the UN in 1992 (*An Agenda for Peace*) had a significant impact on the emerging peace studies agenda.[10] The report emphasized the importance of developing capacity in the four areas of preventative diplomacy, peace-making, peacekeeping and peace-building. In this context attention shifted from the nuclear arms race to focus on ethnicity and the dynamics of identity politics. There were studies of the pitfalls and the potential of armed humanitarian and peacekeeping interventions. There was a significant growth of interest in the theory and practice of mediation and conflict resolution, influenced by the work of authors such as Azar and Burton who suggested that frustrated basic needs were the main drivers of protracted social conflicts. In addition there was a growing interest in the peace-building dimension of intervention in conflict zones by humanitarian aid and development agencies.

---

9   *Harijan*, 28 July 1946.
10 Boutros Boutros-Ghali, *An Agenda for Peace* (New York, 1992).

Important as all this work was, it was very much driven by the priorities of the main actors in the field of international conflict management – governmental and non-governmental agencies. Moreover, criticisms were levelled which echoed those of earlier decades. It was suggested that peace studies was now more concerned with immediate issues of defusing conflict and pacification rather than the longer term project of promoting peace with justice.[11] According to Diana Francis, what was missing from this dominant agenda of peace studies in the 1990s in Britain was the serious engagement with the role of active nonviolence in transforming conflict situations along constructive lines.

Nonviolence and conflict resolution are both concerned with action to overcome violence, transforming the dynamics of the conflict and establishing relationships of respect. But, whereas conflict resolution concentrates on minimizing or ending what is often the secondary violence of armed, or otherwise hurtful, confrontation, the primary concern of nonviolence is to overcome the structural violence of injustice by nonviolent means.[12]

Concluding Observations

The problem confronting peace studies people is the same as that confronting peace activists. Is there a way of reconciling the two modes, a way of combining conviction with responsibility, a way of maintaining the vision of the ideal whilst acknowledging the world-as-it-is? How to address through one's research and teaching the immediate issues threatening the collective well-being of our planet, whilst retaining a deeper commitment to the 'utopian' vision of a world not only without war but also without structural and cultural violence? How to be 'realistic' and 'responsible' whilst remaining 'idealistic' and 'utopian'?

Gandhi depicted himself as a 'practical idealist', and it is in his approach to social change and conflict transformation that the key to this dilemma can be found. In advocating nonviolence as a means of social change and as a guiding principle of individual and collective life he insisted on the continuity between means and ends. Indeed, he argued that there is no fundamental difference between the two: means are ends-in-the-making. If you seek to create a world characterized by truth and nonviolence, then truth and nonviolence must be embodied in the means of change.

A similar conviction can be found in the writings of John Paul Lederach. Observing that many practitioners in the peace-building field are crisis-driven, he has urged that responding to short-term needs must be linked to a long-term vision. In advocating that peace-builders think in 'decades', he has argued:

> This does not mean we think in idealistic but irrelevant terms about peace, thereby making dreams an untouchable utopia. Rather we build from dreams the strategic frameworks

---

11 See, for example, Diana Francis, *People, Peace and Power: Conflict Transformation in Action* (London, 2002), p. 40.

12 Francis, p. 40.

that clarify and concretize the social, political, economic, community, and interpersonal changes those dreams would entail. ... The key in peacebuilding lies not in whether we are proficient at putting out fires, nor in whether we are adept at articulating our hopes. The key lies in whether we are capable of strategically linking the potential in the crisis with the changes needed to move us toward the dream.[13]

In similar vein I would argue that it is vital for the health of peace studies as an intellectual endeavour that the field should embrace modes, minimalist and maximalist. The minimalist approach guided by the ethic of responsibility and responding to immediate threats to our collective well-being needs to sit in creative tension alongside the maximalist approach of those guided by a fundamental commitment to realizing the longer-term vision of a world-without-war. In the history of the British peace movement the tension between war-resisters and pacifists has not always been easy and cordial – but it has been one of the factors that has kept the movement as a whole vibrant. It is also this tension which, I believe, has kept the peace studies 'movement' in Britain lively and energetic. It is to be hoped that as peace studies emerges as a recognized field in new parts of the world, all attempts to establish an orthodoxy that would stifle such a creative tension should be resisted.

---

13 John Paul Lederach, 'Civil Society and Reconciliation' in Charles A. Crocker *et al.* (eds), *Turbulent Peace: The Challenges of Managing International Conflict* (Washington, DC, 2001), pp. 841–54, at p. 846.

Chapter 10

New Themes in Peace Studies

Alan Hunter

Several chapters in this collection show that peace studies has been a growing multi-disciplinary endeavour for at least two generations. Among its important areas of focus have been nonviolence as political philosophy; theories of conflict transformation; peace education; critique of military power including atomic weapons; third party roles to reduce violent conflict; democratic empowerment and nonviolent social movements. As new problems and forms of violent conflict have come to the fore in the past decade, new areas of study have gained prominence including aid-work in conflict zones, interreligious dialogue, asymmetrical war, counter-terrorism and human rights. Chapter 5, for example, introduces a concept of security extended to include gender and environmental violence, arising from a peace studies perspective. This chapter reports on forgiveness, reconciliation and transitional justice, themes that are emerging within mainstream peace studies institutions and publications. It also discusses 'community cohesion' which focuses on peaceful relations within today's diverse and rapidly changing urban environments. For readers' convenience, the bibliography notes some important relevant publications.

Forgiveness

Before the 1990s forgiveness barely appeared in social science research. The concept lies close to the heart of Christianity and is also a component of other world religions; but outside the religious context it was not a mainstream area of study. The situation had changed dramatically by 2005. Scholars had written dozens of books and journal articles on forgiveness, which also featured in hundreds of popular essays, exhibitions, websites and other media. An early catalyst for this development was a book by Lewis Smedes published in 1986.[1] In 1994 the International Forgiveness Institute was established in Madison, Wisconsin, USA. This initiative was followed by a major investment by the Templeton Foundation, which in 1997 sponsored 'The Science of Forgiveness', a research symposium encouraging further analysis of forgiveness. The Foundation committed $5 million to launch a large number of academic studies.[2]

---

1   Lewis B. Smedes, *Forgive and Forget: Healing the Hurts We Don't Deserve* (San Francisco, 1986).
2   <http://www.forgiving.org/>.

Meanwhile, the South African Truth and Reconciliation Commission made a tremendous impact on public opinion world-wide, as a pioneering attempt to resolve some of the bitterness resulting from brutalities in the protracted, violent conflict. Archbishop Tutu, its best-known spokesperson, hoped that the process might preserve the fabric of a working society, if perpetrators confessed to their actions, revealed details of extra-judicial killings and torture, and apologized. Victims or their families might then be able to start coming to terms with the past, and agree to move on without seeking revenge. The 1990s also witnessed many bloody struggles between neighbouring ethnic groups, for example in the former Yugoslavia. Inevitably people wondered whether it would ever be possible for groups to live together again in close proximity after such bloodshed. Some studies questioned the relationship between forgiveness as a personal issue and the broader question of social or political forgiveness: how parties to conflicts could come to forgive and then work together with former enemies.

In the UK, Coventry University started a Centre for the Study of Forgiveness and Reconciliation (now the Centre for Peace and Reconciliation Studies), the University of Leeds ran psycho-therapeutic research programmes, and a group of individuals organized 'The Forgiveness Project' which works with grassroots activities in the fields of conflict resolution, reconciliation and victim support. The Project explained on its website:

> At a time when scenes of atrocity, conflict and crime fill our TV screens and newspapers, when tit-for-tat killings, attacks and counter-attacks seem to grab all the headlines, The Forgiveness Project aims to tell the quieter, less publicized stories of reconciliation. The stories of people who have discovered that the only way to move on in life, is to lay aside hatred and blame.[3]

The intellectual background to forgiveness includes a complex of disciplines, including religion, psychology, philosophy and political science (see Table 10.1). Peace studies, as an interdisciplinary endeavour, reflects all of them.

In the religious dimension, the Abrahamic faiths – Judaism, Christianity and Islam – all have teachings on forgiveness. For example, Judaism distinguishes between interpersonal forgiveness as a social interaction; and forgiveness that God offers to a penitent. The requirements for interpersonal forgiveness are quite stringent. After an offence the transgressor is required to show remorse, to admit the sin to the community, to apologize and offer compensation. Moreover, transgressors who seek forgiveness from the community also have to maintain exemplary behaviour in the future. Even if a situation arises where they could easily commit offences again, and perhaps get away without detection, they have to avoid them. When and if these conditions are met, the victim is encouraged to offer forgiveness. In other words, the perpetrator does not have the right to be forgiven: he or she has to earn it.

---

3   <http://www.forgivenessproject.org>.

Table 10.1   Forgiveness in academic disciplines

Discipline	Main concerns	Typical institutions
Religion	Theological issues (God-human forgiveness) Interpersonal relations	Religious institutions Theology faculties
Philosophy	Moral and ethical concerns Personal responsibility for abuses and forgiveness of abuses	Philosophy faculties
Psychology	Therapy Psychological analysis of resentment and revenge	Psychology faculties Therapeutic groups and agencies
Political science	Symbolic public apologies and forgiveness Dealing with legacies of conflict	Political science faculties NGOs and Truth Commissions

However, final cleansing of sinfulness is not a matter for any person or institution, it is reserved for God. The Jewish Testament describes the ancient ritual of the Day of Atonement, when the high priest would sacrifice one goat at an altar, and lay his hands on a live goat 'and confess over him all the iniquities of the people of Israel, and all their transgressions, all their sins; and he shall put them upon the head of the goat, and send him away into the wilderness'.[4] In modern Judaism the same Day of Atonement is observed, but with fasting and prayer taking the place of animal sacrifice. Christianity developed a body of doctrine about forgiveness based on Jewish ideas, although there is a diverse tradition of interpretation within the numerous churches. The New Testament makes an explicit analogy of Jesus' crucifixion with the Jewish ritual, but emphasizes that this sacrifice is 'once and for all' and brings 'eternal redemption', a kind of forgiveness for the whole of humanity, or at least for those who accept Jesus as saviour.[5]

On the interpersonal level, some Christians believe they are required to forgive a 'sinner' unconditionally, whether or not he repents, apologizes or refrains. Some believe that by doing so they become entitled to God's forgiveness for their own sins: 'For if you forgive others their trespasses our heavenly Father will also forgive you; but if you do not forgive others, neither will your Father forgive your trespasses' (Matthew 6:14–15). In other words, it will benefit us if we can manage to forgive others, because God will respond likewise. Contemporary psychologists might assert a similar sentiment using different language: forgiveness is good for us, because it will help us to move into the future without feelings of anger, pain and resentment.

---

4   Leviticus,16: 6–30.

5   Hebrews, 9: 11–14. The theme of redemption through Jesus' self-sacrifice is also taken up in Ephesians 1: 7–8.

To a greater or lesser extent, Buddhism, Hinduism, Islam and other religions all have teachings to promote forgiveness, for example, 'Say, O my Servants who have transgressed against their souls! Despair not of the mercy of God: for God forgives all sins: for he is Oft-forgiving, Most Merciful';[6] 'Of the sin against the gods, Thou art atonement; of the sin against men, Thou are atonement; of the sin against myself Thou art atonement'.[7]

Philosophers also have considered the issues raised by forgiveness. Immanuel Kant, for example, insisted on a 'categorical imperative': that human beings are worthy of justice, respect and dignity. Often, and especially in conflict situations, these qualities are abused and denied. When another person has treated me without justice, respect or dignity, I may respond by feeling resentment and hatred; or I can choose to exercise a kind of moral virtue, and forgive him. Of course, even if I forgive him, he may still be subject to punishment according to his crime. Forgiveness according to one modern philosopher implies giving up hatred towards a wrongdoer, making 'the decision to see a wrongdoer in a new more favourable light'.[8] Such a decision may be taken by any individual irrespective of religious belief.

Contemporary psychologists have also taken up the question of forgiveness as a research topic and even as a skill that can be taught. A key component is often learning to distinguish between a 'wrongdoer' and the wrong that a person may have committed. It is easy to hate a wrongdoer, and perhaps difficult to ever forgive him or her. However, in a process sometimes called 're-framing' one may perhaps learn to see that individual as essentially a human being, in him/herself worthy of respect, who has taken some bad decisions and committed immoral acts: perhaps because of upbringing, poverty, because of violence suffered, or for some other reason. We may even begin to feel compassion. This kind of feeling may bring relief both to the victim, and to the wrongdoer. Psychological theories of forgiveness may be completely secular, with no connection to religious belief: they may simply argue that forgiveness is, pragmatically, beneficial for psychological well-being.

On the other hand, several writers warn against an easy promotion of forgiveness as a theory. They are particularly concerned that people may feel pressurized – by political expediency or by a current fashion – to forgive a person no matter what crime may have been committed. Yet they would argue that it is often important for one's self-respect to retain a feeling of anger, to refuse forgiveness, to deny comfort to a wrong-doer. There are some crimes which are perhaps just 'unforgivable' and should remain so. The sequelae of brutality can be awful and unfathomable, certainly not offering any easy answers. Simon Wiesenthal's short masterpiece *The Sunflower* offered one effective way to explore the variety of possible responses. The book relates an account of a German soldier seeking forgiveness from a Jew after acknowledging heinous crimes, and then collects short essays and reflections from

---

6   Qur'an, 39: 53.

7   Yajur Veda, 8: 13.

8   Jeffrie G. Murphy and Jean Hampton, *Forgiveness and Mercy* (Cambridge, 1988), p. 84.

individuals of different ages and faiths in response to the question: how would you respond in that Jewish person's position?[9]

Coming from this intellectual heritage, with its general focus on the religious, the individual and the interpersonal, scholars are beginning to address an even more complex issue: what role does forgiveness have in social or political affairs? Cristina Montriel's 'Socio-Political Forgiveness' is a short but thoughtful essay on this question. Forgiveness of course exists as a private matter, between two or a few individuals. But it can also have a social dimension. 'Socio-political forgiveness occurs when a whole group of offended people engages in the forgiveness process ... Public forgiveness takes place in the domain of a conflictual intergroup relationship, not an interpersonal one'.[10] The need for forgiveness arises because in most conflicts atrocities are inflicted by one group upon another, usually mutually.

While in one sense the atrocities are public and collective, in another they are highly personalized and individual: it is individual human beings themselves and their immediate families and friends who suffer. As individuals they may decide whether or not they can ever forgive the perpetrators. What about the collective? Is it possible to pursue the idea that, for example, the Chinese as a people should forgive the Japanese for the events of the 1930s and 1940s? That the Japanese forgive the Americans for the atomic bombs? That any other ethnic group or nation that has suffered, forgive its former enemies?

Montriel makes several relevant points. First, the victims should not be manipulated, by political leaders or anyone else, into having the word 'we forgive' spoken in their names without a genuine process of the victims' involvement. Second, statements of forgiveness can never over-ride the need for social justice, perhaps restitution or compensation. Third, the perpetrators should acknowledge their crimes, and express sincere remorse, in other words, confess and apologize.

We can immediately see difficulties. In most conflicts each side usually sees itself as the victim as well as the perpetrator, so the feeling may arise: why should we, or only we, apologize. Also, apologies are offered by some leaders of a state – a Prime Minister perhaps, a President, or a parliamentary spokesperson. The apology is symbolic, often expressed many years after the conflict, and by someone who quite possibly had no connection with the events themselves. Can this kind of apology ever feel meaningful to the victims and their families and descendants? As we see in the next section, this issue relates to the question of reconciliation: how former warring groups will ever find a means of living together in a harmonious or at least tolerable way.

---

9   Simon Wiesenthal, *The Sunflower: On the Possibilities and Limits of Forgiveness* (New York, 1997).

10   Cristina J. Montriel, 'Socio-political Forgiveness' in Andrew Rigby and Carol Rank (eds), *Peace Review: Journal of Social Justice*, 14/3 (2002): 271–8, at p. 271.

Reconciliation and Transitional Justice

In a text that has become perhaps the best-known work on reconciliation, the American peace studies expert Lederach formulated the idea that reconciliation between former enemies might take place if several factors were brought into public settlements.[11] For example, there needs to be a restoration of justice; truth about the past events needs to be brought to light and acknowledged; peace, security and economic reconstruction need to take place; and the society needs to develop a culture of forgiveness. These four factors will always be to some extent in a state of tension with each other; and also, some cultures, some countries and some regimes will be more interested in pursuing one rather than the others.[12] When there are clear-cut winners and losers in a war between nation-states, the victors will be most likely to impose severe justice on the defeated enemies, for example, execution or long imprisonment for former regime officials. On the other hand, where an internal conflict has ended in a compromise, the emphasis may be on reconstruction, with the priority being to avoid further violence. But whatever the emphasis, the ideal is that a peaceful political solution should replace violent conflict. As Montriel puts it:

> A pluralistic civil society, bent on rectifying social mistakes committed in the past, likewise signals a reconciliatory process. Political dialogue takes centre stage within a civil culture of pluralism. Civilian leaders must be ready to listen and speak with the opposing group. Besides a political culture of dialogue, other signs of reconciliatory pluralism include stronger nonviolent methods for resolving differences and government institutions for reconciliation.[13]

In recent years, reconciliation has often been part of a broader process with important political repercussions which has become known as 'transitional justice'. This term refers to the measures that can be implemented by a new regime when a society is emerging from a protracted conflict. The transitional government may be, for example, taking over after a long period of struggle for democracy against a dictatorship, as, for example, in South Africa, or after a long period of occupation by a foreign country, for example Vietnam after the defeat of the USA, or after civil war, as in several West African countries at present.

In severe conflicts these multi-layered violent struggles may have been going on for decades. For example, when the Chinese Communist Party became the government of China in 1949 it had to deal simultaneously with many legacies: the political movement against Guomindang dictatorship; the national struggle against Japanese occupation; and the military conflict of the Civil War period. The new government in any similar situation faces tremendous challenges. The national

---

11 John Paul Lederach, *Building Peace: Sustainable Reconciliation in Divided Societies* (Washington, DC, 1999).

12 These issues are explored in depth in Andrew Rigby, *Justice and Reconciliation after the Violence* (Boulder, 2000).

13 Montriel, p. 276.

economy may be in ruins, the population traumatized by war, there may be millions of refugees and displaced persons, armies and security services may have mixed loyalties, there may be no tradition of democracy, human rights may be non-existent. How is the new government going to balance the demands of victims for justice, the need for political stability and so many other factors?

In recent years, especially in Africa, we have seen the emergence of a range of techniques that governments may adopt to deal with the difficult and controversial process of restoring some kind of normality. Traditional justice may include the trial and punishment of offenders, reparations, the dissolution of former institutions. More innovative approaches now include Truth and Reconciliation Commissions following the South African precedent, amnesties, institutional reforms, restorative justice, symbolic justice, capacity building, peace education, youth work and cross-community initiatives.

Transitional justice must necessarily be a compromise between two extremes, which can be shown in simple terms as 'punitive justice' and 'reconciliation' (see Table 10.2).

Table 10.2   Justice and reconciliation

Punitive Justice		**Reconciliation**	
Methods:	Investigations	Methods:	Truth commission
	Trials		Reparation
	Punishment		Community re-building
	Purges in institutions		Symbolic justice
			Public apologies
Purposes:	Restore moral order	Purposes:	Exposure of truth
	Satisfy victims		National consensus
	wish for revenge		Economic reconstruction
	End the culture		Avoid further conflict,
	of impunity		especially where former
	Remove abusers from		abusers are still powerful
	positions of power		
	Confirm a rule of law		

After massive social breakdowns into violence, as seen, for example, in Cambodia in the 1970s, Rwanda in the 1990s and Sudan at present, formal punitive justice – the use of police, courts and prisons – would simply be unable to cope with the vast number of abuses, crimes, murders, torture and deaths that unfortunately arose during the course of the conflicts. The way forward that might be found through 'transitional justice' has been expressed as follows:

It is imperative that we seriously re-consider our assumptions about justice, the lens we look through, and develop approaches that do not simply repeat the past (or merely being imported from outside) but offer hope for the future. That hope I believe lies in a vision of justice that puts healing and reparations central, holds offenders genuinely accountable, and gives victims and their families an important role.[14]

Community Cohesion

'Community Cohesion' is a relatively new term that has come to prominence in the UK in the past five years or so. It refers to a set of policies that have become increasingly important in the context of large-scale international migration. Although the term itself may not always be used, policies relating to the cohesiveness, or sustainability or harmony, of communities have become increasingly important in numerous countries, for example those of the EU, North America, Australasia and elsewhere. It applies most specifically to large cities with populations that are diverse in terms of ethnicity, religion, education and/or economic indicators.

Before 2005 it was acknowledged in the UK that relations between the host community and various groups of immigrant populations were tense in some cities, and could occasionally break down into violent confrontations. Governments had commissioned various research initiatives to discover the roots and possible solutions to such issues: one influential report was compiled by Ted Cantle after disturbances in several cities in northern England in 2001.[15] Cantle's team found among other things that different communities – for example Muslim and white working-class – were living in the same city, but in practice had very little contact with each other. They were living, to use a term that is discussed below, 'parallel lives'.

The entire issue became intensified with the catastrophic events of 7 July 2005, when four suicide bombers exploded devices on the London public transport system, killing 52 and wounding some seven hundred victims. It soon transpired that the bombers were resident in the UK, their violent anti-British sentiments had been nurtured in the UK, and despite the intensive surveillance of extremist groups, they had succeeded in building up an infrastructure adequate to detonate a co-ordinated attack 'beneath the radar' of the security services. Important, urgent questions needed answers. On one side, some Muslim speakers, while condemning the bombings, made the point that young people might easily be drawn into such actions while the government persisted with its apparently anti-Muslim foreign policy of, in particular, support for Israel and the US-led invasions of Iraq and Afghanistan. On the other, the government maintained that the bombings had nothing to do with British foreign policy. Their analysis of the bombers' motives was rather sketchy, but Prime Minister Blair apparently regarded them as deluded sympathizers with a global Islamo-Fascist ideology that hates everything democratic and Western.

---

14 Howard Zehr, 'Restorative Justice' in Luc Reychler and Thomas Paffenholz (eds), *People Building Peace: A Field Guide* (Boulder, 2001), p. 334.

15 Ted Cantle, *Community Cohesion* (London, 2001).

Between these two positions, what concerned most people was probably: was the Muslim community in the UK doing everything it could, or doing enough, to prevent a repetition of the bombings; and was the government doing everything it could to secure cooperation? Would it, for example, timetable a withdrawal of troops from Iraq, or decline to support a putative US invasion of Iran or Syria, which seemed to be the next countries in line? Clearly the stakes had become very much higher than the inner-city disturbances of five years earlier.

A working definition used by the UK government is that a cohesive community is one in which:

- there is a common vision and a sense of belonging for all communities;
- the diversity of people's different backgrounds and circumstances is appreciated and positively valued;
- those from different backgrounds have similar life opportunities;
- strong and positive relationships are being developed between people from different backgrounds in the workplace, in schools and within neighbourhoods.

The UK is undergoing fairly rapid change in its population structure in terms of ethnicity and religion. It has long been a destination for immigrants, and likewise because of its colonial history, large numbers of British citizens settled overseas. British life was continually enriched by the influx of, at different periods, Europeans and Russians, Jews, Afro-Caribbeans, South Asians, Chinese, in fact a vast range of peoples from all over the world. After the Second World War new waves of immigration, especially from northern India, Pakistan and the Caribbean, were economically important at times of labour shortages. Legal immigration increased sharply in the 1990s, with an official estimated net inflow of 1 million persons per year through most of the decade according to official figures.[16] By 2004 the total population of the UK was almost 60 million, of which 4.5 million – about 8 per cent – were classified as 'non-white'. The term now widely used to describe all non-white immigrants in public discourse is BME (Black and Minority Ethnic).

Perceptions of existing communities are influenced by perceptions of new arrivals. Therefore, one aspect of government policy in recent years has been the management, or control, of immigration, which in itself is a controversial area. The UK is signatory to various international conventions guaranteeing asylum to those faced with persecution in their own countries. Refugees and asylum-seekers came in several waves especially from the late 1980s, fleeing ethnic conflicts in the Balkans, persecution in Iraq and Afghanistan, civil war in Somalia and Liberia, and many other situations. The press and public opinion has traditionally been quite tolerant of asylum-seekers, yet the popular press in the UK became full of stories – many of them probably true – of 'bogus asylum-seekers', people who could turn up from almost anywhere in the world, spin a yarn about persecution, and then perhaps disappear

---

16 Search within <http://www.statistics.gov.uk>.

into illegal employment in the cities. The government wanted to send a reassuring message to existing UK residents that it would be tough on immigration, restricting the numbers of new arrivals. However, partly because of its chaotic bureaucracy, it never seemed really able to gain a grasp on the situation. By 2004 the government was finally obliged to impose much tighter restrictions on applications which did reduce the number of successful applications, but which also led to allegations that genuine asylum-seekers were being returned to countries where they faced torture or death.

Newspapers also reported that there were very large numbers of illegal immigrants living in the UK. In 2004 Home Secretary David Blunkett openly admitted that he had no idea how many immigrants actually lived in the UK since the illegal ones never registered with the authorities. Some polemicists argued that legal immigration was only the tip of an iceberg. In 2005 police arrested several Turkish men who had allegedly run a smuggling operation that by itself may have brought 'tens of thousands' of Turkish Kurds illegally into the country. By now, dozens of nationalities and ethnic groups have extended family networks in the UK, and it may be relatively easy for them to accommodate new, even if illegal, arrivals.

Several points should be borne in mind here. There is a totally disproportionate concentration of BME population in London and other large cities; and very low numbers indeed in some rural areas. In some urban areas BMEs may account for 20 to even 50 per cent of the total population; in greater London itself, they are estimated to comprise around 30 per cent of the entire population according to some statistics.[17] On the one hand many BMEs report feeling excluded or unwelcome in more traditional, rural areas; on the other the white population may feel excluded from certain urban districts, deeply uneasy about the changing mix of population.

A second point is that ethnic diversity has brought religious diversity. In the 2001 census the UK population reported itself approximately as shown in Table 10.3.

Table 10.3   Reported religious belief in the UK

Religion	%
Christian	70
No religion or no answer	23
Muslim	3
Hindu	1
Other (mainly Buddhist, Jewish or Sikh)	3

Many of those reporting as Christians are in effect nominal Christians, that is, they have family or historical allegiance, but rarely if ever attend religious functions. The main point is the relatively large, and growing, proportion of Muslims, the majority

17 Search within <http://www.monitoring-group.co.uk>.

of whom are immigrants from Pakistan and Bangladesh. Although only 3 per cent of the population, they are enormously influential in some cities, and on the whole very active religiously and socially. In the wave of tension following September 11, and more acutely after the London bombings, the Muslim community was in a potentially dangerous situation, caught between the possibility of a backlash, constant media reporting of Islamic terrorism, and infiltration by Islamist extremists.

A third point is the existence of people, many of them 'White British' who are variously referred to as an 'underclass' or underprivileged, who may live on poor housing estates often on the periphery of big cities. They are often characterized as having low educational achievement, high unemployment and high levels of alcoholism, domestic violence, petty crime, drug abuse and so on. A major priority of the Labour administration which came to power in 1997 was to reform this sector of UK society by providing better opportunities, housing, income and education. By all accounts these initiatives had achieved little by 2005.

Although details differ, the combination of immigration, ethnic and religious diversity, and marginalized communities described above is by no means unique to the UK: similar issues could be highlighted in France, Germany, Australia and numerous other countries. Among larger nations, China is probably unusual in having a highly homogeneous population, with ethnic minorities few in number in comparison to the majority, and for the most part in separate parts of the country. Many experts predict that international migration will become even more intense, driven by factors such as conflicts, environmental disasters, climate change and cheap international travel. Countries like the UK may be seen as favourable alternatives to people caught in desperate circumstances elsewhere.

The UK has historically enjoyed relatively harmonious relations between these large numbers of different ethnic groups. Certainly if one finds oneself in any hospital, school, university, factory or public transport system in a British city, one will be struck by the diverse, easy mingling of all kinds of people in a highly cosmopolitan environment. Nevertheless, from time to time there have been race-related civil disturbances or riots: in the 1980s in Bristol, Birmingham and London; and in 2001 in several northern cities including Bradford and Oldham which eventually led to the Cantle report. In the following years a number of pilot initiatives were launched in UK cities to implement the policy recommendations with a view to improving community relations and mitigating the kind of frictions that had led to the riots. By 2005 metropolitan and county councils were required to mainstream community cohesion as a factor in planning and policy implementation, and in 2006 Cantle and other partners launched the Institute for Community Cohesion at Coventry University. The debate on community cohesion was born; but born into a fast-changing and sophisticated environment with numerous complicating factors. So by 2006 there was by no means unanimity on what is community cohesion, even whether it is desirable, or how it is achievable.

With regard to community cohesion proper, several important issues have been raised. What does it mean to be British – or, one might add, French or Canadian in their respective countries? Should one necessarily speak English, respect the royal family, believe in democracy and freedom of speech? Should there be a shared commitment to a vision of the UK as a place of equal opportunity, shared objectives for the future? Should it be acceptable to educate one's children in, for example, traditional Muslim values as practised in Pakistani villages; or should they be integrated with mainstream British youth? The debate raised the question of 'parallel lives': the fact that some immigrant communities live, work and socialize in certain parts of big cities, and rarely if ever meet a 'white person', or even members of other ethnic groups. Could this be a likely recipe for future social disturbances, where different ethnic groups across a city have no interlinking professional, friendly, family or even sporting links?

Another issue is the relative importance of structural factors as perceived by BMEs themselves, and cultural issues which may be more apparent to the white population. For example, it has long been recognized that racism is deeply embedded in British society, especially in institutions like the police and armed forces. Generally, BMEs may experience fewer professional opportunities, lower education, lower income and poorer housing. There might be subtle or overt discrimination in the workplace, perhaps affecting promotions and salaries. Also, many BMEs had come to the UK to work in industries, like the wool industry in Bradford, or engineering in the Midlands, that suffered recessions from the 1970s onwards. Many of them thus faced both economic downturn and institutional racism; a combination which would re-inforce their low achievement, and quite possibly lead them to an isolated, defensive community posture. Incidentally, it is also important to recognize that many immigrant groups have been extremely successful. There is widespread perception for example that young people from Chinese and Gujarati Hindu families generally perform well in schools and universities, and are often upwardly mobile into highly-paid professional employment. They may also tend to move out of poorer urban areas into more affluent suburbs.

As a generalization, left/liberal thinkers, including many from BME groups themselves, stress structural reasons for community isolation and possible conflict. Remedies should then be along the lines of economic regeneration programmes, cultural training in the police and other institutions, and the implementation of anti-racism policies and laws. As mentioned, UK foreign policy may also play a part in antagonizing some BME groups, especially Muslims. More conservative writers advocate strict immigration controls, relatively low tolerance for single-community ventures – like exclusively Muslim schools – perhaps compulsory examinations in English and respect for the monarchy or other symbols of British tradition. The extremists among them would degenerate into overt racism, with media attacks on Muslims and other groups labelled as enemies.

There is also a spread of opinion, not necessarily along traditional left/right lines, about the extent to which multiculturalism is desirable. Should immigrant groups be encouraged to retain their language, religion, culture, educational preferences; or obliged to conform to a large extent to the practices of the majority around them? If they choose to live and socialize in separate parts of town, should they be encouraged or persuaded in some way to move out? Should religious communities be allowed to set up private schools outside the state system? These issues sometimes become quite sensitive politically, as for example with the ban on headscarves in French schools in the summer of 2004.

A sociologist commenting on the Community Cohesion initiatives of the past few years suggests that they contributed to an:

> unfolding social project of attempting to alleviate disorder, disharmony and discord in these areas characterized by multi-ethnic, multi-faith and multi-cultural communities. However, despite the best of intentions, the process of community cohesion facilitation ... will be presented here as being blighted by three inter-related factors; (1) the practical problems associated with attempting to formulate a public policy of community cohesion on the assumption that common principles and shared values can be founded in multi-ethnic, multi-faith and multi-cultural societies; (2) the relative de-emphasis of material deprivation and socio-economic marginalization in community cohesion facilitation programmes in favour of concentrating on inter-community relationships; and (3) with special reference to Bradford, the criminalization of young male British-Asian 'rioters' in the city is shown to be inconsistent with the rebuilding and re-orientation of social capital from defensive 'bonding' to inclusive 'bridging' in the judicial aftermath that is currently gripping this city.[18]

In other words, progressive cultural policies will no doubt help to form peaceful societies, but they need to form part of a package which also delivers economic growth and prosperity; sensitive police and justice procedures; and policies to take account of a great diversity of views, beliefs and behaviour.

---

18 See Derek McGhee 'Moving to Our Common Ground: A Critical Examination of Community Cohesion Discourse in 21st Century Britain', *Sociological Review*, 51/3 (2003): 376–404. The citation is from the abstract.

Chapter 11

Ethics or Interests?
Blair's Foreign Policy

Liu Cheng

Soon after Tony Blair assumed premiership in 1997, the Labour government announced the adoption of an 'ethical dimension' as the core of British foreign policy for the first time. This new dimension was, apparently, meant to be taken seriously. Michael Williams, special adviser to Jack Straw, told me that 'at least the question of human rights had been mainstreamed and is in our formal foreign policy. At least one person in every embassy in every country is now dedicated to human rights work'.[1] The announcement came as a surprise to both the British administration and public.

With Blair in office, however, Britain soon took part in five international military operations, and continued to export a large amount of military weapons, which went against the Labour Party's ethical foreign policy. Besides this, we are surprised to find that none of these military operations were in line with traditional British military thought: namely, they were undertaken neither to defend national interests nor to counter-attack intruders. During the Iraq War Blair's government emphasized human rights and democracy, trying to give the impression that Britain fought the Iraq War out of concerns for ethics. However, the great majority of the British public and large parts of the Labour Party itself stood firmly against the war, on the grounds that a war would spell disaster for the Iraqis and could lead to a growth in terrorism, further conflict in the region and serious humanitarian repercussions. They believed it was neither in the nation's interest nor in the interest of the Labour Party.

There is, unfortunately, little academic study of British diplomatic and foreign policy in the academic community in China. Before I proceed to my own analysis of New Labour's 'ethical' policies, it may be interesting for readers in the West to understand how Chinese scholars, the Chinese government and the Chinese public feel about international politics and peace. The following observations are my personal reflections, since as far as I know there has been no survey or poll of Chinese attitudes on these questions.

Of Chinese academics specializing in international relations, the majority believe that the United Kingdom has for centuries followed a cautiously pragmatic tradition in its foreign policy; and that the Labour Party has had no particular intent

---

1   Dr Williams kindly met me at the Foreign and Commonwealth Office, 8 December 2003.

to deviate from this tradition. The dominant perspective is that the foreign policies of Conservative and Labour governments are virtually indistinguishable. They would tend to attach little importance to the social-democratic history of elements within the Labour Party, and its occasional flirtation with more radical aspirations. It may be true that on closer scrutiny the early Labour Party embodied socialist principles, for example in its 1918 constitution; one could even say it was rather similar to our Chinese Communist Party in some respects;[2] but we believe that in practice UK foreign policy is based solely on national interest, irrespective of party politics.

The Chinese government has had a rather consistent foreign policy since at least the early 1980s. It has been completely committed to avoiding armed conflict in Asia in particular, since it believed that China needed several generations of international peace to build a modern economy. In this endeavour is has been largely successful. The government formally adopts three guiding principles: non-interference in other countries' affairs; equality of all states irrespective of size; and peaceful resolution of disputes. It believes (perhaps correctly) that Western accusations of human rights abuses in China or elsewhere are usually merely an excuse for interference in domestic issues of other countries; a pretext for selective economic or military force, orchestrated by the USA. The Iraq war is a clear case in point. The Chinese government is well aware of numerous human rights abuses under Saddam Hussein, but believes that similar abuses are taking place in many states including American clients; and they should never be a pretext for an illegal war.

As for a normal Chinese person in the street, I would say they are extremely sceptical about British claims to morality. They might possibly have heard that the UK government appeals to ethical considerations in foreign policy. However, most Chinese people would not hesitate to believe that this is only a transparent disguise: national interest alone determines foreign policy. Britain is perceived as a highly belligerent country which is unlikely to make any essential changes for a long time to come. Participation in the US-led Iraq war, despite world-wide opposition, is taken as evidence. In the eyes of most Chinese, the UK is still a veteran imperialist: although its actual power is nothing compared to its past, for some reason the UK still tries to retain its halo as leader of Empire. Perhaps even the British public, but certainly the two main political parties, cling to past glory.

So, Chinese scholars basically hold that British diplomacy is based on British self-interest, and ethics are merely a veneer. Even in the West, there are few detailed analyses of the Labour Party's foreign policy: as far as I have ascertained, there is not yet a monograph on the history of its evolution. It was not until the Blair government took office that scholars began to pay attention to the Labour Party's handling of foreign affairs; among other issues, the 'ethical dimension' in diplomacy attracts most attention. This chapter starts with an examination of the Labour Party's traditional diplomatic thoughts, and tries to explain the origin and development of the 'ethical dimension' in Blair's political philosophy. It then analyses the influence of

---

2   I have written about this in my book Liu Cheng, *Yingguo gongdang yu gongyouzhi* [The British Labour Party and Public Ownership] (Nanjing, 2003).

the 'ethical dimension' in the several military operations which Blair's government has undertaken.

The Tradition of Labour Party Diplomacy

When the Labour Party first came to power its members may have expected some changes in the relationships that the UK forges with other nations, changes that might give the government a more ethical image. But during the long period before Blair took office the Labour Party had no distinct foreign policy, or at least no long-standing foreign policy derived from social-democratic priorities. This position changed when Blair assumed power. On 12 May 1997, a few days after the establishment of the new government, Robin Cook, the Foreign Secretary, promulgated an 'ethics-centred' diplomatic statement. The text declared:

> The Labour government does not accept that political values can be left behind when we check in our passports to travel on diplomatic business. Our foreign policy must have an ethical dimension and must support the demands of other peoples for democratic rights on which we insist for ourselves.[3]

This was the first time a Labour government had adopted an ethical dimension as a guiding principle while it was in power. In the history of the Labour Party certain Labour politicians, especially those on the left of the party, tended to take ethical stands. Foreign policy, however, cannot be made without consideration of national interests; and whether ethics should take priority over the need of realistic politics remained a debating point inside the Labour Party.[4] This debate sometimes had domestic repercussions when, for example, a dispute over whether the second Boer War was ethical or not led to the split of the Fabian Society. Again the Labour Party met with resolute opposition from the Independent Labour Party when it supported the government's conduct of the First World War: support for the war was considered by many as indicating the Labour Party's abandonment of its ethical standards. Other controversial issues included the policy of appeasement and the increase of armaments in the 1930s; the reform of the British Empire and decolonization from the 1930s to the 1960s; nuclear weapons from the 1950s to the 1980s; and conflicts in the Middle East. These questions all indicated, in different guises, the cognitive dissonance inside the Labour Party over the meaning of ethical diplomacy. However, on the whole it is fair to say that the Labour Party paid little attention to foreign affairs. It was not until the outbreak of the Second World War that the Fabian

---

3   Robin Cook, 'Mission Statement for the British Foreign and Commonwealth Office', 12 May 1997, *Guardian* newspaper website as 'Robin Cook's Speech on the Government's Ethical Foreign Policy', <http://www.guardian.co.uk/indonesia/Story/0,2763,190889,00. html>.

4   Stephen Howe, 'Labour and International Affairs' in Duncan Tanner, Pat Thane and Nick Tiratsoo (eds), *Labour's First Century* (Cambridge, 2000), pp. 119–20.

Society established an International Bureau for the first time, and still to no tangible benefit.

Therefore, in the early Labour government, the main principles of the Labour Party's foreign policy were mainly made by MacDonald and the Union of Democratic Control, which emphasized democratic control over foreign affairs, opposed signing secret treaties with other countries without the agreement of parliament, and insisted on collective safety under a strong international organization, rather than on the traditional British thought of diplomacy as balance of power. When it comes to the colonial problem, it took a firm stand of 'constructive' imperialism and approved of mandates and double mandates by the League of Nations. Meanwhile, Labour Party leaders held that Britain should assume responsibility for the colonized people and the international community by letting the colonies move gradually towards autonomy, and by protecting the aboriginal inhabitants' rights.[5]

In brief, in the early decades of the twentieth century, the Labour Party focused mainly on domestic social and economic problems, with only a few of the members being familiar with foreign affairs. The leaders held sway over diplomatic problems, about which there were seldom discussions. Before 1945 the Labour Party had only been in power twice, on both occasions for only a short period of time, and without gaining a majority of the seats in parliament, which anyway rendered the party unable to put its ideas of ethical diplomacy into practice.

In the general election of 1945 the Labour Party gained a landslide victory, and won a majority of seats in parliament for the first time. Nevertheless, once in power it put aside any thoughts of ethical diplomacy. To give some examples, Attlee's Labour government continued expanding armaments manufacture. On 8 January 1947 the Labour Party decided to develop Britain's own nuclear weapons. Aneurin Bevan, then Foreign Secretary, was convinced that Britain should produce nuclear weapons, whatever the cost.[6] Hugh Gaitskell, at the Labour Party conference in October 1962, opposed joining the Common Market (later the European Union) on the grounds that it would mean 'the end of Britain as an independent state … It means the end of a thousand years of history'.[7] Gaitskell, and the Labour Party, seemed to hesitate between retreating to a Little England and maintaining the empire.

After Harold Wilson took over the leadership of the Labour Party and became Prime Minister, he vigorously supported the idea of a great British empire. In fact, one of his catchphrases was that Britain should be one of the world's great powers, or else it would be nothing. Due to the deterioration of the British economy Wilson's government was forced to depreciate the pound by 14.3 per cent on 8 November 1967. Further, it shifted its focus of defence to Europe, reducing its defence obligations in

---

5 Donald Sassoon, *One Hundred Years of Socialism: The West European Left in the Twentieth Century* (London, 1996), pp. 32–53.

6 Peter Hennessy, *Never Again: Britain 1945–1951* (London, 1993), p. 268.

7 Richard Heffernan, 'Beyond Euro-Scepticism? Labour Party and the European Union since 1945' in Brian Brivati and Richard Heffernan (eds), *The Labour Party: A Centenary History* (Basingstoke, 2000), p. 383.

Asia by transferring to the United States its military roles in the China Sea, the Indian Ocean and the Persian Gulf. Nevertheless, to maintain Britain's strategic independence and global influence Wilson's government completed the Polaris Missile Project and spent more than £400 million annually for military purposes abroad. The ratio of UK defence expenditure to the GDP was higher than in any other Western European country.[8] Hence, some scholars point out that though the Labour Party emphasized internationalism based on ethics, once it come to power its diplomacy demonstrated more 'realist' than idealist characteristics.

After the Labour Party lost the general election in 1979, the left wing of the Party, under the leadership of Michael Foot, gained control of decision-making. From 1979 to 1983 the Labour Party entered a period of so-called 'ideological policy formation', namely, all the Labour Party's policies were to be made according to its value orientation and belief, rather than national interests and public opinion polls.[9] In its 1983 election platform the party promised to establish a social democratic society. Internationally, it viewed the practical task as all-around international cooperation and pointed out that to attain this goal Britain should not turn a blind eye to inequalities in the international community. It proclaimed that seeking peace, development and disarmament was the core of the Labour Party's foreign policy, even pledging unilateral disarmament and negotiations on international disarmament. The Labour Party would establish a non-nuclear defence policy; freeze the production, development and tests of nuclear weapons; not allow any new deployment of missiles in the UK and pull out those that had been deployed. It declared that the next Labour government would put an end to the Trident project, lower Britain's defence expenditure to the level of that of the other main Western European countries, and impose strict controls on the trade of weapons.[10]

The 1983 platform fully demonstrated the idealist trend in Labour Party diplomatic policy. Actually Foot himself was a typical idealist, believing that the Labour Party must change the British people's temporary mood, and prove that the Labour Party essentially was an ethical party, which attached primary importance to core beliefs, even though this commitment might mean electoral defeat.[11] Foot's ideas can be summed up as preferring the Labour Party to lose power, rather than giving up democratic socialism with its ethical content.

In fact, this left-wing aspiration deserved support, since it has been proved time and again that an escalation of weaponry not only does not sustain world peace for long, but also harms economic development. However, as long as the UK insisted on maintaining its global influence in the realpolitik system of international relations, it

---

8   Howe, pp. 140–41.

9   Mark Wickham-Jones, *Economic Strategy and the Labour Party: Politics and Policy-Making, 1970–83* (Basingstoke, 1996).

10   Iain Dale, *Labour Party General Election Manifestos 1900–1997* (London and New York, 2000), pp. 281–4.

11   Richard Coopey, Steven Fielding and Nick Tiratsoo (eds), *The Wilson Governments 1964–1970* (London and New York, 1993), p. 33.

could not deviate from its traditional diplomatic and defensive strategy. Therefore, Foot's undue emphasis on ethics went against the Great Power tradition.

Under Foot's leadership in the 1983 election the Labour Party suffered its biggest defeat since 1918, gaining only 26.7 per cent of the votes and 289 seats. On the issue of defence policy, 50 per cent of the voters sided with the Conservative Party, whereas only 20 per cent supported the Labour Party. The election platform of 1983 thus became the longest suicide note in history.[12]

The debacle prompted the Labour Party to realize comprehensively that idealist diplomatic principles in themselves would only be a liability. Therefore, during the period when Neil Kinnock and John Smith led the party the Labour Party tried to establish the image of being responsible rather than radical, of being realistic rather than pursuing purely ethical idealism. In its platform for the 1987 election the party dropped the pledge of unilateral disarmament; instead, it claimed that it would make efforts to boost technical innovations in the Navy and the Air Force to enhance their effectiveness in battle. And in the platform for the election in 1992 it clearly declared that Britain would preserve its nuclear capability.[13]

As mentioned above, though the Labour Party emphasized ethical content in diplomacy, ethical ideas were not converted into practical policies. Instead, the Labour government pursued a foreign policy that was similar to that of the Conservative Party. And as was proved in practice, an ethics-centred diplomatic ideal did not enjoy the support of the majority of UK voters. The public presumably thought that even if the Labour Party came to power after John Major's Conservative government, it would still stick to the traditional foreign policy. Nevertheless, once Blair took office, Robin Cook, then Foreign Secretary, declared that UK diplomacy would incorporate an ethical dimension: an announcement that came as a real surprise.

Blair's New Diplomacy

Blair's new foreign policy ideas were unexpected. After winning a by-election in May, 1982 Blair became a professional politician and something of a prodigy in the Labour Party. But before taking over the leadership of the Labour Party in 1994, he had no particularly distinctive ideas about international issues, and indeed sought to 'close down foreign policy as a contentious issue'. One of his friends recalled: 'we talked an awful lot of politics in those days, but I can't remember him talking about foreign affairs at all'. Blair had no work experience in any parliamentary group on foreign affairs; even after assuming the leadership he tended to be evasive about diplomatic issues, being afraid of having any negative effect on the Labour Party's electoral prospects. For this reason he may be regarded as the Prime Minister who

---

12 Eric Shaw, *The Labour Party Since 1979: Crisis and Transformation* (London and New York, 1994), p. 12.
   13 Dale, p. 339.

had the least knowledge and experience about diplomacy since the Second World War.[14]

Only on 21 April 1997, the eve of the general election, did Blair give his first important speech about diplomatic issues. However, even on that occasion he did not mention ethics.[15] It is clear that foreign policy was not the focus of the Labour Party's platform in 1997, for although it declared that the Labour Party would base its foreign policy on protecting and improving human rights, it did not provide any details. The whole declaration contained only three sentences (which consisted of 56 words in total) that were related to human rights, and these sentences were not stressed.[16] At this point, Cook showed little interest in diplomacy, but focused almost entirely on economic issues.

Based on all of this, observers were surprised but sceptical about Cook's declaration: perhaps the announcement was only a tactic for self-advancement, namely, by defining his foreign policy immediately after the election victory he pre-empted its definition by others. Did he mean to base government policy on 'his' ideas, which would enhance his own political status and influence? In any case, the ethical content in Cook's declaration did not reflect the underlying historical foreign policy intentions of previous Labour governments.[17]

However, the Labour government confirmed Cook's speech by adopting the 'ethical dimension' as the essence of the Labour Party's foreign policy. On 18 September 1997 George Robinson, the Defence Secretary, pointed out in a speech:

This Government already has a clear and different foreign policy agenda ... We intend Britain's foreign policy to be based on clear ethical principles and not just to be driven by sharp profit ... Nor, in a world which is fast becoming a global village, can we turn our backs on human suffering and economic and social damage, even when our national interests are not directly engaged.[18]

At first Blair made no comments on Cook's speech, maintaining a low-key attitude. As mentioned above, Blair had no real diplomatic experience and was perhaps afraid that too much emphasis on foreign affairs would affect the Labour Party's popularity. Thus, in New Labour's theory of the Third Way, diplomacy did not attract much attention. What is more, in his diplomacy, Blair gave priority to the Anglo-American 'special relationship', trying to reconcile the disputes over the Bosnian crisis and the Northern Ireland issue that had arisen during Major's government. And as early

---

14 John Kampfner, *Blair's Wars* (London, 2003), pp. 5–13.

15 Rhiannon Vickers, 'Labour's Search for a Third Way in Foreign Policy' in Richard Little and Mark Wickham-Jones (eds), *New Labour's Foreign Policy: A New Moral Crusade?* (Manchester, 2000), p. 8.

16 Dale, pp. 378–82.

17 Vickers, p. 106.

18 George Robertson, 'Strategic Defence Review', speech given at the Royal United Services Institute, London, 18 September 1997, search within <http://www.mod.uk>.

as the very month Blair took office, on 19 May 1997, Clinton was invited to 10 Downing Street, where he addressed the British cabinet.

Apart from the 'ethical dimension' Cook's declaration also mentioned Britain's leading role in Europe, and the importance of strengthening the influence of the Commonwealth and the United Nations; however, the UK's relationship with the USA was not included. To make up for this, on 11 November, in Blair's first speech as Prime Minister on foreign policy, he did not even refer to Cook's 'ethical dimension', but stressed the Anglo-American relationship. He pointed out that as long as Britain and America cooperate in solving international problems, all problems could be resolved. The goal of British diplomacy was to strengthen the relationship with the USA on all levels, he said: Britain should act as the liaison between America and Europe, playing a role of global importance. Britain should not reduce its influence on the world stage: 'by virtue of our geography, our history and the strengths of our people, Britain is a global player'.[19]

However, since it had put forward the slogan 'New Labour, New Britain', Blair's government tried to come up with some thoughts on foreign policy of its own, which should be in line with Britain's traditional diplomatic role, as well as with Blair's principle of maintaining the UK's role of leader on the world stage. After a period of careful consideration Blair seems to have discovered that the 'ethical dimension' could meet all those requirements. On 8 January 1999 Blair gave a speech in Cape Town in which he formally integrated the 'ethical dimension' into his political theory.[20] Two months later (22 April 1999) in a speech in Chicago Blair clearly pointed out:

> We live in a world where isolationism has ceased to have reason to exist … We are all internationalists now, whether we like it or not. We cannot refuse to participate in global markets if we want to prosper. We cannot ignore new political ideas in other countries if we want to innovate. We cannot turn our backs on conflicts and violations of human rights within other countries if we want still to be secure. … We are witnessing the beginnings of a new doctrine of international community. By this I mean the explicit recognition that today more than ever before, we are mutually dependent, that national interest is to a significant extent governed by international collaboration and that we need a clear and coherent debate as to the direction this doctrine takes us in each field of international endeavour.[21]

So Cook's declaration on 12 May 1997 was maybe just the first hint of the Labour Party's diplomatic thoughts, while Blair's speech in Chicago convinced people that the Labour Party had adopted an ethical dimension as the core of its diplomatic thoughts.

---

19 Kampfner, p. 17.

20 Tony Blair, 'Facing the Modern Challenge: The Third Way in Britain and South Africa', speech given at The Old Assembly Dining Room, Parliament Building, Cape Town, South Africa, 8 January 1999, search within <http://www.fco.gov.uk>.

21 Tony Blair, 'The Doctrine of the International Community' in Andrew Chadwick and Richard Heffernan (eds), *The New Labour Reader* (Cambridge, 2003), p. 263.

The Practice of the Ethical Dimension

The government's emphasis on the ethical dimension does not interfere with or hinder its selling weapons. The Labour Party holds that the UK should keep its status as a major weapons exporter, and should maintain a powerful defence industry. Arms sales are an important financial resource for the UK, whose economy has been sluggish, and no government would forego such a profitable sector. Blair believes that since the government has an effective arms-sales control, manufacturers can be restrained from unethical transactions.[22] Therefore, British companies continued to sell arms as before to Indonesia, Turkey and Colombia, for example, except for some slight restrictions, such as whittling down 2.4 per cent of the weapons that were to be sold to Indonesia according to the plan of arms sales. In September 1999 the government held the Defence Systems and Equipment International Exhibition as usual, to which it invited guests from many countries. Based on this, the Campaign Against the Arms Trade pointed out that although Cook had put forward a new orientation towards an ethical foreign policy, there was no evidence to indicate that the government's conduct of arms sales is in any significant way different from its predecessors.[23] So, out of concern for Britain's economic interests, Blair's government is not restrained by the 'ethical dimension'. When it comes to military conflicts, how does the government practice its 'ethical dimension'?

In December 1998 the USA blitzed Iraq in a sustained bombing campaign. The UK was the only country in the international community that took part in the US military actions. Blair viewed Iraq as a country ruled by a brutal and vicious dictator, who trampled on international law. He could have argued that participation in the attack on Iraq was in line with the Labour Party's ethical foreign policy. What was bewildering, however, was that in the official statement of the war against Iraq, the word 'ethics' was not mentioned. Lacking widespread support in the international community, the military action looked like a repetition of 'gunboat diplomacy'. What is more, the attack happened during the month of Ramadan, regardless of Muslim religious tradition, which hardly made it possible to convince people that the attack had an ethical drive. Cook did not link the action to ethics, but instead argued for Britain's participation in the war, saying 'No Foreign Minister can be satisfied when events compel the need for military force. The aim of diplomacy can only work if the other side is prepared to negotiate in good faith'.[24] Though the action was not linked to ethics and was not on a large scale, this first military action indicated that the Labour government would not refrain from employing military force, and that using force apparently did not contradict the ethical rhetoric.

---

22 Tony Lloyd, 'Controlling the Arms Trade: A New Agenda for the 21st Century', search within <http://www.fco.gov.uk>.

23 Stuart Croft, 'Ethics, Labour and Foreign Policy' in Colin Itay (ed.), *British Politics Today* (Cambridge, 2002), p. 223.

24 Robin Cook, 'Foreign Secretary's Opening Statement of the Emergency Debate on Iraq', House of Commons, London, 17 December 1998, search within <http://www.fco.gov.uk>, also available at <http://www.fas.org/news/iraq/1998/12/17/981217-cook.htm>.

The military action in Kosovo was a joint action of NATO. This operation provided a chance for the Labour government to advocate its ethical dimension. On 23 March 1999 Blair pointed out in a parliamentary speech that Britain would fight with NATO not for the traditional aim of maintaining the balance of power but 'primarily to avert what would otherwise be a humanitarian disaster for Kosovo'. Three days later he added 'To those who say the aim of military strikes is not clear, I say it is crystal clear. ... We are doing what is right, for Britain, for Europe, for a world that must know that barbarity cannot be allowed to defeat justice'.[25] Cook also emphasized that the military action was in line with ethics, saying the Labour government was going to war not for territorial gain or geo-political influence, but out of concerns for such basic human values as freedom, justice and compassion. The fight for Kosovo conveyed two messages: first, the Labour government could give 'right' as a reason for war; second, the war provided the administration with a precedent for going to war according to an 'ethical dimension'.

The events of 11 September 2001 provided Blair with a new opportunity to adduce ethics as a reason for military operations. He stressed that the Labour government joined the military action against Al Qaeda and the Taliban in Afghanistan with some hesitation. But Blair argued that even if no British citizens died in 9/11, Britain should still take part in the war, and 'we only do it if the cause is a threat to justice'.[26] Blair took the lead in providing evidence that Bin Laden was the planner of the attack. He visited Berlin, Paris, New York and Washington in 40 hours, and then visited Moscow, Islamabad, Delhi and Oman, which made some observers label him the 'US ambassador', or Bush's private envoy. During the visits Blair repeatedly emphasized that the war against terrorism was an ethical obligation.

After 11 September 2001, the unilateralism of the Bush administration was made clear. Subsequently it decided to take pre-emptive military action to overthrow Saddam's regime. Blair approved of Bush's intention, but was still uneasy about two things: first, military actions would violate international law; second, military actions would not gain the sanction of the UN. Morgan, a consultant for democratic affairs, reminded Blair that without the sanction of the UN, going to war in Iraq could lead to a split in the Labour Party and the resignation of several ministers. On 28 September 2002 nearly two hundred thousand people took to the streets to demonstrate against the war in Iraq. Several speakers, including Ken Livingstone, the mayor of London, Tony Benn, a former cabinet minister, and one Labour Party parliamentarian, addressed the crowd in the rally at Hyde Park, where Tony Benn said that no excuse could justify getting Britain involved in a war which its people neither accepted nor wished to see. Without public support Blair had difficulty representing the war as an ethical enterprise. In late September 2002 the Labour Party's convention passed a resolution stating that military action could only be resorted to on condition that political and diplomatic methods had failed; and that

---

25 Tony Blair, 'Television Address to the British Public on the NATO Air Strikes against Yugoslavia', 26 March 1999, <http://news.bbc.co.uk/1/hi/uk/305034.stm>.
26 Kampfner, p. 130.

military operations must be restrained within the limits permitted by international law. Blair explained to Bush privately that without the sanction of the UN Britain would be caught in a real dilemma, which could prevent it from entering the war.[27]

The Bush administration stuck to its guns and decided to act unilaterally. Facing a difficult situation, Blair continued trying to persuade European countries such as France and Germany to support the USA. On one hand he hoped to gain UN sanction; on the other he tried to talk parliament into backing his proposition of entering the US-led war without the sanction of the UN. In fact, by September 2002, when the anti-war movement was at its climax, Blair seemed to cling to six basic ideas on the issue of the relationship between Iraq, the UK and the USA:

1. Saddam was an invader in the past, was a supporter of terrorism at present, and would be a menace in the future;
2. the USA and the UK were both viewed as enemies by Saddam;
3. with 9/11 in mind, people would support the second Iraq war;
4. Bush was determined to initiate the war anyway, and would not be deterred by opposition from anyone;
5. most British people, the Europeans and people of other countries would not approve of the war unless it gained the authorization of the UN;
6. compared to an action endorsed by the international community, unilateral US action was more devastating to world peace and security in the long run.[28]

According to the analysis above, Blair believed that overthrowing the Saddam regime was squarely in line with the Labour Party's 'ethical dimension' in diplomacy; and he also made an accurate estimate of the consequences of acting without the sanction of the UN.

Just before the war broke out Blair decided to risk going to war in support of the Labour Party's 'ethical dimension'. A parliamentary vote on the Iraq war was scheduled for the afternoon of 18 March 2003. Blair pledged that if the bill supporting the Iraq war was vetoed, he would resign at once. It turned out that Blair met with strong opposition in the parliament. One hundred and thirty-nine Labour Party members voted against the bill, constituting the largest revolt in the Labour Party's parliamentary history. 'We should still be working through the UN. We have not exhausted all the diplomatic and political alternatives at this stage. We should not be going to war', said Michael Moore. The Liberal Democrat foreign affairs spokesman said he would have favoured continuing with the UN inspections. However, the bill received resolute support from the Conservative Party. In the debate in parliament Iain Duncan Smith, the leader of the Conservative Party, stated, 'We believe the Prime Minister is acting in the national interest today. This is why he is entitled to our support in doing the right thing'. Former Tory leader William

---

27 Information in this paragraph was reported on the BBC Chinese-language website, <http://news.bbc.co.uk/hi/chinese/news/newsid_2289000/22892131.stm>.

28 Peter Stothard, *30 Days: A Month at the Heart of Blair's War* (London, 2003), p. 87.

Hague said, 'We should take action because it is in the national interest. I believe the Prime Minister and leader of the opposition stood on the right ground in advancing this policy today'.

The parliament vote on the bill would not only decide whether Britain would enter the war, but would also determine Blair's political future. In his last speech before the war Blair pointed out vividly: 'This is not the time to falter. This is the time for this House to give a lead'. People in Iraq are living in 'perpetual fear' while 'we in the UK take our freedom for granted'. So 'if we do act, we should do so with a clear conscience'. There should not be 'rivalry with the US, but partnership'. Blair said: 'Iraq has been supporting terrorist groups'. It would be the 'worst course imaginable' for the UN to fail to act. Taking military action is 'the only sure way to disarm Saddam'.[29] Blair's speech worked, and his motion supporting the use of UK forces in Iraq was passed by a large majority of 412 to 149.

Blair continued to use the ethical dimension argument to garner public support. In a press conference held five days after the war broke out Blair said, 'more than half the Iraqis living in rural areas have no access to safe water. On the latest estimates, up to 400,000 children under the age of five in the centre and south of Iraq have died over the last five years through malnutrition and disease'. Britain attacked Iraq from a moral obligation.[30]

The irony was that Robin Cook, who first put forward the 'ethical dimension' idea, opposed the war against Iraq, and resigned from his post of Speaker of the House of Commons on 17 March, the day before the parliamentary vote on the bill.[31] He said in his resignation speech that the action in Kosovo:

> was supported by NATO; it was supported by the European Union; it was supported by every single one of the seven neighbours in the region. France and Germany were our active allies. It is precisely because we have none of that support in this case that it was all the more important to get agreement in the Security Council as the last hope of demonstrating international agreement ... The legal basis for our action in Kosovo was the need to respond to an urgent and compelling humanitarian crisis. Our difficulty in getting support this time is that neither the international community nor the British public are persuaded that there is an urgent and compelling reason for this military action in Iraq.[32]

Cook's resignation speech indicated that even its first advocate did not see the Iraq war as being in accord with the ethical dimension.

---

29 From BBC News Chinese-language website, <http://news.bbc.co.uk/1/hi/uk_ politics/2862251.stm>.

30 Tony Blair, 'Saddam and his Regime will be Removed', Prime Minister's Press Conference, 10 Downing Street, 25 March 2003, <http://www.number-10.gov.uk/output/page3347.asp>.

31 In Blair's second term, Cook became the Speaker of the House of Commons and Jack Straw took over Cook's post as Secretary of FCO.

32 Cook's resignation speech at <http://news.bbc.co.uk/1/ni.uk-politics.2859431.stm>.

Three other ministers had resigned before the parliamentary vote. At the last moment before the war Jack Straw handed in a secret memo, hoping to persuade Blair to inform the USA that Britain would only provide moral and political support and would not send troops to the battlefield.[33] However, Blair had already resolved to go to war against Iraq. Blair's determined support for the war caused many to view it as Blair's war, rather than a war of Britain or of the Labour Party.[34] In a poll after the war Blair's rating dropped below that of the Labour Party's, the first time this had happened since Blair had assumed leadership of the party ten years earlier.

In conclusion, Blair's new foreign policy ideas are based on some knowledge of the world's political situation and globalization. In Blair's eyes, the boundary of national interests is no longer the British Isles, and an 'ethical dimension' has become the synonym of 'national interests'. As the Foreign and Commonwealth Office (FCO) report put it, 'as the global agenda of shared concerns lengthens, more and more issues will be dealt with collectively in ways that will further challenge traditional interpretations of state sovereignty'.[35]

Of course, ethics and war are not two essentially contradictory concepts, since 'just' wars are widely regarded as moral ones. Throughout British history both the Conservative Party and the Liberal Party initiated and took part in many wars. Protecting British interests and independence has always been the driving principle of mainstream foreign policy among all British political parties. George Canning, a Tory Prime Minister, put it clearly: 'Every nation for itself, and God for us all', while the catchphrase of Whig Prime Minister Lord Palmerston noted that 'England had no permanent friends or enemies, only permanent interests'.[36] Almost by definition, they could not consider that a war fought for national interests was unethical.

Seeing itself as representing the interests of the working class, the Labour Party in its early years had distinctive political ideas, and its foreign policies were tinged with democratic socialism, stressing ethics while condemning wars. Though it practised pragmatic foreign policies after coming to power, it did not shed all its traditional ideals and policies, from which the internal debate derived. After Blair took over the leadership the Labour Party tried to resolve the dilemma between principles and practice in international relations: the changes and development of the world situation seemed to provide a chance for reconciliation between ethics and interests.

As far as Blair was concerned, the starting point and the goal of British foreign policy should be to maintain the UK's leading position in the world. However, Britain's real economic and political clout was inexorably in decline. Blair's most

33 BBC News Chinese-language website, <http://news.bbc.co.uk/hi/chinese/news/newsid_2769000/27698731.stm>.

34 Kampfner, p. 351.

35 Foreign and Commonwealth Office, *UK International Priorities: A Strategy for the FCO*, presented to Parliament by the Secretary of State for Foreign and Commonwealth Affairs by Command of Her Majesty, December 2003 (London, 2003), p. 24.

36 Croft, p. 218.

promising alternative to resolve this quandary, knowing the limits of British power, was to cooperate unconditionally with the USA, whilst proclaiming ethics and morality. This stance perhaps indicates that Blair has succeeded in driving out the former, old-style idealism of the Labour Party left. For him, an ethical dimension is not only the justification for war, but also equates with national interests. Therefore, the content of this Blairite ethical dimension is wide and varied, and different from Cook's ethical dimension which held a comparatively narrow meaning. That is why Blair accepted Cook's choice of term, ethical dimension, and is also why their opinions over the Iraq war clashed. Nonetheless, Blair's judgement is that the Iraq war was in accord with the ethical dimension of the Party's foreign policy; an interpretation that is still widely questioned by people in and outside the party.

To summarize my own findings, I personally believe that the tradition of British foreign policy undoubtedly has had moral aspects which we should appreciate. For example, I would say that some decolonization processes were conducted in a moderate way. However, the emphasis on morality rarely translates into actual policies, and moreover, it does not attract the support of voters. It may be true to say that many British people oppose the war in Iraq, not only on ethical considerations but also because they believe that such military action damages British interests.

One of the most important reasons why Blair emphasizes moral standards is his attempt to generate a new image for the Labour Party, which would say goodbye to 'old Labour' on the one hand and preserve traditional Labour values on the other. However, there is also a deep motivation of self-interest embedded in Blair's 'moral' foreign policy, the essence of which is to protect and expand national interests. He thus inherits and furthers the pragmatic British foreign policy tradition, of which the key problem is how to maximize the fulfilment of national interests. To be frank, I personally appreciate Blair's talent and ability. His leadership created many extraordinary changes in the Labour Party which could then win several elections against the Conservatives. But he has also initiated a great tragedy. It is so ironic that by appealing to morality, he has involved the UK's armed forces in an illegal, immoral and vastly destructive war. Moreover, the great majority of people believe that in fact he had no particular moral purpose in mind, but simply a crudely sycophantic pro-US position.

Overall, I believe that explicit moral standards could have some impact on international affairs if they are well-oriented; but they should never be closely linked with war, or become an excuse for war. I believe that a responsible government, especially in today's rapidly globalizing world, will not ignore tragic incidents in other countries. But there should be no third-party interference through unilateral actions which lack international support and a UN mandate. We have to find the historic roots of problems as soon as possible, and solve them structurally instead of superficially. As a first step, we should strengthen the function of the UN, and respect its decisions made by a majority instead of a cabal of powerful countries.

Chapter 12

Exploring Conflict and Harmony: Hong Kong and Macao

Lin Yuan

Introduction

Since re-unification with the People's Republic of China, political developments in the Hong Kong Special Administrative Region (SAR) have been quite different from those in the Macao SAR. There have been numerous conflicts in Hong Kong, whereas in Macao the government is generally seen as having been successful, the residents support it, and the overall situation is harmonious. In studies of conflict various writers have argued that conflict may have simultaneously constructive and destructive functions; and harmony does not simply mean peace, but tolerance of differences, even of clashes. Conflicts and harmonies on the political scene cannot be explained in simplistic terms.

Political conflicts in Hong Kong have been expressed mainly through large-scale demonstrations organized by democratic groups on Re-unification Day (1 July) and New Year's Day. These rallies have become a stage on which political demands are expressed, and have apparently reflected the desire of Hong Kong residents for democratic reforms. The demonstrations have made top news stories, and the slogans and the number of participants have been taken as indicators of public opinion. Defiant expressions by rival political camps even led to physical attacks on each other. Assemblies are guaranteed by law as a fundamental right of the residents of Hong Kong. In fact, they serve as a kind of punch-bag for residents to express their dissatisfaction with government policies, and as a channel for their political demands. When these rallies proceed peacefully with rational slogans, and the objective is to send messages of public opinion rather than a mere venting of sentiments, they could play a positive role. However, when they are conducted because of the need of different political camps to occupy newspaper inches, they could have a negative impact on the political scene. For example, after recent rallies, the demand for universal suffrage for the election of the Chief Executive and all seats of the Legislative Council has been continually increasing. If the administration were to act precipitously in response to these demands, attempting to seek a superficial peace, it may not result in a happy ending. The question now facing intellectuals, and people from all walks of life, is how best to seek for a way in which residents will be able to strive for democracy in an effective manner, without jeopardizing stability and prosperity.

The political development of Macao has been relatively harmonious since re-unification. On the one hand this achievement is thanks to a series of favourable factors, namely the wise leadership of the SAR Government, rapid economic development and improved public security. On the other hand it is also due to a unique 'association culture'. Association culture comes from a tradition of consensus politics in governance, an emphasis on patriotism and love for Macao and a social atmosphere which prioritizes harmony. For five years after re-unification residents have been satisfied with the SAR Government, testament to the success of Macao's political development model.[1]

Most political participation in Macao is streamed through the associations, which are different from political parties. Since associations have become the voices for different sectors and strata of society, several political élites have arisen from them, controlling the political development of Macao. Although democratic groups did emerge from some 'new associations' in the 1980s, traditional associations with businessmen at the core have continued to dominate the political scene. In terms of scale and momentum, the democratic movement is still in a weak position. The kind of demonstration politics that has appeared in Hong Kong does not even exist in Macao.

Reviewing the history of Macao, it is not difficult to discover the reason for its special ability to balance conflicts and strive for development, with harmony as the pre-requisite. In this small territory people of different ethnicities, religions and cultural backgrounds have lived together for centuries. During the period of Portuguese administration Macao maintained harmony between the Chinese and Portuguese populations. After re-unification the numerous associations and élites demonstrated the functions of integration, reflecting the ability of Macao to safeguard a harmonious social development through its unique governance model. Being a small community, the association culture penetrates all aspects of Macao's political, economic and social spheres, and fosters political élites who are able to use interpersonal networks of *guanxi* (relationships) to balance different power bases. Certainly there are other objective political and economic factors that have created the external conditions for Macao's stable development. The peaceful transfer of power from Portugal to China in 1999 also allowed continued development in a stable manner. Owing to its conditions, Macao had to rely fully on mainland China. After re-unification Macao has benefited largely from the implementation of the 'One Country, Two Systems' principle and the Basic Law, as well as a series of economic support measures from the Beijing government. In the first decade of the twenty-first century the major problem facing Macao has become how to co-ordinate between the demand to make Macao more open and democratic, and the maintenance of the

---

1   Opinion polls show that the Chief Executive of the Macao SAR, Edmund Ho Hau Wah, frequently receives about 80 per cent support.

existing harmony. The democratic development of Macao lags behind neighbouring regions such as Hong Kong, Taiwan and even the People's Republic of China.

Studying conflict from a perspective adopted in economics, we ought to find a way to achieve a win–win situation through a rational distribution of resources, avoiding damage as far as possible, and also avoiding gains to one side at the expense of the other. Political conflicts should also aim for a win–win situation, or at least for a reduction of destructive, negative effects. Damaging consequences to the governing, the governed and all interest groups should be reduced to a minimum; the concept of harmony should be used as a guideline for participants to manage conflicts, so they are able to cope with both conflicts and harmonies during the process of political development. This chapter presents the principles of conflict and harmony for political development. Through reviewing the existing literatures, it attempts to explore the relations between the two and the best way to balance them in the case of Hong Kong and Macao SARs.

Conflict and Harmony

Writers in the Western sociological tradition have produced a number of studies on conflict in the past fifty years or so. Parson's 'structural functionalism', Turner's 'politics of conflict', Bentley's 'group conflict' and Dahrendorf's 'harmony and conflict' theories are four of the more influential. After a brief review of these, I go on to mention more general ideas about harmony, including some reflections from Chinese culture.

From the mid-1940s Parsons' structural functionalism was dominant in conflict theory.[2] Parsons argued that the values of the members of a society are decisive in maintaining social integration and stabilizing social order. Conflict is regarded as 'morbid' in a healthy society, and mechanisms to eliminate conflicts are positively sought. The social system proposed by Parsons tends to be balanced, with the negative effects of conflicts emphasized: conflicts are regarded as destructive forces.

Following the dissolution of the temporary stability after the Second World War, and the emergence of a series of conflicts in the mid- and the latter half of the 1950s, some sociologists began to express their doubts about the viability of Parson's theory. These sociologists absorbed ideas of conflicts earlier proposed by Marx, Weber and Simmel, to revise the bias of structural functionalism. In his work, *Functions of Social Conflict*, Coser initiated the use of the term 'conflict theory'. He opposed Parsons' merely negative appraisal of conflict and argued that conflicts contain both positive and negative functions. He argued that under certain conditions conflicts can guarantee social continuity, reduce polarity, prevent the rigidity of a social system, enhance the adaptability of social organization and promote integration. Coser proposed that the functions of conflict, particularly reducing polarity and promoting social integration, can be benign rather than merely catalytic in societal breakdown.

---

2   Talcott Parsons, *Social System* (New York, 1951).

Turner constructed a relatively complete system of conflict theory, especially its relation to social integration.[3] Turner describes political development as the outcome of a series of regulated struggles for political power between interest groups. He argues that conflict involves a political force attempting to deprive, control, damage or eliminate another political force. In a pure form, political conflicts may be wars that aim to harm opponents by assimilation, destruction or other means. In the real world, however, the struggles are usually restricted by political objectives: in this sense, confrontational political actions aim to attain fundamental goals rather than just to harm enemies. The opponents are regarded as 'political competition'. Some political competitors gradually integrate. The objective is to convince and prove to the opponents, or to people in general, the legitimacy, correctness and attractiveness of the opinions of a political force.[4]

Another suggestion, Bentley's theory of group conflict, is that conflict and harmony operate in cycles.[5] Although his group theory is based on the perspective of conflict, the ideas of balance and unity emerge throughout the process of conflict. Bentley argues that all well-organized groups embody some form of unity, related to the tradition of the pursuit of stability under democratic conditions. Constrained by the culture of a democratic political tradition, group conflicts are usually moderate, and are negotiated by elections. Here unity is a kind of a disorganized interest. This interest could be latent or even conceptual, and although it is not always explicit, it is essential. It is a standard against which people analyse, select and judge. It is a kind of 'rule of the game' of group conflict, or a general politico-cultural consensus between the norms of personal freedom and dignity, and the justified integration of conflicts, democratic model and welfare system.

Finally, Dahrendorf argues that social reality has two sides: stability, harmony and consensus on the one side; change, conflict and coercion on the other.[6] Sociology needs not only a harmonious social model but also a conflictive social one. Sociology, therefore, should depart from the 'utopia' of balance and harmony as constructed by Parsons, and should instead construct a general conflict theory. He also argues that a social organization does not seek a balanced social system, but a coercive, co-ordinated organic whole. The different positions within a social organization possess authority and power in different quantities. Such an inherently unequal distribution of power has triggered society to split into two opposing quasi-groups – the ruling and the ruled. Under certain conditions, quasi-groups are organized in the form of visible interest groups and devote themselves as collective actors in open group conflicts, which will result in the redistribution of authority and power, as well as a temporary stability and harmony of society. However, this also signals the beginning of the

---

3   Jonathan H. Turner, *The Structure of Sociological Theory* (California, 1991).

4   Jonathan H. Turner, Leonard Beeghley and Charles Powers, *The Emergence of Sociological Theory*, 5th edn (Duxbury, 2001).

5   Arthur Bentley, *The Process of Government* (Bloomington, 1949).

6   The ideas are mainly elaborated in Ralf Dahrendorf, *Class and Class Conflict in Industrial Society* (Stanford, 1959).

institutionalization of the roles of the new rulers and the new ruled. In this way, the crisis of conflicts hides within harmony. When the situation matures, the members of society will re-organize for another round of conflicts to strive for power. The reality of society is a cycle between conflict and harmony, and the dialectic of power and resistance moves history forward.

Tensions between conflict and harmony have been observed by many writers in the past. Harmony may be simply viewed as the opposite of conflict. In Western philosophy an early topic was the harmony of numbers. Pythagoras saw numbers as the origins of all things of creation. He argued that all natural phenomena and patterns are determined by numbers: they have to obey the harmony of numbers, or mathematical relationships. A second meaning of harmony is the combination of different tones in music. The intervals produce harmony when they enjoy a certain mathematical ratio.

Harmony in political development is a metaphorical extension of these two basic meanings. As music pursues audible harmony, politics pursues social harmony, which implies social justice, so that each member of society can enjoy life without having too many uncertainties, with basic security guaranteed. The concept also dates back to Pythagoras who said, 'There must be justice. Injustice destroys order and harmony. This is the biggest evil'. Many Western thinkers thereafter expressed their views on justice and harmony along these lines. The descriptions of social harmony by Western political philosophers have often been based on social discords. In other words, they sought for and designed a theoretical concept to help people achieve social harmony in the face of specific problems. The ideal and metaphor of a harmonious society has been an important factor, from Plato's *Republic* to Rousseau's *Social Contract*, from Adam Smith's 'economic harmony' to Green's new liberalist idea on 'political harmony' and Rawls' idea of justice.

On the other hand, Marx argued that endless conflict and not stability is the normal state of a polity and that it is impossible for politics to develop without conflict, until reaching the Marxist utopia.[7] Marx specifically saw history as a series of class conflicts, a process by which the rule of one class is replaced by another. He argued that endless conflicts are inevitable as they serve progress. John Dewey also noted the benign consequences of conflicts, saying, 'Conflict is the gadfly of thought. It stirs us to observation and memory. It instigates to invention. It shocks us out of sheep-like passivity, and sets us at noting and contriving ... Conflict is the *sine qua non* of reflection and ingenuity'. In India Gandhi recognized the need for conflict to oppose injustice, but he would only countenance nonviolent struggle, returning good for evil and moving the hearts of the people through love and forgiveness. Gandhi's ideal, particularly in process rather than outcome, was for a more harmonious approach than that of Marx, accepting conflict but rejecting violence.

Most Chinese believe the term 'conflict' usually implies struggles and violence, carrying negative connotations, while 'harmony' is linked to tolerance, stability

---

7   Lewis Coser and Robert K. Merton, *Introduction to Sociology*, 3rd edn (San Diego, 1991).

and balance, having a positive significance. From the political point of view, many Chinese scholars believe conflict is perhaps inevitable but certainly undesirable. They may delve into peace studies in order to preach tolerance and peaceful coexistence. Therefore, an unbalanced view of conflict has arisen because most thinkers in the Chinese cultural orbit have tended to value only 'harmony' (*he*) as a positive concept; as a corollary, they see conflict as something inherently evil or destructive or at least undesirable. Of course this view would be approved by governments, who tend to favour policy implementation without opposition. The same might be said about Chinese patriarchy in clan or extended family settings.

It is quite hard to find any Chinese discussions on conflict to compare with the spirited and positive debates about different aspects of harmony. In ancient Chinese philosophy, the concept of harmony is usually designated by the ideogram *he* (harmony, peace) which has several meanings. First of all, *he* implies full respect to creativity and diversity by integrating different aspects of life. It seeks unity between divergence and conflict. Second, *he* indicates the achievement of the best state of interpersonal relations. You Zi, a follower of Confucius, proposed that propriety (*li*) and harmony (*he*) were the two most important aspects of interpersonal relations. Mencius emphasized that a united people (*ren he*, or harmony between people) would be more powerful and more significant than timeliness (*tian shi*) and favourable terrain (*di li*).

Harmony, *he*, also indicates the ideal relationship between an individual and society. Thinkers before the Qin Dynasty (before 221 BCE) regarded *he* as the highest principle of political ethics, as that which politics is supposed to achieve. In the early text *Shangshu* (usually known in English as *Documents of the Elder*, or *Classic of History*), there is a phrase, 'To be able to unite the clans, one must be able to enlighten them with outstanding virtues. Only when the nine degrees of clans are in harmony, the civilians are settled. When the civilians are enlightened, the states are in harmony. Thus the people in the country enjoy universal peace because of the emperor'. What the verse emphasizes is first manage one's own clan well, to achieve harmony and single-hearted unity between members; and then to manage and co-ordinate the social relations of one's own state and the states of others. Thus the subjects of the country are friendly to each other, as in a family. The social ideal is one in which families are harmonious and the country is peaceful. All are able to obtain what they need, and to contribute their best without conflict. Harmony is definitely a major component in any Chinese utopia.

In Chinese thought, the terms 'Heaven' (*tian*) and the 'Way' (*dao*) signify both the changing nature of the universe and the wish to pursue harmony in this world; humanity (*ren*) is the intent to pursue harmony within the conflicted society by cultivating one's own mind, which means a noble individual (*junzi*) must practise non-attachment in thought and self-restraint in behaviour.

The *Zhonyong* (the Doctrine of the Golden Rule) refers to these qualities, where human beings would care for their society and vice versa. The unifying (*he*) and the changing (*yi*) are harmonious in evolution, the essence of the universe and thought.

As a concept, the doctrine of *Zhongyong* implies levels of communication between humans and nature or society.

After 1949 and especially after the early 1980s the Chinese government appealed to the term 'Harmonious Society' as a new concept in social reconstruction. The slogan of the 'Harmonious Society' raises the aspiration for democracy, rule of law, equality, justice, sincerity, amity, vitality, stability and harmony between humanity and nature. It needs to insist on the fundamental interests of people as the starting point, and also to meet the growing material and cultural demands of the public in general. This would hopefully ensure citizens' economic, political and cultural rights in a practical manner enhance harmonious coexistence between people and nature and achieve co-ordination between socio-economic development and population, resources and the environment.

It can be seen above that conflict and harmony are two facets of political development, like the black fish and the white fish in the *taiji* icon. These two facets are the different functions of motivation and cohesion. Harmony and unity interpenetrate through conflict, and harmony requires conflict as a reference of antithesis. The two are mutually reinforcing. Whether political conflicts cause benevolent motivation or vicious destruction is not a given. It is, rather, dependent on how the issues are handled by participants and governors, and how rights and interests are to be rationally coordinated and distributed. In real life, therefore, it could be restrictive in a developmental sense if conflict or harmony is used merely to promote democracy, progress and political development; or merely to maintain peace and stability. Political participants should learn how to use conflict and harmony as tools to avoid the destructive consequences of conflicts, and to explore the most amenable ways to achieve coordination and coexistence between different political forces. This is the best choice to achieve and promote maximized political benefit and development.

Conflicts and Democracy in the Hong Kong SAR

Political conflict and social turmoil in the Hong Kong SAR has attracted international attention. It reached some intensity because of the active development of party politics after re-unification, because of divergent understandings about democratization, and because of the relatively radical actions such as massive, high profile demonstrations. For example, responding to an appeal by the Civil Human Rights Front, which opposed national security legislation in compliance with article 23 of the Basic Law, some half a million residents of Hong Kong took to the streets on 1 July 2003, the sixth anniversary of the handover of sovereignty of Hong Kong to China. This was the biggest rally since the one on 4 June 1989. The scale of the rally was unprecedented, shocking Hong Kong and the world. On New Year's Day 2004 an assembly was held with 100,000 people attending, demanding that the government draw up a timetable for Hong Kong's political reform; to adopt universal suffrage of the Chief Executive by 2007 and all seats in the Legislative Council by

2008. On the same day the Concern Group for Hong Kong's Free Economy and the Hong Kong Securities and Futures Industry Staff Union formed a Union for Defending the Stability of Hong Kong, and organized a rally 'against politicians rioting Hong Kong'. On 1 July 2004 several hundred thousand people took to the streets again, demanding full democracy. Due to the tsunamis in South Asia in 2005, a rally against collusion, demanding distributional equity and universal suffrage by 2007 and 2008 was called off by the democrats.

The powerful democratic camp in Hong Kong is mainly backed by middle-class and party organizations. Following the exchange of the Joint Declaration between mainland China and the United Kingdom on the question of Hong Kong and the drafting of the Basic Law during the period of transition in the 1980s, debates on such sensitive subjects as the political system, human rights, freedom and democracy ignited the political consciousness of the middle class and the intellectuals. Political discussion groups were formed to voice opinions on the political system and governance of Hong Kong. A political participation system began to take shape by holding regular elections at the Urban Councils and the District Councils. These organizations were allowed to receive training from grass-roots democratic elections, thus transforming them into political participatory organizations.

Following the decision to introduce directly-elected seats in the Legislative Council in 1991, many political organizations expanded to become political parties.[8] Party politics began to flourish. However, owing to the 'China factor', structural constraints, and limited public support, political parties in Hong Kong played a relatively limited role in the political institutions before 1997.[9]

Under the guarantee of the Basic Law and the principle of 'Hong Kong people governing Hong Kong' after re-unification, political parties in Hong Kong have gained more important functions in the process of political reform and democratic development. Two major political groups, the Democratic Alliance for the Betterment and Progress of Hong Kong (DAB) and the Democratic Party of Hong Kong, have emerged, along with other parties, such as the Liberal Party and Article 45 Concern Group.

The widely divergent understandings on many fundamental issues in Hong Kong have directly caused endless political disputes. For example, the pro-government camp appreciates the Beijing government's argument on the understanding of democratic development in Hong Kong, saying that democracy in Hong Kong has been greatly improved after re-unification; in British times the Governor held all power in his hands. The democrats still insist that democracy in Hong Kong is too limited, arguing that only half of the 60 seats in the Legislative Council are directly elected, and that the Chief Executive is elected by an 800-member

---

8   Owen H.H. Wong, 'Cover People and Deformed Objects in Politics: On the So-Called Political Parties in Hong Kong', *A Sketch of Political Organizations in Hong Kong* (Hong Kong, 1993), p. 5.

9   J. Tak-man Lam, 'Party Politics in Hong Kong during the Political Transition', *The American Asian Review*, 15/4 (1997): 71–95.

committee composed of pro-Beijing professionals and business executives. In many demonstrations the democrats have insisted on striving for universal suffrage in 2007 and 2008. Another example is slogans like 'resistance to communism through democracy' or 'resistance to communism through opposing China' as part of the democracy demands in Hong Kong. Those who oppose these slogans argue that these democrats, who equate democracy with anti-China and anti-communist ideas, do not only impede the smooth transition to full democracy in Hong Kong, but also trigger the emergence of potentially vicious political conflicts.

Therefore, democratic development in Hong Kong after re-unification is characterized by conflicts. Rallies and assemblies have become the symbols of the political culture. Although the territory has so far maintained its peaceful and rational tradition, it is difficult not to feel the hidden tensions that are about to erupt. A report submitted by Donald Tsang, the then Chief Secretary, to the Chief Executive in April 2004 reads,

> Many problems arose when Hong Kong had to face the most serious cyclical and structural economic difficulties in forty years. Coupled with avian flu, SARS and the controversy surrounding the implementation of Article 23 of the Basic Law, a considerable level of grievances has accumulated within the community. As a result, the community have doubts and concerns about the Government. In turn, this has led to expression of dissatisfaction in various ways.[10]

If the themes of the rally in 2003 were rather broad and varied, in 2004 more acute demands for an early universal suffrage and complete democratization were proposed. Those participating in the 1 July rally in 2003 were strongly dissatisfied by the poor administration of the Hong Kong government as well as its poor handling of the SARS outbreak and the harsh anti-subversion bill. The 1 July rally in 2004, on the other hand, demonstrated the desire to realize full democracy in Hong Kong. A survey commissioned by the daily newspaper *Ming Pao* in Hong Kong of 610 participants in the 2004 rally showed that 92 per cent wanted full democracy immediately.

Is political conflict the best and the most effective way to satisfy such a strong demand for democracy? We can learn something from the experience of the democratic development in Taiwan, characterized by increasing conflicts between clans, unsightly physical and language violence, the distrust of the public towards the impartiality of the authorities, and antagonism between supporters of the different political groups. The progress of democracy in Taiwan has been achieved – or marred – by these radical means. The presidential election in Taiwan in 2004 began with a scene comparable to a commercial gangster movie, and ended with the refusal by the losing camp to accept the election results. Yet despite these massive controversies in the election, the major political powers on the island still followed a peaceful path of resolution through the judiciary. Force was not used to refute the results: conflicts

---

10 Constitutional Development Task Force, Hong Kong SAR Government: *The Second Report of the Constitutional Development Task Force – Issues of Principle in the Basic Law Relating to Constitutional Development* (Hong Kong, 2004), p. 16.

were resolved within a nonviolent, constitutional and legal framework. Compared to the bloodshed in earlier political conflicts on the island, the presidential election in 2004 can be regarded as a step forward. However, democratic progress obtained by this means has been expensive, and it will not be easy to heal the social antagonisms between the clans.

From another angle, although the conditions for Hong Kong to exercise democracy are perhaps better than Taiwan, would Hong Kong be able to find a better development path than Taiwan? The enthusiasm of Hong Kong residents for political participation is far less than that of the Taiwanese; but Hong Kong has a relatively sound legal system and widespread respect for the rule of law. There have been no confrontations between the clans or major grievances against the government's high-handedness. The major divergence for Hong Kong for now is the difference of opinions on democratization, as well as dissatisfaction with a lack of efficiency in governance. However, this political conflict in Hong Kong, characterized by demonstrations, reflects that the community still requires further political maturity. A politically mature society not only upholds such fundamental values as democracy, freedom, justice and the rule of law, but also possesses rational politicians and voters. If politics in Hong Kong remains at the level of slogans and radical personal attacks, with a lack of calm rational thinking, it may only trigger a fanatic political farce, and will eventually bring an upsurge of populism and social unrest.

The current political conflicts have not yet caused serious damage. If the Hong Kong residents can combine harmony with conflicts, they may achieve positive results with half the effort of a confrontational approach. A wise use of conflict is not to resort to force, but to tolerate any negative effects of conflict and resolve them in a dialectical way. Before democracy is fully realized demonstrations will continue to be the main avenue for people to express their anger. But instead of condemnations and attacks, they should transform rallies into peaceful, rational, creative political activities with Hong Kong characteristics. It is more beneficial for the healthy development of democracy in Hong Kong to transform the destructive forces and to minimize damage to its international image and social stability. Different political groupings in Hong Kong need understanding and tolerance, and less distrust, of each other. They should concentrate on how Hong Kong's political reform should be designed, how élites and grass-roots could unite to seek a fair distribution of social resources and the maximization of social interests.

Political Harmony in the Macao SAR

After re-unification the Macao SAR implemented the principles of 'One Country, Two Systems', 'Macao People Governing Macao' and 'High Degree of Autonomy', and its political development has also been relatively stable. The SAR Government adopted a successful positioning by developing tourism and gaming industries as the flagship sector of Macao, whilst also coordinating other industries. The Beijing government also adopted efficient measures in a Closer Economic Partnership

Arrangement (CEPA) and a permit scheme to allow mainland residents to visit Macao individually (Individual Traveller Scheme). These measures have stimulated a rapid economic development in the Macao SAR, with the annual GDP growth rates in double digits for the past two years. Meanwhile, favourable conditions such as the significant improvement of public security after re-unification, a stable community and popular support for re-unification have also played roles in creating advantageous conditions for stable political development.

In general, democratic development in Macao has lagged behind that of Hong Kong, Taiwan and even mainland China. This is because party politics has not yet been formed, and the influence of the democratic camp, represented by the newly-emerged associations in the 1980s, has been constrained in the face of the dominance of the traditional associations.

Associations play an important role in Macao's society. Its characters seem to be the crucial function for the social development of Macao and might be a unique type in the world. According to official statistics, 2,400 associations have been registered in the territory, which has a population of only half a million. The groupings of associations include charitable clubs, countrymen societies, industry societies, communions, political groups and so on. With the funds and subsidies from the Macao Government, these associations organize cultural festivals, educational and voluntary activities as well as political activities, thus enhancing governance and avoiding social conflicts within the mini-society.

Moreover, the relatively traditional and conservative political culture and the weak political consciousness among the population have resulted in a low level of political participation. Only recently has the rapid economic development stimulated the emergence of the middle class which may become the principal force striving for democracy in Macao. Should there be changes in the balance of power between all forces in political participation, the political environment will also inevitably change, thereby breeding the possibility of political conflicts. How stability and harmony can be maintained while searching for a harmonious approach to democratic development is a question that requires deep consideration.

Democracy in Macao has developed to some extent through the participation in political groups of the middle class among the Chinese population. The economic boom in the 1980s changed the social structure of Macao, creating a middle class of professionals and well-educated young people. The Chinese representatives who wanted to be in politics began to display their talents, breaking the control of the Macanese in the Legislative Assembly. Alexandre Ho was elected into the third Assembly in 1984 through direct elections, and his group scooped three out of the six directly-elected seats in the fourth election in 1988. The middle classes in Macao had become a political force that could not be ignored, although the monopoly of traditional associations still constrained their influence.

The establishment of the election system in Macao's Legislative Assembly opened the doors to the Chinese for political participation, and an early form of democratization emerged in Macao. During the process the emergence of the new associations broke the inherent monopoly of the traditional associations and the Macanese community. They stimulated diversification of political forces and symbolized development and progress of democratization. 'New associations' means the Chinese associations that were formed independently from the traditional associations in the 1980s. Members of these associations were mainly those who were born and bred locally in the 1950s. A majority of them were new middle class, and had a strong sense of belonging to Macao. They positively strived for more political participation, with hopes to achieve a genuine 'Macao People Governing Macao'.[11] In these associations two groups had contributed greatly to the democratization in Macao, the 'livelihood camp' and the 'democratic camp'.

The development of the 'livelihood camp' began in the 1980s. This group mainly focused on care of the community and service to the population, especially new immigrants and grass roots organizations. The 'livelihood camp' did appeal to democracy but mainly emphasized improvement of livelihood: they argued that the improvement of livelihood of the population would naturally lead them to understand the importance of democracy; they were elaborating an indirect catalytic effect. These measures attracted much praise from the population and forced traditional associations to respond positively by investing in their relations with the grass roots. The democratic camp which emerged at the end of the 1980s focused more directly on promoting democracy. It includes both grassroots activists and professional people. For example, legislators from the 'democratic camp' are working hard to seek collaboration with legislators from other camps to enhance the power of the Legislative Assembly in monitoring the Government.

During the period of transition democracy had been developed to a certain extent. However, unlike Hong Kong, Macao neither expressed deep worries about its future nor began fierce debates on how the political system should be developed after re-unification. Political development remained stable and there were no confrontations or active political participation. Apart from such specific factors as the role of the associations, defects also exist, such as the lack of understanding of democracy, limited space and imbalances in political participation. Owing to the influence of the relatively traditional and conservative political culture, political consciousness is weak among Macao's population. Their understanding of democracy remains at the level of feeling it is the duty of the government to listen to public opinions and to take care of their interests.[12] An elected government, the essential requirement for Western-style democracy, does not appear to be valued in Macao's community, hence voices for universal suffrage are extremely subdued. It can be seen that a civil society did not accompany the democratic development in Macao. Intellectuals, even in the younger generation, have not yet publicly demanded more political space and full direct election to the Legislative Assembly. A baseline of the democratic activists has been to avoid angering the central government. Some academics argued that the community of Macao is clearly depoliticized, and the media has taken a pro-

---

11 Herbert Yee et al., The Political Culture of the Chinese in Macau (Macao, 1993), p. 20.
12 Yee, p. 55.

government stance by rarely providing readers with news and information that are critical of government policies. This has resulted in the current weak function of the media in monitoring the government.

Huntington has pointed out that social motivation and political organizations as well as institutional support must be compatible with each other.[13] In a fully democratized society the pressure for social motivation and political participation will increase. Political organizations and systems must change accordingly in order to endure these pressures, to maintain a stable society and to realize democracy. Macao is currently facing such pressures and has to consider how government policies and the relevant systems and institutions should be changed in order to fulfil the increasing needs of democratic participation. Changes in political environment as well as balances between all political forces may possibly result in unprecedented political conflicts. Optimistically, some conflicts and changes will inject motivation and vigour into Macao's political development, will break the political pattern of the past 20 years – which traditional associations have dominated – and will promote the maturity and advancement of the democratic force in Macao. However, if social and political conflicts were given free reign to develop in themselves, negative effects could also arise. Conflicts need to be guided and used, but not suppressed by force. They should not be upgraded to bloodshed and violence, but their positive functions are to be elaborated. The view of harmony should be used to guide conflicts.

It is difficult for a society to develop and strengthen if only one voice is heard: singularity only brings monotony and political bleakness, an unsustainable situation. To promote democratic development, unprecedented conflicts and clashes may have to emerge. To elaborate the idea of harmony a higher level of tolerance and stability is required: in other words, a state of inclusive differences within a harmonized society. The fruit of the history of Macao is the creation of the 'Macao spirit' that entails toleration and integration between plural ethnicities and cultures. This spirit will hopefully radiate new vitality in the post-independence era. Macao had already paid a bloody price in its early stage of democratic development and the experiences in Hong Kong and Taiwan have also provided much to learn from. The positive functions of conflicts and the tradition of tolerance can safeguard a harmonious socio-political environment and promote political reform and democratization. Acknowledgement of tolerance, stability and dissonance will provide another beneficial lesson for Macao to implement successfully the principle of 'One Country, Two Systems'.

Conclusion

The Hong Kong and Macao SARs have their distinctive features in their respective political and democratic development. Both SARs have now entered the second terms of government. Political reform, universal suffrage and legislation are all on

---

13 Louie Kin-sheun, *A Preliminary Exploration of the Politics and Political System of Hong Kong* (Hong Kong, 1987), p.19.

the agenda. The serious divergence on how these issues should be handled in Hong Kong, expressed by noisy demonstrations, does not bring any substantial progress in leading them to resolution. Learning from the experience of Hong Kong, Macao has adopted a delaying tactic. However, these problems are also a good test for the SAR governments. Both the international community and mainland China are waiting for their responses.

Although the word democracy is frequently discussed, different groups twist and abuse the interpretation of the term itself in order to gain support. In our highly globalized world, governments and oppositions should not pursue democratization only through conflicts, and especially not through violence. They should bear in mind the need to safeguard social stability and balance. Democracy provides rules on conflict management. If a community sees democracy as a forum where they physically fight for their demands, society may divide from within. If the government adds too much pressure for the sake of reaching consensus, society may be crushed from above.

Conflicts must be resolved within certain boundaries, and compromise is reached by integrating an impulse to harmony with the expression of different demands. There is no singular or easy route to resolving conflict. Emphasizing one side at the expense of the other may destroy the overall balance of society. Democracy is not an automated machine which will run itself after the correct commands and programmes have been input. A democratically-developed society requires support from people upholding different political pacts, who also recognize the inevitability of conflict and the necessity for harmony and tolerance. Citizens, associations and political parties must at least be willing to tolerate the differences between each other, and acknowledge the rights and points of view of their opponents. They should understand each other in a spirit of compromise. Seen from this perspective, democracy should be realized as a process encompassing both conflict and harmony. This mechanism is applicable in the environments and soils of different political cultures. Harmony can be understood as the most complicated and the most perfect organizational mechanism. It is a logic that governs the existence and development of things. It is an order of tolerance and function. Thus harmony includes everything, the one in everything and everything in the one. Democracy emphasizes effectiveness. Any points of view and methods to resolve problems cannot be examined by rigid ideologies but by experimentation in the real world. The real world can review, amend, accept or reject any points of view and methods to highlight weaknesses and emphasize strengths.

Although the majority of the residents of Hong Kong and the democrats have voiced their strong desire to elect all members of the Legislative Assembly as well as the Chief Executive by universal suffrage, such a desire should not be realized at the expense of the stability and prosperity enjoyed by the population in the past decades. Crude competition based on mere political considerations will adversely affect any economic and political developments. Democratic forces in Macao, on the other hand, still need time to develop. Macao should seize the current opportunity of a prosperous environment to launch democratic politics and to seek diversification in democratic development. A harmonious order is advantageous for Macao's politics and democracy, but conflicts should also be allowed to exist to a certain degree. In other words, Macao should avoid reducing itself to an unsustainable political environment, but should pursue a state of inclusive differences within a harmonized society. In sum, the Hong Kong and Macao SARs should each pursue their own best-suited paths towards democracy. The key is how to conduct this in an incremental manner. Elster and Slagstade argue that democracy is a contingent outcome of conflicts.[14] This author hopes the two SARs can be witnesses to successful processes of democratization and political reforms that are jointly promoted by conflict and harmony.

---

14 Jon Elster and Rune Slagstade, *Constitutionalism and Democracy* (Cambridge, 1988).

Chapter 13

Towards Peace with Justice: Developing a Peace Centre in Australia

Stuart Rees

Distinguishing between 'Peace' and 'Peace with Justice'

The creation of the Centre for Peace and Conflict Studies at Sydney University came in response to students' protest that teaching in that large university covered almost every subject except peace. The process involved consultations between representatives of three groups: students, university staff and members of the public with longstanding interests in pacifism and peace. Following those consultations, the objectives of a Centre for Peace and Conflict Studies were written. The basic objective was: 'To promote understanding of and the means of attaining peace with justice'.

In defining these objectives, the distinction between peace and peace with justice became central to the Centre's identity and activities. Consistent with accounts in peace studies literature, peace was seen as an absence of hostilities, an end to a conflict, perhaps signified by the calling of a truce or the signing of a treaty.[1] Peace could always be regarded as an important achievement but could not guarantee that conflict would not resume, in particular if the causes of conflict had not been addressed.

The objective, 'peace with justice', confronted questions about the causes of conflict and the quality of people's lives. Such issues were addressed years ago by my colleague Andrew Rigby when he insisted, 'the question is what are we fighting for not what are we fighting against?'[2] Our answer to his question produced a wide interpretation of any future Centre's tasks.

In the initial years, this interpretation involved us in addressing conflict in personal affairs rather than in international relations, in addressing issues arising from social and economic rather than foreign policy. Social policy questions which involved peace with justice included equal access to health care and to opportunities in higher

---

1   Johan Galtung, *Peace By Peaceful Means* (Oslo, 1996); Johan Galtung and Carl G. Jacobsen, *Searching For Peace* (London, 2000); Andrew Rigby, *Justice and Reconciliation, after the Violence* (Boulder, 2001).

2   Andrew Rigby, 'Be Practical, Do the Impossible: The Politics of Everyday Life' in Chester and Rigby (eds), *Articles of Peace* (Bridport, 1987), pp. 90–105.

education, fairness in the treatment of juveniles convicted of offences and the task of reconciliation with Australia's indigenous peoples. We regarded peace with justice as synonymous with equality of opportunity in policies affecting the quality of people's lives. We also paid attention to equity or fairness in the administration of those policies. In these respects we mounted the argument that discrimination against people because of age, ethnicity, religion or disability was unjust and should be addressed as part of a peace agenda. The attainment of human rights and, as far as possible, the promotion of nonviolence would be a major responsibility in the Centre's work.

The question, 'what is the relationship between human rights and peace with justice?' affected our discussions about priorities. Efforts to understand and promote human rights revealed experiences of citizens in their daily lives and the concept 'citizenship' became a key topic in our interpretation of peace. To be a citizen of any country depends on opportunities to participate freely in public life. In local and in international terms, the full experience of citizenship could be regarded as similar to a concern with the needs and interests of a common humanity. The lessons of the tsunami disaster come to mind: we share a fragile planet and the needs of peoples are linked. The Indian poet Rabindranath Tagore expressed this principle of interdependence more eloquently: 'No civilized society can thrive upon victims whose humanity has been permanently mutilated .... Those we keep down inevitably drag us down'.[3]

Deliberations about this Centre's objectives had produced a trinity of ideas which we regarded as synonymous with peace with justice in any context or country. These ideas represent values about the way we should treat one another and about our attitudes towards more vulnerable citizens. Those three ideas are human rights, nonviolence and a common humanity. The following account of the Centre's development and activities reflects the influence of these ideas. It also reflects the fact that the Centre was an autonomous unit, run by its staff and volunteers, making its policy and management decisions democratically but operating within the framework of the University of Sydney.

Stages of Development

The Centre's development can be marked in terms of stages, each characterized by projects concerned with education about social justice. Over ten years four stages or projects overlapped. During those ten years the Centre's staffing evolved from volunteers to part time staff to a combination of full time employees, part timers and volunteers. As the costs of paying staff increased, so too did the Centre's relationship to our sources of income, to Sydney University and to other public institutions. In common with world-wide community development, the task of raising money to cover the costs of an organization which was increasing in size and ambitions

---

3   Cited in Louis Fischer, *The Life of Mahatma Gandhi* (London, 1997).

hindered the progress of the work which was the Centre's main responsibility. Raising money could so easily displace the task of working for peace with justice, means could become ends. Unless you have a wealthy patron who respects your autonomy, there seems to be no escape from this means and ends dilemma.

The four stages were:

1. advocacy on social justice issues;
2. the writing and publication of books;
3. the creation of the Sydney Peace Prize;
4. the design of post-graduate courses in peace and conflict studies, the enrolment and teaching of students.

The last of our projects, namely the enrolment of students, is usually the first to evolve elsewhere. The fifty post-graduate students now enrolled at Sydney University's Centre for Peace and Conflict Studies generate energy, ideas and income. Yet the Centre's identity and reputation had evolved before the students arrived. They inherited a legacy of commitment to peace with justice on domestic as well as on international issues. That commitment derived from the achievements of the previous three stages.

Advocating Social Justice

Taking action against injustice, which in turn reflected how key staff members interpreted the goal of peace with justice, was influenced by our areas of expertise. I was previously a Professor of Social Work and Social Policy. The university students who participated in the social action projects were mostly studying social work.

In this initial stage three projects demonstrate the Centre's priorities. We contributed to a campaign to defend policies of universal health insurance across Australia.[4] We were saying that access to high standard health care according to need and irrespective of the ability to pay should be a characteristic of a civil society. It was therefore a peace with justice issue. Secondly, we organized campaigns against the possession of guns. We advocated nonviolence. We supported strict gun controls. Thirdly, we were concerned about the war in Bosnia and the increasing prejudice in Australia against Serbs. We organized seminars to educate ourselves and a wide public about the competing interests in that cruel civil war.

We have recently been investigating human rights abuses in the West Papua province of Indonesia and together with Sudanese residents of Sydney have organized a peace march and rallies to raise public awareness of the killings in the Darfur region of Sudan.

---

4   Stuart Rees and Leonie Gibbons, *A Brutal Game* (Sydney, 1985).

Writing and Publishing Books

To complement these social action projects the Centre conducted research in order to compile significant books about social justice, human rights and nonviolence. We were aware that university authorities were impressed by scholarly activities. They were seldom impressed by departments which only took social action and who were therefore not considered scholarly. On the other hand we were conscious of students' criticism of academics that they usually behaved like lions in the classroom but as lambs on the streets. They did not have the courage of their convictions, or, in more vernacular terms, academics were said to talk the talk but seldom walk the walk. From its very beginning the Centre for Peace and Conflict Studies built a reputation for having the courage of its convictions, for taking action on social issues. This action involved the organization of public meetings, writing to the press, arranging scholarly conferences and playing an active part in public debate.

The books which gave the Centre a scholarly reputation, which sold well and provided income from royalties, addressed several issues: (1) the consequences of free market economic policies and the advocacy of more equitable policies;[5] (2) the social costs of the violence associated with efficient but inhuman forms of management, whether in social welfare agencies, in the conduct of private industry or in scientific research;[6] and (3) the responsibilities of the world of business to take human rights seriously.[7] The latter book examined the interrelationships between international law and the interests of business, between social science analysis and the claims of lawyers, between the perspectives of women and indigenous peoples and the assumptions of people in traditional positions of power.

The brief description of one of the books in this Centre's series is provided in order to emphasize that the production of significant publications depended on cooperation with colleagues from a wide range of university disciplines. For example, my social science background derived from education in sociology and political science, in social work and social policy. My chief collaborators in these books were Gordon Rodley, who was a distinguished chemist and physicist, Frank Stilwell, a professor of economics and Shelley Wright, an international human rights lawyer. Study and advocacy about peace with justice is an interdisciplinary activity which demands respect for the theoretical base of disciplines but not their boundaries. Enquiries into the meaning of peace and the means of attaining that goal require researchers and educators to be international in outlook and never parochial. This challenge to cross discipline boundaries and to seek inspiration from any source has also characterized the last book in the Centre's series, my

---

5   Stuart Rees, Gordon Rodley and Frank Stilwell (eds), *Beyond the Market: Alternatives to Economic Rationalism* (Sydney, 1993).

6   Stuart Rees and Gordon Rodley, *The Human Costs of Managerialism: Advocating the Recovery of Humanity* (Sydney, 1995).

7   Stuart Rees and Shelley Wright, *Human Rights, Corporate Responsibility* (Sydney, 2000).

analysis of the ways in which power can be used to liberate people and to envision how human rights and peace with justice can be attained.[8] The subtitle of the book is 'exercising power creatively'. In writing the book a major source of inspiration derived from the work of poets over several centuries and from many countries, each joined in a common endeavour to oppose wars, to express human dignity and to champion nonviolence. Chinese poets have been no exception. For example, as a protest against war and in praise of nonviolence the legendary poet and philosopher of Daoism Lao Tzu once wrote:

> Where troops have encamped
> There will brambles grow;
> In the wake of a mighty army,
> bad harvests follow without fail.

Lao Tzu was also concerned about ways to implement the virtues which he depicted in his poetry, in particular the significance of self-examination to achieve reconciliation with others. He wrote in a tradition which other champions of the philosophy and practice of nonviolence have followed, including Mahatma Gandhi, Dag Hammarskjold the second Secretary General of the United Nations and His Holiness the Dalai Lama.

Lao Tzu wrote:

> I have just three things to teach:
> simplicity, patience, compassion.
> These three are your greatest treasures.
> Simple in actions and in thoughts,
> you return to the source of being.
> Patient with both friends and enemies,
> you accord with the way things are.
> Compassionate toward yourself
> you reconcile all beings in the world.[9]

Creating the Sydney Peace Prize

The third significant initiative in this Centre's development concerned the creation of the Sydney Peace Prize. The work associated with a jury's selection of Prize recipients and the organization of Peace Prize events, held in the first week of November each year, became the responsibility of a newly created Sydney Peace Foundation (SPF), which is an arm of the Centre and provides generous funds for staff

---

8   Stuart Rees, *Passion for Peace: Exercising Power Creatively* (Sydney, 2003).
9   Translated in Stephen Mitchell, *The Enlightened Heart: An Anthology of Sacred Poetry* (New York, 1992).

salaries. Although the Director of the Foundation is also the Director of the Centre, for financial and administrative purposes, the two organizations are separate.

Two issues prompted this initiative. First, we wanted to interest a large public in peace with justice. Secondly, we wanted to involve that huge constituency which has considerable influence in politics and public life but which is usually ignored when social justice and peace are discussed. We decided to ask representatives of business corporations to share in the promotion of a Peace Prize. To do so we established partnerships with business corporations. They pay a $15,000 per year fee to become a partner of the Peace Foundation and in turn receive advertising publicity and free tickets for the Peace Prize events which include the annual City of Sydney Peace Prize Lecture.

The Peace Foundation is an alliance of business, media, academic and community sector representatives. Its executive committee meets monthly to determine the choice and conduct of each year's activities, including well publicized seminars on peace with justice issues. For example, the public seminar in 2004 was given by former Australian Foreign Minister Gareth Evans on humanitarian intervention as a challenge to state sovereignty. His co-authored report on this subject is arguably the world's most important recent document on intervention to protect the vulnerable and to promote and show respect for human rights.[10] I mention the Evans seminar to highlight the Peace Foundation's commitment to peace education and to emphasize that it is not preoccupied with the award of the Peace Prize. Nevertheless the Foundation's reputation derives mostly from its choice of Peace Prize recipients and their presence in Sydney each November. The following list names recipients of the award together with the titles of their lectures and depicts diversity and common themes.

1998, Professor Muhammad Yunus, *Peace is Freedom from Poverty*
1999, Archbishop Emeritus Desmond Tutu, *Peace through Reconciliation*
2000, Xanana Gusmao, *Peace Building: A Challenge for East Timor*
2001, Sir William Deane, *Peace with Justice: Australia's Indigenous People*
2002, Mary Robinson, *Peace by Attaining Human Rights*
2003, Hanan Ashrawi, *Peace in the Middle East: An Humanitarian Imperative*
2004, Arundhati Roy, *Peace and the New Corporate Liberation Theology*

Negotiations to interest business corporations in the Peace prize are not easy. Their support is sorely tested when controversies arise which become public knowledge. Such a controversy arose in 2003 when the Sydney Peace Prize was awarded to the Palestinian academic and human rights activist Dr Hanan Ashrawi. Accounts of those events have been given, though most of that story has yet to be told.[11] The

---

10 International Commission on Intervention and State Sovereignty, *The Responsibility to Protect* (Ottawa, 2001).

11 Antony Loewenstein, 'Taking Back the Power: Hanan Ashrawi' in Margo Kingston (ed.), *Not Happy John* (Camberwell, Australia, 2004); Stuart Rees, 'Vilification Nation: The

popularity of the Peace Prize awards and the lecture which is given in a large theatre on the night before the award ceremony are apparent from the fact that tickets for the lecture are sold out within days of going on sale. A large public is thirsty to hear from distinguished world citizens about peace, that most precious commodity.

Teaching Post-graduate Students

The fourth stage of development concerns the design of peace studies units for post-graduate students. Through the Centre, the University of Sydney now offers a certificate, a diploma and a masters degree in Peace and Conflict Studies. From four units of study students can obtain a certificate, from six units they obtain a diploma, from eight units including a 12,000 word thesis they obtain a Master of Arts degree and from twelve units including a 25–30,000 word thesis they obtain a Master of Letters. Most students proceed by graduated steps to the masters degree. There is one core course called Understanding Peace: The Issues, which all students must complete. Apart from that one compulsory unit, students are free to choose from approximately twelve courses, eight of which would be taught in any one academic year. These courses have been supplemented with a full range of research degrees.

The range of choices open to students shows that the Centre's work has moved from a concern with domestic issues to analyses of international relations, from conflict resolution over local controversies to an examination of internationally sponsored peace negotiations. The first course to be taught was called Resolving Conflicts in Organizations, a topic which reflected our concern that unresolved conflicts occurred within the walls of organizations and had destructive effects on people's lives. We were concerned as much with working out ways to resolve conflicts as with diagnosing their cause. That course is still popular with students but the peace studies curriculum is now much more diverse and ambitious. It includes units on the Reform of the United Nations and on Clashes Between Civilizations, on Peace and the Environment, on Non Violence and Social Change, on Peace Journalism (sometimes called Media Building Peace) and on Cultures of Violence.

One of my interests is in the unit called Passion, Peace and Poetry. As indicated in the reference to Lao Tzu, efforts to express nonviolence and to promote peace with justice come in many forms, perhaps music and dance, pottery and poetry, painting and literature, drawing and street theatre. Educators have an opportunity to consider how these art forms can be used in peace advocacy and in peace education; reference to passion in the title of the course conveys the enthusiasm which has characterized the work of many artists. For example, an important Australian contributor to an understanding of peace was the poet Judith Wright. She was a campaigner for the rights of Australian Aborigines and she drew inspiration from the beauty of the Australian environment.[12] Here are four lines from her poem called

---

Hanan Ashrawi Affair', *East West Arts, Australia and Beyond*, inaugural issue (September–November 2004): 61–6.

12 Judith Wright, *Collected Poems* (Sydney, 1994).

'The Flame Tree', which is blood red in colour and often stands out as a symbol of life even in barren places:

> How to live I said as the flame tree lives?
> – to know what the flame tree knows; to be
> prodigal of my life as that wild tree
> and wear my passion so?

Conclusion

The experience of striving for peace with justice is like a journey which never ends. You have to keep assessing where you are today and what your direction will be tomorrow. Identifying the conflicts and tensions on this journey should provide an apt summary of factors which continue to affect the direction and achievements of the Centre at Sydney. I will list those conflicts. They could be posed as questions.

1. Is a Centre for Peace and Conflict studies a small business, a university department, a non-governmental organization, or an autonomous self governing group of staff and supporters who engage in all these activities and more?
2. How do you avoid means becoming ends, that is, when fund raising takes precedence over research and advocacy?
3. How do you avoid having too many projects and too few resources?
4. Do you take stands on most peace with justice issues or do you compromise in order to avoid offending your financial patrons?
5. Do you teach large numbers of under-graduate students and so increase your income and size, or do you insist that peace studies should remain a post-graduate area of study, available to limited numbers of students?

Struggling to answer these questions can be a catalyst for future ideas. The questions cannot be ignored. The very conflicts and contradictions within all five points are inherent in the study and the advocacy of peace with justice.

Chapter 14

A Peaceful Solution:
British Parliamentary Reforms

Qian Chengdan

Transformation of political system is an essential aspect of social transition; in modern times such transformation has also been the occasion of numerous conflicts. In modern societies political systems have always mutated in step with social changes. Various social strata, classes, professional groups, political forces, ideologies and so on may fundamentally disagree with each other on questions of whether, how, to what extent and at what time a change should be implemented. Thus the transition process will certainly give rise to serious conflicts, especially so when the changes touch the real core of a system. From the perspective of modernization it is quite natural to expect constant confrontation between traditional and modern groups, and between traditional and modern cultures: there is so great a divergence between traditional and modern politics that a new system can stabilize only after a long period of correlation and mutual adaptation.

Conflicts are the norm at a time of social transition, and no society could escape them. Yet there are numerous ways to resolve conflicts: different countries exercise different choices. In general there are two patterns of conflict resolution, one violent, the other peaceful. A violent solution leads to wars, disorders and internal disturbances, while a peaceful solution can avoid all these, keeping the overall situation mainly free from violence while the system undergoes changes. In recent history we have witnessed both patterns, which have universal significance and applicability. When we talk about peaceful resolutions of conflicts, we should consider domestic as well as international conflicts. Domestic conflicts are in some ways even more numerous and subtle, where a single mishandling may lead to profound disturbances.

Britain succeeded, on the whole, in finding a peaceful path to political reform, making it a model of the pattern for peaceful transformation of a political system. The British pattern is worth special attention because Britain's experiences offer to other countries an example of how peaceful transition can be made. Its example is the more notable as Britain is the earliest 'modernized' country of the world.

The British people achieved this peaceful solution through practical experiments which started as early as the seventeenth century, when Britain became the first nation to attempt political transformation into a modern state. Yet the first attempts were in fact violent. Only after learning many lessons in their first attempts did the British people gradually realize first, that conflicts are inevitable in the course of political transformation; but also that these conflicts can be handled peacefully. Three events are key to understanding the British peaceful solution: the seventeenth century English Revolution, the Glorious Revolution and the First Parliamentary Reform. In this chapter I focus mostly on the latter, because I take the success of the Reform as the symbol that the peaceful solution to political transformation in Britain had at last been found.

In the seventeenth century Britain experienced a Revolution and a Glorious Revolution, by which absolute monarchy was overcome and political power began to diffuse: that is, to diffuse from one person – the king – to a group of persons – the aristocracy – who, through the control of the parliament, dominated the country. The Glorious Revolution was a nonviolent process characterized by a compromise within the ruling élite, that is, between the king and the parliamentary magnates, and between aristocratic groups. While it is true that this power diffusion marked the beginning of transition to a modern political system, the Glorious Revolution did not in itself guarantee further peaceful solutions of conflicts in the future, because it seemed to be a coincidence: war would have broken out if John Churchill and his troops had not switched sides. Later, when the populace rose up to demand political rights from the ruling élite, was it assured that another compromise, rather than another violent revolution, would be worked out? That was the situation that Britain would face in the course of the Industrial Revolution.[1]

The Industrial Revolution brought about great changes in both economic and social dimensions, thus paving the way for further political changes. Although the political system in Britain had been the most developed in a modern sense up to the end of the eighteenth century, and had been taken as example by many European countries – for instance by France – it became far less successful in accommodating the economic and social reality as industrialization developed in depth. The new reality was characterized by the emergence of two new social classes: the middle class as a whole and the working class, who obtained their social identity during the progress of industrialization. For the middle classes, factory owners included, the political system became more and more preposterous because it no longer responded to the changing distribution of wealth as the Industrial Revolution shifted the balance of wealth in their favour; while the working class, as the existing system became less and less tolerable, attributed their poverty to the faults of the system. Thus from the 1760s through to the nineteenth century, political movements aiming at parliamentary reform began to take shape both among the middle classes and among the working class. These were the reform movements.

The pre-reform parliamentary system was indeed outdated, with hardly a tinge of real democracy. The historian Cannon comments: 'To these developments [that is, new social changes] the electoral system made no acknowledgement. Outwardly it remained exactly as it had been, each anomaly and oddity preserved. In practice it

---

1   Christopher Hill's *The Century of Revolution 1603–1714* (Edinburgh, 1961) is recommended as both narrative and analysis. For the Glorious Revolution and John Churchill, see Lord Macaulay, *History of England* (Reprint, Whitefish, NT, 2003).

was more narrow and oligarchic than ever. The year 1761 can, in many respects, be regarded as the peak of aristocratic power, before it was challenged by liberal and popular movements'.[2] Nevertheless, compared with the rest of the world, the British system was quite advanced. Other European powers such as France, Russia, Austria and Spain were without exception under the reign of monarchical absolutism, in which the monarch's will was the law of his realm and the monarch could act with no constraint. The British system was highly praised by many European radicals, and was valued with evident pride by the British ruling class. The ruling élite declared that the British system had been perfectly formulated since the Glorious Revolution, and that any change could lead to intolerable disasters. Thus it was hard to change the system and if there had been no Industrial Revolution it would doubtless have lasted much longer. But the Industrial Revolution held sway, making change inevitable. Rapid economic growth and, consequently, drastic changes in social structure made the political system more and more incompatible with current needs. The parliamentary system became a discordant remnant of the past, posing not only a threat to the order and stability of the country but also a hindrance to Britain's long-term evolution. If reforms were not properly managed, the political system could have become a dangerous threat to the nation's well-being.

What was the systemic weakness? After the Glorious Revolution the electoral system was well enough suited to a society dominated by the landed classes, the aristocracy, when landed property was the predominant form of social wealth. But it would also block the only channel through which newly emerging classes could participate in government. At a time when the Industrial Revolution was changing the proportion of wealth distribution and the balance of social forces, the 'old system', as it was then called, became degraded into a mere tool for the landed aristocracy to maintain its vested interests. Under the 'old system' the franchise, which had been maintained for several centuries, would not be adjusted to suit the changing situations; and the distribution of parliamentary seats, in use since the Middle Ages, no longer reflected the real importance of various constituencies. Up to the early nineteenth century only around 3 per cent of British adult males were eligible to vote, and even they were enfranchised not by wealth or personal qualifications but by ancient rights; while of the 202 electoral boroughs in England, about half had a population with fewer than 200 residents. Middle-class and working-class people were excluded from franchise, while newly emerging industrial cities and business centres, such as Manchester, Birmingham or Leeds, whose populations all reached 500,000 or more, did not even have a single seat in the parliament. The prolonged existence of the old electoral system would only sharpen social conflicts, causing an unnoticed risk of decline. At the same time, the voting practices were highly corrupt. The purchase of votes was commonplace, patronage was essential. In some places there were fixed prices for a vote and the exchange of votes for money was a matter of common knowledge. Vivid contemporary portrayals of electioneering typically depict widespread drunkenness and subsequent disorder. The poor sold their votes

---

2   John Cannon, *Parliamentary Reform, 1640–1832* (Cambridge, 1973), p. 49.

for money, while the ruling élites bought the votes as an investment in power and for accumulation of interests through power.[3]

Even if it was acknowledged that the 'old system' was more or less reasonable in a society where landed property was the most important form of wealth – because the aristocracy was the owner of land – how could the system continue when land no longer represented the source of wealth? The monopoly of government by the aristocratic oligarchs, hence the exclusion of other social groups from political rights, became increasingly unbearable, especially when industrialization made Britain the most prosperous country in the world. Change was inevitable.

On the other hand, since Britain was the first country to be industrialized it was also the first country to experience the problems of modern social transition. One of the most acute was the intensification of social conflicts. The differentiation of society, especially the polarization of economic status, sharpened social contradictions. During the process of industrialization British society was increasingly divided by identities of social classes based on differentiation of economic interests and by their realization of this differentiation: social classes achieved class-consciousnesses. The most prominent social results of industrialization were to make Britain a 'class society' and to provoke confrontations among social classes. Differentiation and confrontation then caused a further problem: if the political system must be changed, would any change bring about a total disintegration of the society? In other words: in the midst of profound social change, could a peaceful resolution be achieved that would avoid violent civil conflict?

Social polarization was shocking. The wealth gap was so extreme that the communist leaders Karl Marx and Friedrich Engels claimed British society was splitting into two antagonistic camps, two conflicting classes – the bourgeoisie and the proletariat.[4] The radical William Cobbett recognized this polarization in the 1830s when he cried out in alarm: 'We are marching towards a country where there are only two classes, that is, the employers and the humble dependents'.[5] Even Benjamin Disraeli, later a Conservative prime minister, admitted that Britain was a country with two nations – one poor, the other rich – between which there was an unbridgeable gap.[6]

Economically, the polarization was evident during the Industrial Revolution. Take wealth distribution as an example. In 1801 1.1 per cent of the wealthiest people had 25 per cent of the national income, while in 1848 1.2 per cent of the wealthiest people had 35 per cent of the national income. In 1867, when the Industrial Revolution had been accomplished, 2 per cent of the wealthiest people possessed 40

---

3   For abuses of the 'old system', see Edward and Annie G. Porritt, *The Unreformed House of Commons* (Cambridge, 1903).

4   Karl Marx and Friedrich Engels, *The Manifesto of the Communist Party* (Harmondsworth, 2002).

5   Edward P. Thompson, *The Making of the English Working Class* (London, 1963) p. 759.

6   Hampden Jackson, *England since the Industrial Revolution, 1815–1948* (London, 1976), p. 76.

per cent of the nation's income. Compared with this, the percentage of wealth that the working people had in proportion to the national income fell from 42 per cent in 1803 to 39 per cent in 1867, while their overall number in relation to total population increased. It was very obvious that with the progress of the Industrial Revolution, the disproportionate distribution of wealth had made the wealthy wealthier and the poor poorer, widening the gap between them. This gap was perhaps greater than in any other part of the world at the time, when we take into consideration the much greater total amount of wealth produced by industrialization.

It was not difficult to see how industrialization created a society of savage economic polarization in which wealth was distributed among the upper and the middle classes, and in which the working people were often deprived of even a basic livelihood. At the same time another polarization split the nation, between 'those with rights' and 'those without rights'. Although the middle classes and the working class were worlds apart economically they were both excluded from the franchise: this was indeed the characteristic feature of the 'old system'.

The franchise qualifications under the 'old system' had a touch of the absurd since even extremely wealthy individuals were not necessarily entitled to vote, especially when they were enriched by industry or business rather than by landed property. At the same time, some persons who were born with an archaic status could have the franchise even if they were penniless. The only purpose of this absurd system was to keep parliamentary votes in as few hands as possible, especially in the hands of the landed classes, so as to prevent other classes from sharing political power. Before the parliamentary reform in 1832 the majority of the working-class and middle-class population was denied the right to vote and was politically powerless. Two results came from this strange situation: one, the middle and the working class shared a common purpose, namely to fight against the monopoly of government by the landed aristocracy and to strive for their own rights; two, if the landed classes made an alliance with the wealthier people of the society – the middle classes – on the basis of property, their joint strength would enable them to reject working-class demands, and at the same time to avoid turmoil. But for this to happen the middle classes had to be enfranchised. This unique situation before the 1832 parliamentary reform provided a chance to change the system peacefully, without disastrous confrontation.

The middle classes played an important role in the struggles for reform before 1832. Their organized movements began with the 'Wilkes Affair' in the 1760s, when the slogan 'Wilkes and Liberty' became the platform for a reform campaign.[7] Wilkes's supporters later on founded a reform organization, the Society for Constitutional Information (1780), which was afterwards recognized as the forerunner of modern political organizations. The Society agitated for parliamentary reform and launched widespread activities such as petitions, publications, propaganda tours and even

---

7 For the details of the affair, see George Rude, *Wilkes and Liberty* (Oxford and New York, 1962). John Wilkes was an MP who attacked the King in person in issue 45 of his journal *North Briton*. Wilkes was ejected from parliament and persecuted by the government, actions which initiated the middle-class reform movements.

public meetings. Their activities were further stimulated by the outbreak of the French Revolution, when the middle-class radicals were backed up by working-class elements, bringing about genuine mass campaigning that Britain had never seen before.[8] During the agitation in early 1830s the middle classes played a leading role in the upsurge of mass movements: among other political organizations they established the National Political Union and the Birmingham Political Union. These organizations, cooperating with those constituted primarily by the working-class radicals, initiated large-scale mass activities demanding parliamentary reform. They easily organized huge meetings attended by tens of thousands or even hundreds of thousands of people, and delivered petitions with tens of thousands of signatures. At the most critical moment of the reform campaign middle-class leaders such as Francis Place put forward a slogan: 'To Stop the Duke, Go for Gold', attempting to reach their aim through economic coercion. This campaign put great pressure on the anti-reform Tories who were about to form a government. It was later commented, not without truth, that the anti-reformists were forced into submission by the threat of the middle classes to withdraw gold.[9]

The middle-class campaign for franchise was generally waged in a moderate and nonviolent way.[10] Their campaigns were characterized by peaceful means such as organizing meetings, delivering petitions and threatening to exert economic coercion. There was almost no tendency to violence or conspiracy. The reason for this lay in the fact that their economic importance was fully recognized by the aristocrats who monopolized the state power; and as long as their political demands were acknowledged and accepted, even partly (as in the case of the Reform Bill of 1832), the new rich were happy to form an alliance with the old political élites. Their anger could be defused comparatively easily, provided that the aristocracy agreed some measure of compromise.

After the 1832 Reform a major part of the middle classes obtained the franchise and became 'those with rights'. Their aim to participate in government was to a large extent realized, so the fight for their own rights was basically concluded. Now the political system was strengthened with an enlarged social base that comprised not only the landed classes but also a large portion of the middle-class men whose wealth had skyrocketed during the Industrial Revolution. In short, the upper and middle classes formed a union to rule the country. The middle-class men now were not only financially successful, their newly acquired franchise also enabled them to enjoy a corresponding political prestige. They had no need for further agitation and

---

8 For mass movements during the period of the French Revolution, see Harry T. Dickinson, *Liberty and Property: Political Ideology in Eighteenth-Century Britain* (London, 1977) and Carl B. Cone, *The English Jacobins* (New York, 1968).

9 For details, see Michael Brock, *The Great Reform Act* (London, 1973).

10 To understand the middle-class reform movements Simon Maccoby's two books are useful: *English Radicalism, 1762–85* (London, 1955) and *English Radicalism, 1786–1832* (London, 1955).

left the battleground almost exclusively to the working class. Of course, at this time and until the early twentieth century women had no voting rights.

Before the advent of industrialization there were hundreds of thousands of hand workers in Britain. A large social group, their crafts earned them a reasonably comfortable life. But naturally during the process of industrialization, hand-made products were gradually replaced by machine-made ones, and consequently hand workers were deprived of their means of living. They suffered a disastrous decline in terms of economic and social status, becoming main victims of industrialization. It is entirely understandable that in the early stages of industrialization hand workers, rather than the factory workers, were the most active in demanding relief, raising grievances and defending their traditional privileges, for which purposes they had a tendency to launch their own political organizations and involve themselves in political movements. In fact, from the London Corresponding Society (LCS) founded at the end of the eighteenth century, to Luddism, and further to Chartism in the mid-nineteenth century, the mainstream of the working-class radicalism was primarily the hand-workers demands.[11]

Compared with the claims of middle-class radicals, whose purpose was to raise their political status which was disproportionately low when compared to their already formidable economic strength, the working-class radicals started their reform demands from a different perspective: they were eager to create a political change that would induce an improvement in their economic conditions. They saw parliamentary reform as such a change. Although the political element was important, their ultimate aim was rather to improve economic condition. For instance, the leaders of the LCS believed that it was due to unfair and unequal representation in the House of Commons that the labouring poor were reduced to a miserable life.[12] How could this evil be redressed? The answer was to reform the parliament.[13] Thus it could be seen that although the LCS fixed an eye on political rights, the economic concerns were what mattered most to them. The same was true with the later Luddist and Chartist movements: the working-class people put forward a good many political demands, yet their ultimate aim was improve their economic condition.[14]

As to the means of their struggles the working people resorted not only to the conventions, petitions, demonstrations and mass meetings which had also been adopted by the middle-class radicals, but also to riots, conspiracies and even

---

11 The best work on working-class radicalism is Edward P. Thompson, *The Making of the English Working Class* (London, 1963).

12 For the LCS, see Albert Goodwin, *The Friends of Liberty* (Cambridge, MA, 1979) and Thompson (1963).

13 See 'Address from the LCS to the Inhabitants of Great Britain, 6 August 1792' in Mary Thale (ed.), *Selections from the Papers of the London Corresponding Society* (Cambridge, 1983).

14 For Luddism, see Malcolm I. Thomis, *The Luddites* (Hamden, CT, 1970); for Chartism, see Dorothy Thompson, *The Chartists* (London, 1984). It is obvious that Chartism was a political movement aiming at improvement of working-class conditions. The Luddite movement was a machine-breaking outburst whose links with Radicalism are less clear.

intended armed uprisings. Indeed, it could be seen that in the decades when working-class radicalism was on the rise, both peaceful and violent means were used. When peaceful means failed, they resorted to violence; when violent struggles failed as a result of government repression, peaceful tactics would be resumed.

However, due to the unique British traditions, peaceful struggles formed the mainstream of working-class radicalism, as we see from the LCS. Since the day of its foundation it held routine correspondences with similar groups, and undertook joint actions with the middle-class organizations. The LCS printed and distributed a great number of leaflets and pamphlets to publicize their platform of reform and to politicize the general population. Despite different opinions among themselves concerning the best means, the peaceful wing always maintained an upper hand, mainly resorting to petitions, meetings, demonstrations and so on. In May 1793 the LCS and other organizations launched a petition movement during which 36 petitions were presented to parliament from across the nation. Many of them were rejected by parliament on the pretext that they did not conform to certain stylistic rules. Nevertheless, a petition with 6,000 signatures, presented by the LCS, was accepted, read and put on record to be discussed. But when all petitions fell on deaf ears the LCS decided to initiate a new action.

In imitation of the French National Assembly, the LCS called for a National Convention to be held in Scotland. It was convened in November 1793. The LCS was the leading body, although many other organizations, including the Society for Constitutional Information, sent representatives. All speakers demanded universal suffrage and annual parliaments, and called for joint actions by all reform organizations, creating a serious threat to the authorities, since a French style of revolution was the nightmare of the government. The convention was repressed, its leaders arrested and sent in to exile abroad. After a short period of inactivity the LCS began to adopt a new method, mass rallies. In 1795 two such meetings were held in London with a hundred thousand people or more attending, demanding that reforms be undertaken and that the government be responsible to the people. These peaceful protests were once again repressed when the King was assaulted on his way to attend a ceremonial opening of parliament. The government seized on the incident as a reason to pass two bills which forbade any combination of over 50 people and which authorized local magistrates to arrest anyone at will without legal procedure. The passage of the two bills marked the failure of peaceful means. After that the violent wing of the LCS came to the fore, weaving conspiracies and preparing uprisings. Some people even tried to collaborate with the United Irishmen, a secret Irish group which aimed to overthrow British rule in Ireland. Although the LCS disappeared at the end of the eighteenth century, this violent tradition extended to the first years of the nineteenth, and even to the time of Luddism.

Yet as soon as the political atmosphere became favourable, for example after the Napoleonic wars and during the Chartist movement, the peaceful tradition rose again to form the mainstream of British politics, though violence usually followed any deterioration in conditions. In 1848, when Europe was swept by revolutionary storms, the Chartists in Britain launched another upsurge. They prepared a petition with about two million signatures to present to parliament, and on 10 April staged a massive popular meeting on Cannington Common with up to 150,000 people attending. The government appointed the Duke of Wellington, the hero of Waterloo, to command an army in case a revolution occurred, but at the same time they permitted the Chartists to continue their agenda, including presenting their petition. The government's anxiety in fact proved to be ungrounded, for it never occurred to the Chartist leaders to make use of the situation for a revolution. The meeting ended peacefully, the petition was delivered without turmoil – to avoid any possible turbulence and bloody confrontation, the Chartist leaders called off the scheduled procession in line with a government request, and then themselves went to parliament to deliver the petition.

Bearing all this in mind, we see that a peaceful tendency dominated in both middle-class and working-class traditions. But how could this tendency become tradition? One condition was crucial, and that was an open channel between social classes through which compromises could be made. The situation in France was completely different: it was a typical example of making change through violent confrontations. In fact, before 1789 there might still have been some hope of peaceful reform, yet under the *ancien régime* there was no channel of communication, classes could not take part in dialogue. The king and aristocracy refused to listen to the people, an intransigent posture which gave the bourgeoisie no choice, if they insisted on their rights, but to ally with the *sans-culottes*. Failure to compromise brought on bloody confrontations, and once the first bloodshed occurred, hatred accumulated. Thus France went from one revolution to another until in the 1870s some accommodation was at last made. It contrasted sharply with British history after the Glorious Revolution.

In constructing the channel of communication, one British group was especially noteworthy, namely the Whig aristocracy. The Whigs advanced their own economic reform agenda as early as the 1770s and 1780s, and they proposed bills in parliaments to make themselves leaders of the parliamentary reform movement. At the time of the French Revolution, when the tide of reform movements was on the upsurge and Britain was terribly torn between reformers and anti-reformers, the Whig Party maintained its reformist tradition, even though many members themselves left the party and joined the Tories. They even formed a 'Society of the Friends of the People' which worked alongside the Society for Constitutional Information and the LCS. From then on they always sympathized with reformist initiatives, and whenever possible they worked hard to protect lower-class reformers from too harsh government suppression.[15] Such a group with reformist attitudes among the aristocratic élites was of vital importance to a possible compromise because it served as a bridge between the élites and the people, and prevented conflicts from escalating

---

15 For the Whigs attitude toward reform, see Frank O'Gorman, *The Whig Party and the French Revolution* (Oxford, 1967), and Austin Mitchell, *The Whigs in Opposition, 1815–1830* (London, 1967).

into bloody confrontations, thus making it possible to carry out the parliamentary reforms in a peaceful way.

On the other side, British conservatism was not totally opposed to any form of change. Edmond Burke and William Pitt Jr, the most ardent counter-reformists during the period of the French Revolution, had themselves advocated economic reform. In the 1820s the governing Tory Party split into different factions when a liberal camp, headed by George Canning and Robert Peel, began to implement many reform measures. The Duke of Wellington himself, who was to lead the Tories against the Reform campaign from 1830 to 1832, actually made a fundamental change in the British constitution when his government emancipated the Catholics. Earl Grey noted, wisely, that the Whigs should provide a check on the existing system, find out its faults, and improve it, to avoid political calamity. The ruling élites gradually took it as a kind of common sense that they should take initiatives to avoid revolution of the French style. Thus the Whigs, and later on both parties, supported some kind of reform agenda, an attitude which became characteristic even of British conservatism.

Considering the above, we can understand how a compromise could be made in the years 1830 to 1832 when Earl Grey and his Whig Party were in power. In 1829 the Wellington government, under pressure from the Irish Catholics, allowed the passage of the Catholic Emancipation Act. The Duke made this concession to avoid war, although it enraged Tory extremists who, in the following year, overthrew the government by joining forces with the Whigs and some liberal Tories. Earl Grey was called to form a new government, which immediately initiated the Reform process by putting forward a Reform Bill. The Bill was passed in the Commons but rejected by the Lords. Very soon, the nation roared into angry action with an outburst of political organizations supporting the reform. Middle- and working-class radicals united for the common cause, which pushed the Whig government to propose another Bill which was again rejected by the Lords in which the Tories had a majority. This action dramatically aggravated the situation and plunged the nation into crisis. People at large launched a continuous wave of demonstrations and protests to demand reform. Violence broke out in places, and a major confrontation seemed unavoidable. For fear that the failure of reform would trigger off a revolution, the Whig Government decided to lead the reform to a success. When a third Reform Bill passed the House of Commons in March 1832 and faced another rejection from the Lords, Grey requested the King to confer enough pro-reform peers as were necessary to overwhelm the anti-reform Tory majority.

The political confrontation turned white-hot when this request was refused and the Duke of Wellington was called to form a Tory government. All reformist forces now came together to struggle for a common cause, and the real possibility of a revolution loomed large. Both the middle-class and the working-class radicals began to take action: some decades later it transpired that they had even been organizing a revolutionary conspiracy. When activists called on businessmen to withdraw gold from the banks, they pulled out half of the reserve of the Bank of England within three days. Facing a determined, politically active populace, the King had no choice but to submit. Grey was recalled, Wellington acknowledged defeat, and the Tory's enterprise was absolutely hopeless. Their only means to oppose the Reform would have been to fight a civil war: but they decided to give up that option in order to keep their majority in the Lords. They chose to absent themselves when the Upper House was in session, and let the Bill pass unopposed. On 7 June 1832, after 18 months of fierce conflict, the Reform Bill was signed into law by the King and entered into force. The first parliamentary reform had finally succeeded.

Though a small step towards democracy, the Reform meant that the aristocracy lost its monopoly on power, and the newly enfranchised social strata gained some influence on state affairs. In this respect, one can say that the Reform was a step forward, although too small a step to meet popular expectations. In the following decades the aristocracy kept their dominance over parliament and state politics. Only a comparatively few people – the upper and central sectors of the middle classes – were enfranchised by the Reform, while other classes gained nothing despite their determined support for reforms over several decades. Here we see a phenomenon similar to the Glorious Revolution: a compromise in which both sides were partially satisfied, so that it seemed there had been no losers. With this result the Great Reform, restricted as it was, led Britain in the direction of peaceful democratic change, in an irreversible process.

What makes peaceful change possible? Under what circumstances does it become a reality? The British experience demonstrates circumstances under which peaceful transition may be made. On the one hand, we see the reformists' persistent and arduous struggles. On the other, even those who hated the reforms eventually approached change with an open mind, making wise and timely concessions when they became unavoidable. It seems a lesson from history, then, that the reforming forces should harbour no aspiration to change suddenly the social order with a single deadly blow; while the conservative forces should not harbour illusions that their world can survive forever without progress. Both sides, knowing that changes are surely to come in the long run of history, should be willing to compromise when conflicts occur; but the crucial issue for a peaceful change often lies with the attitude of those in power – whether they can keep abreast of the times to meet demands for reform.

Afterword:
Aspirations for Peace Studies in China

Liu Cheng

We find an abundance of peaceful thought in Chinese traditions. The Middle Way, the basic principle of action delineated by Confucius, harmoniously unifies *ren* – benevolence – with *li* – correct behaviour. The essence of *ren* is to love others. It is the highest internal standard, to act honourably when handling relationships among people, while *li* functions as a kind of external norm for one's behaviour. Confucian doctrine shows some resemblances to Aristotle's thought, in that both reckon it significant to mediate reasonableness and sensibility through a Middle Way. Confucianism advocates a moral, peaceful ideal, namely that interpersonal and also international conflicts should find resolution through moral means rather than by war, even if war be the 'Just War' proposed by some Christian thinkers. Confucius was the first prophet in China to put forward the ideal as 'to convince others by morality', laying the foundation for the subsequent Confucian mode of resolving disputes. This ideal demonstrated such enormous power in politics that it could even substitute violent mechanisms, like criminal laws or military power, in governing a country. Meanwhile, Daoist thinkers also developed flexible or compromising ideas on peace. As Johan Galtung, the founder of peace studies puts it: 'thoughts of peace and violence coexist in Daoism, warning people to be prepared for danger in times of safety', and he specially emphasizes that peace studies is as practical a science as medicine, using Chinese traditional medicine as an excellent analogy. Therefore he has adopted the principle of maladjustment and rebalancing between *yin* and *yang* in his writings.

I opened the course 'Peace Studies' at Nanjing University in 2003 after completing a graduate course in Coventry University's Centre for Peace and Reconciliation Studies. Up to now about three hundred students from arts and science faculties have attended our programme in Nanjing. One student wrote after a class: 'It can not be denied that the Peace Studies course has exerted an influence on my life. I have really acquired something which is not offered by other traditional methods when I try to tackle problems through peaceful means'. 'On the course', another student wrote, 'I always meet a dilemma. I want to believe or try to convince myself that these theories could be realized, but at the same time I often feel depressed when faced with big differences between theory and reality'. Another student thought that the Peace Studies course could serve as 'a little spark which can kindle a great fire'. Reactions of Chinese university students – showing a variety of different concerns and evaluations – have proven that it is both necessary and urgent to progress peace research in China.

Our peace research in China started in 2000, when cooperation was formally established between the World History Study Section in the History Department of Nanjing University and the Centre for Peace and Reconciliation Studies in Coventry. From 2002 one or two Chinese lecturers each year attended advanced studies on peace studies in Coventry University. Up to 2005 our researchers made considerable contributions: the first Chinese translation of Rigby's monograph *Justice and Reconciliation After the Violence*; papers on peace studies published in journals such as *Foreign Social Science, Journal of Nanjing University* and *Academia Bimestris*; four edited volumes of *Peace Archives*; and three Peace Studies courses for both under- and post-graduate students in Nanjing University. In addition, the university began to recruit post-graduates and doctoral candidates on peace research in 2004, and a new under-graduate textbook *Peace Studies* will be published in 2006. As a formal start-up for peace research in China, the International Symposium on Peace Studies in March 2005 received wide coverage and allowed more Chinese academics to understand the implications of peace studies, enormously advancing teaching and research in the area.

Meanwhile in these early stages, peace studies in China also confronts many challenges. First, until now peace studies has not had any special research organization or academic major in any Chinese university. Although Nanjing University has been working hard on building up a special centre for peace research, the final decision is still in question, as is its funding. Secondly, another problem is whether or not peace studies can obtain full recognition from academic circles. As is well known, China suffered a century of humiliation by foreign powers, 'being beaten for lagging behind' as the expression goes. Many academics may believe that peace studies only states some ideals, but does not offer any achievable reality. Third, in a developing country like China, graduates majoring in peace studies will soon encounter the fierce realities of the job market, where they may suffer compared to those with qualifications in IT, management or engineering.

However, China is a nation which loves peace and opposes violence. Despite the Ming dynasty's technological and military capacity to invade other countries, Zheng He's peaceful overseas voyages formed a strong contrast to those that opened Western colonialism, to give one example. Since the foundation of the People's Republic of China the government has adhered to the foreign policy of non-intervention based on 'Five Principles of Peaceful Coexistence' and focused on peaceful rather than violent means to settle disputes. In the twenty-first century the new leaders have announced the 'Peace Rising' path of China on its way to becoming a great power. In other words, peace and development have always been the two main targets for both the Chinese government and people, an aspiration which is largely shared in the peace studies agenda.

Another Chinese government target is the construction of a 'Harmonious Society' characterized as follows: to accelerate economic development with an emphasis on the individual human being; to advocate a new-style modernity with 'twofold gains' in human efforts to transform the natural environment; to promote a society based on the values of equality and justice in which all exert their ability and live on good terms with others; and to build a society with a robust legal system and orderly management. All these could also fall into the category of peace research.

China's further development will surely always need a peaceful international surrounding and a stable domestic environment. Nevertheless, new contradictions and conflicts have come to the surface with globalization and modernization. Peaceful methods to eliminate divergences and to conciliate conflicts, as the core of peace studies, will be worthwhile as both theoretical study and practical activity. Peace studies' fundamental value is peace, which is testified through the application of theory into practice. I personally hope that one effect of our classes is that students who have experienced peace education will show more inclination to solve problems by peaceful means.

We have good reasons to believe that, now it has been initiated, peace studies in China will never come to a halt. Universally, the goal of the peace studies is consistent with the basic interest of all humankind, including Chinese people. Specifically, it is part of our heritage, the ancient profound Chinese culture that has made and will make great contributions to the further development of peace studies.

Bibliography

Abu-Nimer, Mohammed, *Dialogue, Conflict Resolution and Change: Arab–Jewish Encounters in Israel* (Albany: State University of New York Press, 1999).

Ameglio, Pedro, 'Defensa noviolenta de una ciudad contra las megatiendas Costco-Comercial Mexicana' in Úrsula Oswald (ed.), *Resolución noviolenta de conflictos en sociedades indígenas y minorías* (México DF: Böll, 2004), 405–65.

Armendáriz García, Lorenzo, 'El proceso organizativo del pueblo rom en América: un camino para ser visible' in Úrsula Oswald (ed.), *Resolución noviolenta de conflictos en sociedades indígenas y minorías* (México DF: Böll, 2004), 159–72.

Baechler, Günther, 'Environmental Degradation and Violent Conflict: Hypotheses, Research Agendas and Theory-Building' in Mohamed Suliman (ed.), *Ecology, Politics and Violent Conflict* (London: Zed Books, 1999).

——, K.R. Spillmann and Mohamed Suliman (eds), *Transformation of Resource Conflicts: Approach and Instruments* (Berne, Switzerland: Peter Lang, 2002).

Beck, Ulrich, *Políticas ecológicas en la edad del riesgo* (Barcelona: El Roure, 2001).

——, *La sociedad de riesgo: Hacia una nueva modernidad* (Buenos Aires: Paidós, 1998).

Bennhold-Thomsen, Veronika and Maria Mies, *The Subsistence Perspective: Beyond the Globalized Economy* (London: Zed Books, 1999).

Blair, Tony, 'The Doctrine of the International Community' in Andrew Chadwick and Richard Heffernan (eds), *The New Labour Reader* (Cambridge: Polity Press, 2003).

Bloomfield David, Teresa Barnes and Luc Huyse (eds), *Reconciliation after Violent Conflict: A Handbook* (Stockholm: IDEA, 2001).

Bogardi, Janos and Hans Günter Brauch, 'Global Environmental Change: A Challenge for Human Security – Defining and Conceptualising the Environmental Dimension of Human Security' in Andreas Rechkemmer (ed.), *UNEO – Towards an International Environment Organization – Approaches to a Sustainable Reform of Global Environmental Governance* (Baden-Baden: Nomos, 2005).

Boulding, Elise, *Cultures of Peace: The Hidden Side of History* (New York: Syracuse University Press, 2000).

—— (ed.), *New Agendas for Peace Research: Conflict and Security Reexamined* (Boulder: Lynne Rienner, 1992).

Boulding, Kenneth, *Stable Peace* (Austin: University of Texas Press, 1978).

——, 'Twelve Friendly Quarrels with Johan Galtung', *Journal of Peace Research*, 14/1 (1977):75–86.

——, 'National Image and International System' in James N. Rosenau (ed.), *International Politics and Foreign Policy* (New York: Free Press, 1969), 422–31.

———, *The Image: Knowledge in Life and Society* (Ann Arbor: University of Michigan Press, 1956).

Boutros-Ghali, Boutros, *An Agenda for Peace* (New York: United Nations, 1992).

Brauch, Hans Günter, 'Environment and Human Security: Towards Freedom from Hazard Impact', *InterSecTions*, 2 (Bonn: UNU-EHS, 2005).

———, 'Threats, Challenges, Vulnerabilities and Risks in Environmental and Human Security', *Source*, 1 (Bonn: UNU-EHS, 2005).

———, 'Security and Environmental Linkages in the Mediterranean: Three Phases of Research on Human and Environmental Security and Peace' in Hans Günter Brauch, P.H. Liotta, A. Marquina, P.F. Rogers and M. El-Sayed Selim (eds), *Security and Environment in the Mediterranean: Conceptualising Security and Environmental Conflicts* (Berlin: Springer, 2003).

———, *Entwicklungen und Ergebnisse de Friedensforschung (1969–1978): Eine Zwischenbilanz und konkrete Vorschläge für das zweite Jahrzehnt* (Frankfurt: Haag and Herchen, 1979).

———, G. Bräunling, R. Hermle, W. Mallmann (eds), *Friedensforschung in Skandinavien: Informationen, Material und kritische Reflexionen* (Heidelberg: AG Konflikt- und Friedensforschung am IPW an der Universität Heidelberg, 1969).

Brock, Michael, *The Great Reform Act* (London: Hutchinson University Library, 1973).

Brock-Utne, Birgit, *Educating for Peace: A Feminist Perspective* (New York: Pergamon Press, 1985).

Brogan, Patric, *World Conflicts* (Lanham: Scarecrow Press, 1998).

Cadena Barquin, Félix (ed.), *De la economía popular a la economía de solidaridad: Itinerario de una búsqueda estratégica y metodológica para la construcción de otro mundo posible* (México DF: Centro Lindavista y Unión Europea, 2005).

———, 'Aprender a emprender: La economía de solidaridad como alternativa a la globalización excluyente' in Úrsula Oswald (ed.), *Soberanía y desarrollo regional: El México que queremos* (México DF: UNAM, 2003), 285–300.

Calva, José Luis, 'Balance de las políticas públicas: la economía mexicana bajo el consenso de Washington' in Úrsula Oswald (ed.), *Soberanía y desarrollo regional: El México que queremos* (México DF: UNAM, 2003), 143–72.

Cannon, John, *Parliamentary Reform, 1640–1832* (Cambridge: Cambridge University Press, 1973).

Cantle, Ted, *Community Cohesion* (London: Home Office, 2001).

Carmichael, Kay, *Sin and Forgiveness: New Responses in a Changing World* (Aldershot: Ashgate, 2003).

Carmody, Denise L. and John T. Carmody, *Peace and Justice in the Scriptures of the World Religions* (New York: Paulist Press, 1988).

CEPAL, *Balance preliminar de la economía en América Latina* (Santiago de Chile: CEPAL, 2004).

Chang, Iris, *The Rape of Nanking: The Forgotten Holocaust of World War II* (Harmondsworth: Penguin, 1998).

Chomsky, Noam, 'A Century Later', *Peace Review*, 10/3 (1998): 313–21.

Cone, Carl B., *The English Jacobins* (New York: Scribners, 1968).

Consortium on Peace Research, Education and Development (COPRED), *Global Directory of Peace Studies and Conflict Resolution Programs* (Fairfax, VA: George Mason University/COPRED, 2000).

Coopey, Richard, Steven Fielding and Nick Tiratsoo (eds), *The Wilson Governments 1964–1970* (London and New York: Pinter Publishers, 1993).

Cordera Campos, Rolando, 'Economía y política en el cambio democrático mexicano' in Úrsula Oswald (ed.), *Soberanía y desarrollo regional: El México que queremos* (México DF: UNAM, Coltax, Canacintra, 2003), 114–39.

Cortés, Hernán, *Cartas de relación* (Madrid: Historia 16, 1985).

Cox, Caroline and Roger Scruton, *Peace Studies: A Critical Survey* (New York: Institute for European Defense and Strategic Studies, 1984).

Creel, H.G., *Confucius and the Chinese Way* (New York: Harper, 1960).

Croft, Stuart, 'Ethics, Labour and Foreign Policy' in Colin Itay (ed.), *British Politics Today* (Cambridge: Polity Press, 2002).

Curle, Adam, *Making Peace* (London: Tavistock Press, 1971).

Dale, Iain, *Labour Party General Election Manifestos 1900–1997* (London and New York: Routledge, 2000).

De la Rúa, Diana, 'Pueblos originarios y resolución de conflictos' in Úrsula Oswald (ed.), *Resolución noviolenta de conflictos en sociedades indígenas y minorías* (México DF: Böll, 2004), 101–8.

Diamond, Jared, *Guns, Germs, and Steel* (New York: W.W. Norton, 1997).

Díaz Fonseca, Eliezbel, 'Empleo de nueva tecnología de información conmo alternativa para la educación en las zonas rurales de Cuba' in Úrsula Oswald (ed.), *Resolución noviolenta de conflictos en sociedades indígenas y minorías* (México DF: Böll, 2004), 357–69.

Dickinson, Harry T., *Liberty and Property: Political Ideology in Eighteenth-Century Britain* (London: Weidenfeld and Nicolson, 1977).

Doise, W., *Levels of Explanation in Social Psychology* (Cambridge: Cambridge University Press, 1986).

Du Toit, Pierre, *South Africa's Brittle Peace: The Problem of Post-Settlement Violence* (New York: Palgrave, 2001).

Dussel Peters, Enrique, 'Políticas de competitividad sectorregionales o regionales-sectoriales? Hacia una propuesta de políticas privada y pública de fomento' in Úrsula Oswald (ed.), *Soberanía y desarrollo regional: El México que queremos* (México DF: UNAM, Coltax, Canacintra, 2003), 205–16.

Economist, Pocket World in Figures, 2005 edn (London: Profile Books in association with *The Economist*, 2004).

El Colegio de México, *Historia de México* (México DF: Colmex, 1972).

Estete, Miguel de, 'El descubrimiento y la conquista del Perú', *Boletín de la Sociedad Ecuatoriana de Estudios Históricos Americanos*, 1 (1918): 300–350.

Fischer, Louis, *The Life of Mahatma Gandhi* (London: HarperCollins, 1997).

Foreign and Commonwealth Office, *UK International Priorities: A Strategy for the FCO*, presented to Parliament by the Secretary of State for Foreign and Commonwealth Affairs by Command of Her Majesty, December 2003 (London: TSO, 2003).

Francis, Diana, *People, Peace and Power: Conflict Transformation in Action* (London: Pluto Press, 2002).

Fromm, Erich, *The Art of Loving* (New York: Harper & Row, 1956).

Fuentes, Patricia (ed.), *The Conquistadors* (Norman: University of Oklahoma Press, 1933).

Fukuyama, Francis, *The End of History and the Last Man* (New York: Free Press, 1992).

Gaitán, Iván Mauricio, 'Resistencia civil indígena en zonas de conflicto armado en Colombia' in Úrsula Oswald (ed.), *Resolución noviolenta de conflictos en sociedades indígenas y minorías* (México DF: Böll, 2004), 71–95.

Galtung, Johan, *Peace by Peaceful Means: Peace and Conflict, Development and Civilization* (London: Sage Publications, 1998).

——, *Peace by Peaceful Means* (Oslo: PRIO, 1996).

—— (ed.), *Essays in Peace Research*, vol. 6, *Transarmament and the Cold War* (Copenhagen: Christian Ejlers Forlag, 1988).

——, 'What is Meant by Peace and Security? Some Options for the 1990s' in Johan Galtung (ed.), *Essays in Peace Research*, vol. 6, *Transarmament and the Cold War* (Copenhagen: Christian Ejlers Forlag, 1988), 61–71.

——, *Environment, Development and Military Activity: Towards Alternative Security Doctrines* (Oslo: Norwegian University Press, 1982).

——, 'Violence, Peace and Peace Research' in Johan Galtung (ed.), *Peace: Research, Education, Action*, vol. 1, *Essays in Peace Research* (Copenhagen: Christian Ejlers Forlag, 1975); originally published in *Journal of Peace Research*, 6/3 (1969): 167–91.

—— and Carl G. Jacobsen, *Searching For Peace* (London: Pluto Press, 2000).

García, Emilio Plutarco, 'Conflictos agrarios y pueblos indíos: de la contrarreforma agraria a los llamados focos rojos' in Úrsula Oswald (ed.), *Resolución noviolenta de conflictos en sociedades indígenas y minorías* (México DF: Böll, 2004), 261–74.

Giddens, Anthony, *Beyond Left and Right: The Future of Radical Politics* (Stanford: Stanford University Press, 1994).

——, *Modernity and Self-Identity: Self and Society in the Late Modern Age* (London: Polity Press, 1991).

Gil, Lise, 'Una nueva generación de tratados para el pueblo innu, Canadá y Québec' in Úrsula Oswald (ed.), *Resolución noviolenta de conflictos en sociedades indígenas y minorías* (México DF: Böll, 2004), 109–16.

Glasl, Friedrich von, *Konfliktmanagement: Ein Handbuch zur Diagnose und Behandlung von Konflikten für Organisationen und ihre Berater* (Stuttgart: Verlag Freies Geistesleben, 1994).

Gluckman, Max, *Custom and Conflict in Africa* (Oxford: Blackwell, 1956).

Goodwin, Albert, *The Friends of Liberty: The English Democratic Movement in the*

Age of the French Revolution (Cambridge, MA: Harvard University Press 1979).

Gopin, Marc, *Between Eden and Armageddon: The Future of World Religions, Violence, and Peacemaking* (New York: Oxford University Press, 2000).

Govier, Trudy, *Forgiveness and Revenge* (London: Routledge, 2002).

Graves, Robert, *The Greek Myths* (2 vols, Harmondsworth: Penguin, 1960).

Habermas, Jürgen, *Kommunikatives Handeln und detranszendentalisierte Vernunft* (Stuttgart, 2001).

——, *La constelación posnacional: ensayos políticos* (Barcelona: Paidos, 2000).

——, *Más allá del Estado nacional* (México DF: FCE, 1998).

Han Hongwen, *Ershi shijide heping yanjiu: lishixing kaocha* [Peace Research in the Twentieth Century: A Historical Investigation] (Beijing: Dangdai Zhongguo chubanshe, 2002).

Harris, Ian, 'Peace Studies in the United States at the University and College Levels' in Ake Bjerstedt (ed.), *Peace Education: Global Perspectives* (Stockholm: Almqvist & Wiksell International, 1993).

Hayter, Teresa, *Open Borders: The Case against Immigration Controls* (London: Pluto Press, 2000).

Heffernan, Richard, 'Beyond Euro-Scepticism? Labour Party and the European Union since 1945' in Brian Brivati and Richard Heffernan (eds), *The Labour Party: A Centenary History* (Basingstoke: Macmillan, 2000).

Hein, Laura and Mark Selden (eds), *Censoring History: Citizenship and Memory in Japan, Germany, and the United States* (Armonk, NY: M.E. Sharpe, 2000).

Helmick, Raymond G. and Rodney L. Petersen, *Forgiveness and Reconciliation* (Radnor, PA: Templeton Foundation Press, 2001).

Hennessy, Peter, *Never Again: Britain 1945–1951* (London: Jonathan Cape, 1993).

Hesse, Barnor (ed.), *Un/settled Multiculturalisms* (London: Zed Books, 2000).

Hill, Christopher, *The Century of Revolution, 1603–1714* (Edinburgh: Thomas Nelson and Sons, 1961).

Hogg, M.A. and D. Abrams, *Social Identification: A Social Psychology of Intergroup Relations and Group Processes* (London: Routledge, 1988).

Homer-Dixon, Thomas F. and Jessica Blitt (eds), *Ecoviolence: Links between Environment, Population, and Security* (Lanham: Rowman and Littlefield, 1998).

Howe, Stephen, 'Labour and International Affairs' in Duncan Tanner, Pat Thane and Nick Tiratsoo (eds), *Labour's First Century* (Cambridge: Cambridge University Press, 2000).

Hunter, Alan and John Sexton, *Contemporary China* (Basingstoke: Macmillan, 1999).

International Commission on Intervention and State Sovereignty, *The Responsibility to Protect* (Ottawa: International Development Research Centre, 2001).

International Network of Peace Museums, *Newsletter of the International Network of Peace Museums*, 12 (February 2000): 17.

Jackson, Hampden, *England since the Industrial Revolution, 1815–1948* (London: Greenwood Press, 1976).

Jahn, Egbert, 'Friedens- und Konflitkforschung' in Andreas Boeckh (ed.), *Internationale Beziehungen*, vol. 6 of Dieter Nohlen (ed.), *Lexikon der Politik* (7 vols, Munich: C.H. Beck, 1994).

Jessup, John E., *An Encyclopedic Dictionary of Conflict and Conflict Resolution, 1945–1996* (London: Greenwood Publishing Group, 1998).

Johnston, Douglas and Cynthia Sampson, *Religion, the Missing Dimension of Statecraft* (New York: Oxford University Press, 1994).

Juergensmeyer, Mark, *Terror in the Mind of God: The Global Rise of Religious Violence* (Berkeley: University of California Press, 2000).

Kaldor, Mary, Helmut Anheier and Larlies Glasius (eds), *Global Civil Society Yearbook 2002* (Oxford: Oxford University Press, 2003).

Kampfner, John, *Blair's Wars* (London: Free Press, 2003).

Kaplan, Marcos, 'Globalización, política y Estado' in Úrsula Oswald (ed.), *Soberanía y desarrollo regional: El México que queremos* (México DF: UNAM, Coltax, Canacintra, 2003), 41–82.

Keltner, John W., *The Management of Struggle: Elements of Dispute Resolution through Negotiation, Mediation and Arbitration.* (Cresskill, NJ: Hampton Press, 1994).

Koestler, Arthur, *The Yogi and the Commissar* (London: Macmillan, 1946).

Kritz, Neil J. (ed.), *Transitional Justice* (Washington, DC: United States Institute of Peace, 1995).

Kritzinger, Klippies, 'Introduction' in Gerrie Lubbe, *Believers in the Struggle for Justice and Peace* (Johannesburg: WCRP, 1988).

Kyoto Museum for World Peace at Ritsumeikan University, 'Inscription', *Academeia*, 21 (1999): 1.

——, *Jousetsu Tenji Shousai Kaisetsu* [Detailed Manual on Permanent Exhibition] (Kyoto: Kyoto Museum for World Peace, 1997).

Labedz, Leopold (ed.), *Poland under Jaruzelski: A Comprehensive Sourcebook on Poland during and after Martial Law* (New York: Scribners, 1984).

Lagarde y de los Rios, Marcela, *Claves feministas para la autoestima de las mujeres* (Barcelona: Horas y Horas, 2000).

——, *Los cautiverios de las mujeres: madresposas, monjas, putas, presas y locas*, unpublished doctoral thesis, National University of Mexico, 1990.

Lao Tzu, *Tao Te Ching* [translated into English by D.C. Lau] (Harmondsworth: Penguin, 1963).

Lederach, John Paul, 'Civil Society and Reconciliation' in Chester A. Crocker *et al.* (eds), *Turbulent Peace: The Challenges of Managing International Conflict* (Washington, DC: United States Institute of Peace, 2001).

——, *Building Peace: Sustainable Reconciliation in Divided Societies* (Washington DC: United States Institute of Peace, 1999).

Liu Cheng, *Yingguo gongdang yu gongyouzhi* [The British Labour Party and Public Ownership] (Nanjing: Jiangsu renmin chubanshe, 2003).

Loewenstein, Antony, 'Taking Back The Power: Hanan Ashrawi' in Margo Kingston (ed.), *Not Happy John* (Camberwell, Australia: Penguin, 2004).

Lópezllera Méndez, Luis, 'La economía social y solidaria como factor de desarrollo equitativo e incluyente' in Úrsula Oswald (ed.), *Soberanía y desarrollo regiona: El México que queremos* (México DF: UNAM, Coltax, Canacintra, 2003), 336–59.

Lubbe, Gerrie, *Believers in the Struggle for Justice and Peace* (Johannesburg: WCRP, 1988).

Luo Cunkang, 'The Anti-Japanese War Museum in Beijing', *Muse: Newsletter of the Japanese Network of Museums for Peace*, 11 (June 2004).

Macaulay, Lord, *History of England from the Accession of James II (1861)* (reprint, Whitefish, MT: R.A. Kessinger, 2003).

Maccoby, Simon, *English Radicalism, 1762–85* (London: George Allen and Unwin, 1955).

——, *English Radicalism, 1786–1832* (London: George Allen and Unwin, 1955).

Mandela, Nelson, *Long Walk to Freedom*, 9th edn (London: Abacus, 1997).

Marini, Ruy Mauro, *Teoría de la Dependencia en América Latina* (México DF: Siglo XXI eds, 1975).

——, *El secreto intercambio desigual* (México DF: Ediciones Era, 1973).

Martin, Laurence and John Garnet, *British Foreign Policy: Challenges and Choices for the Twenty-First Century* (London: Pinter, for the Royal Institute of International Affairs, 1997).

Martínez, Ifigenia, 'Planeación del desarrollo regional y de los sectores estratégicos y prioritarios' in Úrsula Oswald (ed.), *Soberanía y desarrollo regional: El México que queremos* (México DF: UNAM, Coltax, Canacintra, 2003), 233–46.

Martínez Cuevas, Judith, 'Los pueblos originarios y la reconquista a través de la cultura' in Úrsula Oswald (ed.), *Resolución noviolenta de conflictos en sociedades indígenas y minorías* (México DF: Böll, 2004), 96–100.

Marx, Karl and Friedrich Engels, *The Manifesto of the Communist Party* (first published 1848, new edn Harmondsworth: Penguin, 2002).

McCarthy, Ronald M. and Gene Sharp, *Nonviolent Action, A Research Guide* (London and New York: Garland Publishing, 1997).

McCullough, Michael E., Kennith I. Pargament and Carl E. Thoresen, *Forgiveness: Theory, Research, and Practice* (New York and London: Guildford Press, 2000).

McGhee, Derek, 'Moving to Our Common Ground: A Critical Examination of Community Cohesion Discourse in 21st Century Britain', *Sociological Review*, 51/3 (2003).

Mekenkamp, Monika, Paul van Tongeren and Hans van de Veen (eds), *Searching for Peace in Central and South Asia* (Boulder and London: Lynne Rienner, 2002).

Menchú, Rogoberta, 'Culturas indígenas, cosmovisión y futuro' in Úrsula Oswald (ed.), *Resolución noviolenta de conflictos en sociedades indígenas y minorías* (México DF: Böll, 2004), 49–62.

Mercado, Monina A. (ed.), *People Power: The Philippine Revolution of 1986: An Eyewitness History* (Manila: S.J. Foundation, 1986).

Mial, Hugh, Oliver Ramsbotham and Tom Woodhouse, *Contemporary Conflict Resolution* (Cambridge: Polity Press, 1999).

Mies, Maria, *Patriarchy and Accumulation on a World Scale*, new edn (North Melbourne, Vic.: Spinifex Press; London: Zed Books, 1998).

—— and Vandana Shiva, *Ecofeminism* (London: Zed Books, 1993).

Minow, Martha, *Between Vengeance and Forgiveness: Facing History after Genocide and Mass Violence* (Boston: Beacon Press, 1998).

Mitchell, Austin, *The Whigs in Opposition, 1815–30* (Oxford: Oxford University Press, 1967).

Mitchell, Stephen, *The Enlightened Heart: An Anthology of Sacred Poetry* (New York: Harper Perennial, 1992).

Møller, Bjørn, 'National, Societal and Human Security Discussion: A Case Study of the Israeli–Palestine Conflict' in Hans Günther Brauch, P.H. Liotta, Antonio Marquina, Paul F. Rogers and Mohammad El-Sayed Selim (eds), *Security and Environment in the Mediterranean: Conceptualising Security and Environmental Conflicts* (Berlin: Springer, 2003).

Montriel, Cristina J., 'Sociopolitical Forgiveness' in Andrew Rigby and Carol Rank (eds), *Peace Review: Journal of Social Justice*, 14/3 (2002).

Moscovici, Serge, 'The History and Actuality of Social Representations' in Gerard Duveen (ed.), *Social Representations: Explorations in Social Psychology* (Cambridge: Polity, 2000).

——, 'Social Consciousness and its History', *Culture and Psychology*, 4 (1998): 411–29.

——, 'Social Psychology and Developmental Psychology: Extending the Conversation' in G. Duveen and B. Lloyd (eds), *Social Representations and the Development of Knowledge* (Cambridge: Cambridge University Press, 1990).

——, 'The Phenomenon of Social Representations' in R.M. Farr and S. Moscovici (eds), *Social Representations* (Cambridge: Cambridge University Press, 1984).

——, *Social Influence and Social Change* (Cambridge: Academic Press, 1976).

Murphy, Jeffrie G. and Jean Hampton, *Forgiveness and Mercy* (Cambridge: Cambridge University Press, 1988).

Myrdal, Alva, *War, Weapons and Everyday Violence* (Manchester: University of New Hampshire Press, 1977).

—— and V. Klein (eds), *Women's Two Roles* (London: Routledge & Kegan Paul, 1968).

Myrdal, Gunnar, *El estado del futuro* (Mexico: FCE, 1961).

——, *The Political Element in the Development of Economic Theory* (*Teoría económica de regiones subdesarrolladas*, 1968) (Mexico: FCE, 1953).

Nussbaum, Martha C. and Amartya Sen, *The Quality of Life* (Oxford: Oxford University Press, 1993).

Nygren, Anders, *Agape and Eros* [translated from Swedish by Philip S. Watson] (Philadelphia: Westminster Press, 1953).

O'Connell, James, 'Approaches to the Study of Peace in Higher Education: The Tensions of Scholarship' in Tom Woodhouse (ed.), *Peacemaking in a Troubled World* (Oxford: Berg, 1991).

O'Gorman, Frank, *The Whig Party and the French Revolution* (London: Macmillan, 1967).

Oswald, Úrsula (ed.), *Resolución noviolenta de conflictos en sociedades indígenas y minorías* (México DF: Fundación Heinrich Böll, 2004).

——, 'Sustainable Development with Peace Building and Human Security' in M.K. Tolba (ed.), *Our Fragile World: Challenges and Opportunities for Sustainable Development*, forerunner of *The Encyclopedia of Life Support Systems* (2 vols, Oxford: Eolss Publishers, 2001).

——, *Peace Study from a Global Perspective: Human Needs in a Changing World* (New Delhi: Maadhyam Book Services, 2000).

—— and M. Lourdes Hernández, *El Valor del Agua: una Visión Socioeconómica de un Conflicto Ambiental* (Tlaxcala, Mexico: Coltlax, 2005).

Parekh, Bhikhu, *Rethinking Multiculturalism: Cultural Diversity and Political Theory* (Basingstoke: Macmillan, 2000).

——, *The Future of Multi-Ethnic Britain* (London: Profile Books, 2000).

Pizarro, Pedro, *Relación del descubrimiento y conquista de los reinos del Perú* (Lima: Universidad Católica de Lima, 1978).

Polensky Gurwitz, Yeidckol, 'Prólogo' in Úrsula Oswald (ed.), *Soberanía y desarrollo regional: El México que queremos* (México DF: UNAM, Coltax, Canacintra, 2003), 33–8.

Porritt, Edward and Annie G. Porritt, *The Unreformed House of Commons: Parliamentary Representation before 1832* (Cambridge: Cambridge University Press, 1903).

Powers, Roger S. and William B. Vogele, *Protest, Power, and Change: An Encyclopedia of Nonviolent Action from ACT-UP to Women's Suffrage* (London and New York: Garland Publishing, 1997).

Preiswerk, Roy, 'Could We Study International Relations as if People Mattered?' in Gordon Feller, Sherle Schwenninger and Diane Singerman (eds), *Peace and World Order Studies: A Curriculum Guide* (New York: Transnational Program of the Institute for World Order, 1981).

Prescott, William H., *History of the Conquest of Mexico* (New York: Harper and Brothers, 1843).

Rawls, John G., *Political Liberalism* (Cambridge: Cambridge University Press, 1990).

Reardon, Betty A., *Sexism and the War System* (New York: Syracuse University Press, 1996).

Rees, Stuart, 'Vilification Nation: The Hanan Ashrawi Affair', *East West Arts, Australia and Beyond, Inaugural Issue* (September–November 2004): 61–6.

——, *Passion for Peace: Exercising Power Creatively* (Sydney: UNSW Press, 2003).

—— and Leonie Gibbons, *A Brutal Game* (Sydney: Angus and Robertson, 1985).

Rees, Stuart and Gordon Rodley, *The Human Costs of Managerialism: Advocating the Recovery of Humanity* (Sydney: Pluto Press, 1995).

—— and Frank Stilwell (eds), *Beyond the Market: Alternatives to Economic Rationalism* (Sydney: Pluto Press, 1993).

Rees, Stuart and Shelley Wright (eds), *Human Rights, Corporate Responsibility* (Sydney: Pluto Press, 2000).

Reychler, Luc and Thomas Paffenholz (eds), *Peace Building: A Field Guide* (Boulder: Lynne Rienner, 2001).

Richards, Howard, *Understanding the Global Economy* (New Delhi: Maadhyam Book Services, 2000).

Richardson, Lewis Frye, *Statistics of Deadly Quarrels* (originally published privately on microfilm, 1950), edited by Quincy Wright and C.C. Lienau (Pittsburgh: Boxwood Press, 1960).

——, 'Contiguity and Deadly Quarrels: The Local Pacifying Influence', *Journal of the Royal Statistical Society*, 115/2 (1952): 219–31.

——, 'Chaos, International and Inter-Molecular', *Nature*, 158 (1946): 135.

——, *Generalized Foreign Politics: A Study in Group Psychology* (Cambridge: Cambridge University Press, 1939).

Rigby, Andrew, *Justice and Reconciliation after the Violence* (Boulder: Lynne Rienner, 2000).

——, 'Be Practical, Do the Impossible: The Politics of Everyday Life' in Gail Chester and Andrew Rigby (eds), *Articles of Peace* (Bridport: Prism Press, 1987).

——, 'Peace News, 1936–1986' in Gail Chester and Andrew Rigby (eds), *Articles of Peace: Celebrating Fifty Years of Peace News* (Bridport: Prism Press, 1986).

—— and Carol Rank (eds), 'Symposium: Forgiveness and Reconciliation', *Peace Review: Journal of Social Justice*, 14/3 (2002).

Ríos Martínez, Maribel, 'El temascal: una terapéutica alterntiva en las relaciones sociales' in Úrsula Oswald (ed.), *Resolución noviolenta de conflictos en sociedades indígenas y minorías* (México DF: Böll, 2004), 467–79.

Rogers, Paul and Oliver Ramsbotham, 'Then and Now: Peace Research – Past and Future', *Political Studies*, 47 (1999): 740–54.

Rojas Aravena, Francisco, 'Repensando la Seguridad en América Latina: Nuevas Demandas Conceptuales' in Mario Salinas and Úrsula Oswald (eds), *Culturas de paz, seguridad y democracia en América Latina* (México DF: CRIM-UNAM, Coltlax, CLAIP y Fundación Böll, 2003).

Rude, George, *Wilkes and Liberty* (Oxford, Clarendon Press, 1962).

Ruiz Duran, Clemente, 'Reposicionando el desarrollo: del esquema central a la recuperación de lo local' in Úrsula Oswald (ed.), *Soberanía y desarrollo regiona: El México que queremos* (México DF: UNAM, Coltax, Canacintra, 2003), 415–34.

Salinas, Mario and Úrsula Oswald (eds), *Culturas de paz, seguridad y democracia en América Latina* (México DF: CRIM-UNAM, Coltlax, CLAIP y Fundación Böll, 2003).

Sassoon, Donald, *One Hundred Years of Socialism: The West European Left in the Twentieth Century* (London: I.B. Tauris, 1996).

Saviñón, Diez de Sollano, 'Dos procesos que confluyen en uno: desarrollo regional y solución de conflictos' in Úrsula Oswald (ed.), *Resolución noviolenta de conflictos en sociedades indígenas y minorías* (México DF: Böll, 2004), 369–80.

Schimmel, Solomon, *Wounds not Healed by Time* (Oxford: Oxford University Press, 2002).

Schmid, Herman, 'Politics and Peace Research', *Journal of Peace Research*, 3 (1968): 217–32.

Sen, Amartya, *Inequality Reexamined* (Cambridge: Harvard University Press, 1995).

Senghaas, Dieter, *Der strukturelle Imperialismos* (Frankfurt: Suhrkamp, 1978).

Serrano Oswald, Serena Eréndira, 'Género, migración y paz: incursiones a una problemática desde una perspectiva multidimensional e incluyente' in Úrsula Oswald (ed.), *Resolución noviolenta de conflictos en sociedades indígenas y minorías* (México DF: Böll, 2004).

——, 'Changes of Women's Social Identity in Modern Mexico', unpublished Master's dissertation, Department of Social Psychology, London School of Economics and Political Sciences, 2003.

——, 'Exploring a Socio-cultural Social Psychology: A Potential for Regional Studies', paper presented at the 18th Pacific Regional Science Conference, Acapulco, Mexico, July 2003.

Sharp, Gene, *The Politics of Non-violent Action* (Boston: P. Sargent, 1973).

Shaw, Eric, *The Labour Party Since 1945: Old Labour, New Labour* (Oxford: Blackwell, 1996).

——, *The Labour Party Since 1979: Crisis and Transformation* (London and New York: Routledge, 1994).

Shenkar, Oded, *The Chinese Century: The Rising Chinese Economy and Its Impact on the Global Economy, the Balance of Power, and Your Job* (Philadelphia: Wharton School Publishing, 2004).

Shiva, Vandana, *Staying Alive: Women, Ecology and Development* (London: Zed Books, 1988).

Shriver, Donald W., *An Ethic for Enemies: Forgiveness in Politics* (Oxford: Oxford University Press, 1995).

SIPRI (Stockholm International Peace Research Institute), *SIPRI Yearbook 2004: Armaments, Disarmaments and International Security* (Oxford: Oxford University Press, 2004).

Smedes, Lewis B., *Forgive and Forget: Healing the Hurts We Don't Deserve* (San Francisco: HarperCollins, 1986).

Smith, Charlene, *Mandela* (Cape Town: Struik, 1999).

Solomos, John, *Race and Racism in Britain* (Basingstoke: Macmillan, 2003).

Stephenson, Carolyn, 'New Approaches to International Peacemaking in the Post-Cold War World' in Michael Klare (ed.), *Peace and World Security Studies: A Curriculum Guide* (Boulder: Lynne Rienner, 1994).

——, 'The Evolution of Peace Studies' in Daniel Thomas and Michael Klare (eds), *Peace and World Order Studies: A Curriculum Guide*, 5th edn (Boulder: Westview Press, 1989).

Stiglitz, Joseph E., *Globalization and Its Discontents* (New York: W.W. Norton, 2002).

Stothard, Peter, *30 Days: A Month at the Heart of Blair's War* (London: HarperCollins, 2003).

Tanaka, Yuki, *Hidden Horrors: Japanese War Crimes in World War II* (Boulder: Westview Press, 1996).

ter Haar, Barend J., 'Rethinking "Violence" in Chinese Culture' in Göran Aijmer and Jos Abbink (eds), *Meanings of Violence: A Cross Cultural Perspective* (Oxford: Berg, 2000).

Terrill, Ross, *The New Chinese Empire: And What It Means for the United States* (New York: Basic Books, 2003).

Thale, Mary (ed.), *Selections from the Papers of the London Corresponding Society* (Cambridge: Cambridge University Press, 1983).

Thomas, Hugh, *Conquest: Moctezuma, Cortés, and the Fall of Old Mexico* (New York: Simon Schuster, 1993).

Thomis, Malcolm I., *The Luddites* (Hamden, CT: Archon Books, 1970).

Thompson, Dorothy, *The Chartists, Popular Politics in the Industrial Revolution* (London: Temple Smith, 1984).

Thompson, Edward P., *The Making of the English Working Class* (London: Gollancz, 1963).

Thompson, W. Scott and Kenneth M. Jensen (eds), *Approaches to Peace: An Intellectual Map* (Washington, DC: The United States Institute of Peace, 1991).

Touraine, A., *Actores sociales y sistemas políticos en América Latina* (Santiago: Publicaciones OIT, 1987).

UNDP (United Nations Development Programme), *Report on Human Development* (London: UNDP, 1996–98).

United Nations, *Peace Museums Worldwide*, Archives of the League of Nations, Geneva, United Nations Publications on Peace Series, 1st edn (Geneva: United Nations, 1995); 2nd edn, in association with the Department of Peace Studies, University of Bradford (Geneva: United Nations, 1998).

van den Dungen, Peter, 'Peace Education: Peace Museums' in Lester R. Kurtz (ed.), *Encyclopedia of Violence, Peace and Conflict* (3 vols, San Diego: Academic Press, 1999).

Vickers, Rhiannon, 'Labour's Search for a Third Way in Foreign Policy' in Richard Little and Mark Wickham-Jones (eds), *New Labour's Foreign Policy: A New Moral Crusade?* (Manchester: Manchester University Press, 2000).

Wallensteen, Peter, 'The Origins of Peace Research' in Peter Wallensteen (ed.), *Peace Research: Achievements and Challenges* (Boulder and London: Westview Press, 1988).

—— and Margareta Sollenberg, 'Armed Conflict and Regional Complexes, 1989–97', *Journal of Peace Research*, 35/5 (1998): 621–34.

Wallerstein, Immanuel (ed.), 'Heritage of Sociology and the Future of the Social Sciences in the 21st Century', *Current Sociology*, 46/2 (1998).

Wang Zhicheng, *Hepingde kewang: dangdai zongjiao duihua lilun* [Eager for Peace: Contemporary Theories of Inter-Religious Dialogue] (Beijing: Zongjiao wenhua chubanshe, 2003).

Warren, Karen J. (ed.), *Ecofeminism: Women, Culture, Nature* (Bloomington: Indiana University Press, 1997).

Weber, Max, 'Politics as a Vocation' in Hans Gerth and C. Wright Mills (eds), *From Max Weber* (London: Routledge & Kegan Paul, 1967).

Wickham-Jones, Mark, *Economic Strategy and the Labour Party: Politics and Policy-Making, 1970–83* (Basingstoke: Macmillan, 1996).

Wien, Barbara (ed.), *Peace and World Order Studies: A Curriculum Guide*, 4th edn (New York: World Policy Institute, 1984).

Wiesenthal, Simon, *The Sunflower: On the Possibilities and Limits of Forgiveness* (New York: Schocken Books, 1997).

Wolfers, Arnold, 'National Security as an Ambiguous Symbol' in Arnold Wolfers, *Discord and Collaboration: Essays on International Politics* (Baltimore: Johns Hopkins University Press, 1962).

Worthington, Everett L., *Dimensions of Forgiveness: Psychological Research and Theological Perspectives* (Radnor, PA: Templeton Foundation Press, 1998).

Wright, Judith, *Collected Poems* (Sydney: Angus & Robertson, 1994).

Wright, Quincy, *A Study of War* (Chicago: University of Chicago Press, 1st edn 1942, 2nd edn 1965).

Index

For Product Safety Concerns and Information please contact our EU
representative GPSR@taylorandfrancis.com
Taylor & Francis Verlag GmbH, Kaufingerstraße 24, 80331 München, Germany